| DATE | | | |
|---|---|---|---|
|  |  |  |  |
|  |  |  |  |
|  |  |  |  |
|  |  |  |  |
|  |  |  |  |
|  |  |  |  |
|  |  |  |  |
|  |  |  |  |
|  |  |  |  |
|  |  |  |  |
|  |  |  |  |
|  |  |  |  |
|  |  |  |  |

# Soviet Labour and the
# Ethic of Communism

By the same author

*The End of Social Inequality? Class, Status and Power under State Socialism* (1982)

*State and Politics in the USSR* (1985)

*Soviet Economy and Society* (1985)

*Labour and Employment in the USSR* (Wheatsheaf Books, 1986)

# Soviet Labour and the Ethic of Communism

## Full Employment and the Labour Process in the USSR

David Lane

*Professor of Sociology*
*University of Birmingham*

WHEATSHEAF BOOKS

WESTVIEW PRESS
Boulder, Colorado

First published in Great Britain in 1987 by
WHEATSHEAF BOOKS LIMITED
A MEMBER OF THE HARVESTER PRESS PUBLISHING GROUP
*Publisher: John Spiers*
16 Ship Street, Brighton, Sussex

and in the United States of America by
WESTVIEW PRESS, INC.
5500 Central Avenue, Boulder, Colorado 80301
*Frederick A. Praeger, Publisher*

© David Lane, 1987

*British Library Cataloguing in Publication Data*

Lane, David
  Soviet labour and the ethic of communism.
  1. Labor supply—Soviet Union
  I. Title
  331.12'5'0947        HD5796

  ISBN 0−7108−0278−1
  ISBN 0−7108−0283−8 Pbk

  WESTVIEW PRESS
  ISBN 0-8133-0624-8
  LCN 87-50799

Typeset in 11pt Times by Woodfield Graphics, Fontwell,
Arundel, West Sussex

Printed in Great Britain by Billing & Sons Ltd, Worcester

# Contents

# Acknowledgements

This work has been facilitated by the support of the British Economic and Social Research Committee (Grant F230085) which provided the author with one term's study leave and one year's research assistance, mainly in the form of Sheila Marnie who gave excellent help. My thanks also to Linda McLeod who also assisted with the research for a short period and to Mike Berry who saved me from making many mistakes. I would also like to acknowledge the support of the Kennan Institute, Washington D.C. for a month's visiting Fellowship and to the University of Illinois at Urbana Champaign for the facilities of their summer research lab. The Alexander Baykov Library at Birmingham University, the Library of Congress and the Radio Liberty Archives were invaluable sources of literature.

# Introduction: The Labour Process

On 13 March 1930, Michail Shkunov, A Moscow plumber, finally got a job. When he left the labour exchange, the doors closed and Soviet commentators pronounced that this event symbolized the end of mass unemployment in the USSR. Since that time, the provision of regular paid labour and a permanent occupation for all who are able to work has been one yardstick which has been used to legitimate Soviet society as a socialist state. This book seeks to discover the extent to which this claim is true and whether there are any systemic features of Soviet society in distinction from capitalism which lead to the provision of full employment.

Almost all research in the West on employment (or unemployment) and the labour process is based on capitalist market-type societies. Levels of unemployment are seen to derive from the working of the market economy: to be the result of structural insufficiencies in demand, of the overpricing or immobility of labour or—as seen by Marxist critics—to be consequent on the laws of capitalist accumulation creating a reserve army of idle people. Employment and the labour process in socialist states must be seen in a completely different economic, ideological and political context. It will be established in this book that the Soviet economy is one of full employment with the highest rate of paid employment known to history. This is considered to be a consequence of the operation of the economic mechanism and political system. In distinction from market economies, it will be shown that in the socialist economy there is no effective propensity to increase the profitability of capital by reducing labour costs.

The contemporary 'labour process' approach emphasizes the role of labour as the creator of wealth in the context of the

1

exploitation of labour through the competition of capitals. Numerous policies are seen to stem from this in the eyes of western labour process writers.[1] Exploitation of workers by capital prevents work from being the expression of a human need; coercion of labour by management is ensured by depriving workers of control—'scientific management' and automation lead to deskilling, to dependency on management, to redundancies and a pool of surplus labour which enfeebles the political resistance of workers.

This kind of approach cannot be applied without considerable modification to socialist states. It is not appropriate here to explain the Soviet economic system[2] but some of the major distinctions from market capitalism may be noted. The competition of capitals is replaced by administrative direction of accumulation; wholesale and consumer prices are fixed by planning organs. Output and product mix is not determined by market conditions and demand but by an administratively assigned economic plan. From the point of view of the enterprise, the output plan is the main indicator of success. There is a quasi-labour market in which the price of labour may respond to shortages within fairly strict wage differentials laid down by the planners and the total wage fund is given to a production enterprise. There is little incentive to reduce labour costs or the number of workers employed; on the contrary, the enterprise's interest is served by the inflation of the wage fund. In this context, the quasi-labour market operates at the industry and enterprise level. Full employment and the absence of administrative restrictions on mobility between jobs give rise to labour mobility between enterprises. To maintain a large and reliable workforce, enterprises seek to reward their employees with better facilities to earn wages and provide payments in kind. This gives rise to the differentiation of conditions and opportunities not as under capitalism on the basis of a monopoly of skill or by bargaining position but by the industry and enterprise in which a person works.

Turning from the economic mechanism to the political and ideological spheres, there are also major dissimilarities between the USSR and the West. The government accepts responsibility for the provision of occupations for the population of working age and for a job thought appropriate for the worker. Marxist—Leninist ideology regards work not only as an instrumentality to provide income to meet needs, but as a human need in itself. A priority of policy and one which confers legitimacy on the leadership is to provide employment—albeit, if necessary, at the expense of efficiency. Trade unions operate on an industry-wide basis and their prime job is to fulfil the plan—to increase output—rather than to support some sectional interest. The Communist Party plays an administrative role unknown to political parties in western societies: it functions not only to integrate the worker but also seeks to stimulate the efficiency of management and the productivity of the employee.

It will be shown in the chapters that follow that the Soviet economy is one of full employment and labour shortage. This affects the labour process by strengthening the position of labour *vis-à-vis* management, and weakening the 'control' of management. It leads to a 'slack' labour regime, with infractions of labour discipline such as absenteeism and low effort. In order to improve efficiency and labour productivity, the economic planners and management have to devise new and different methods of labour motivation. These involve collective financial incentive schemes, the use of moral stimulation, the development of a collective consciousness on the part of the workforce, and greater reliance on administrative control. A dilemma facing the Soviet economic and political leadership is whether it can increase efficiency in general and labour productivity in particular within the confines of a full-employment economy.

The approach taken in this book departs from the labour process paradigm associated with the followers of Braverman. First, it takes into account the dominant ideology defining the values which work and non-work have for the dominant classes and groups. Since the time of the Reformation, it has been widely held that work is a major component in the ethic of capitalism. Work, however, in its modern form of paid employment is an instrumentality, it is a means to the achievement of income. This, in turn, is seen to provide satisfaction in terms of standard of living or status by occupation. While it is true that some commentators see paid labour as being psychologically and socially desirable, in the West policy-makers tend to give priority to the provision of income as a substitute for work for those who are voluntarily (e.g. the sick, young and old people, much domestic labour) or involuntarily 'unemployed' (i.e. those actively 'seeking paid labour' but unable to get it). It is hypothesized in this study that policy-makers in socialist states have a different attitude to the use of labour. Many western Marxists regard paid labour as alienating and seek to transcend it under socialism by the substitution of leisure[3] for work. The writings of Marx and Lenin will be cited to show that they regarded labour as being part of human liberation. This element of Marxism, it is argued, provides an ideological environment which conditions policy-makers to give priority to providing employment (rather than income) in Soviet society.

Secondly, labour history has its own particular dimension which shapes popular aspirations to work of workers and non-workers. Historically, Soviet industrialization has placed great store on mobilizing labour as an econonic resource; hence the value of work could be interpreted as an effect of the economic system in its legitimation of wage labour. It might therefore be regarded not as a fundamental value in Marxism, but as an instrumentality (similar to the 'Protestant work ethic') to induce people to accept a system of paid labour. The work culture of Tsarist Russia, shaped by the relatively short working year of the traditional peasant and inherited by Soviet power, has to be taken into account.

Thirdly, I consider that prominence has to be given to the political and economic system based on public ownership of property and which accepts responsibility for the level of economic activity, including investment and employment. In the absence of a market, administrative politics in the USSR dominate economics, and administrative solutions have to be found for economic problems. One must attempt to discover the forces which drive a socialist economy. Under the present conditions of Soviet planning, industrial enterprises are not subject to the constraint of a market, they are not threatened by bankruptcy or takeover. They seek to maximize output, and wage cost is relatively unimportant. One must consider whether a full-employment economy is simply the result of intentional decisions by the government or whether the operation of the economic mechanism creates a surplus of jobs in relation to the labour supply. There are obvious economic inefficiencies involved in a low-wage/high-employment economy: we shall investigate the extent to which *under* employment and low productivity are systemic properties of Soviet planning and the scope for improvement.

The book describes the context of the labour process and attempts to locate various theoretical approaches in an empirical context. The book has the following plan. In the first chapter, I consider the nature of the dominant value system of Marxism—Leninism as it has developed in the Soviet Union with respect to labour and employment. In Chapter 2, I outline the evolution of a full-employment labour economy in the Soviet Union and the extent to which one may say that 'full employment' has been achieved. Next I consider the ways that the labour force is allocated to jobs and the mobility of labour. Various forms of unemployment are analysed in Chapter 4 including 'frictional' movements due to turnover and structural unemployment as found in certain geographical regions. In Chapter 5 our concern is with labour productivity and administrative measures to improve it. In Chapter 6 we turn to consider the under-utilization of labour and the phenomenon of 'labour shortage' and the effects of technological change with respect to redundancy or what I have termed 'displacement' (*vysvobozhdenie*). In Chapter 7 some conclusions are made concerning the Soviet labour market. Next we examine the 'brigade' system of work organization devised to increase the efficient use of labour. Finally, I attempt to generalize about the labour market, full employment and a shortage economy by locating labour in a system of societal exchanges. These are: the resource mobilization system, the political support system, the loyalty solidarity commitment system, the labour consumption market system, the allocative standard system and the authority legitimation system. While these systems are common to all societies, the Soviet one does not function in the same way as under capitalism. Its peculiarities and interests promoting full employment are described in the last chapter.

## REFERENCES

1. The best known is H. Braverman, *Labor and Monopoly Capitalism*, (New York: Monthly Review Press, 1974). Other influential books are: C.R. Littler, *The Development of the Labour Process in Capitalist Societies* (London: Heinemann, 1982) D.M. Gordon, R.Edwards and M. Reich, *Segmented Work, Divided Workers* (Cambridge: Cambridge University Press, 1982).

2. See David Lane, *Soviet Economy and Society* (Oxford: Blackwell, 1985), Chs 1−3; A. Nove, *The Soviet Economic System* (London: Allen and Unwin, 1977).
3. For example, G.A. Cohen, *Karl Marx's Theory of History*, 1978, (Oxford: University Press), Chapter II.

# 1 Soviet Marxism and the Ending of Mass Unemployment

## WORK AND EMPLOYMENT IN SOVIET IDEOLOGY

In their approach to the labour process, the leaders of the USSR have been influenced in their policy and thinking by Marxist assumptions. For Marx, the maintenance and reproduction of material life is the prime human need. In a well-known passage in *The German Ideology*, Marx writes: 'The first historical act is . . . the production of material life itself. This is indeed . . . a fundamental condition of all history, which today, as thousands of years ago, must be accomplished every day and every hour merely in order to sustain human life.'[1]

In Marxist thought it is labour that creates value, i.e. it is the labour power that is embodied in a good or service that gives it social value. The labour theory of value is the linch-pin holding together work, production and output. Use-values are produced by conscious or purposeful human activity: such activity may be defined as work. The notion of work not only connotes physical or mental activity but also social relationships which are formed in the process of working. Work has two social aspects. First, it fulfils a social need on the part of the worker—it uses mankind's creative power. Expending such effort is man's 'life-activity'.[2] What distinguishes the human race from other species is the ability to transform nature to a world of its own making. The second aspect of such activity is that the goods and services produced are consumed. Material and spiritual human needs are met through the consumption of goods and services. Production and consumption are both aspects of the fulfilment of needs in the Marxist conception of human beings.

7

In Marxist theory, the kind of activity or work that characterizes a society (and the requisite structure of needs) is dependent on a given mode of production. The labour process in pre-capitalist societies was linked to the direct satisfaction of needs; the typical peasant laboured to fulfil his or her material and spiritual wants, and to pay taxes. Employment and unemployment are concepts which only have meaning in a society which has a market for labour. In peasant societies the division of labour activity into employment and unemployment does not occur. There is no wage labour. There is no sharp demarcation between work and leisure. The social relations engendered by work focus on family activity. If the harvest fails, the peasant starves, but he or she is not unemployed. If the family increases in size, all take part in tilling the soil, reaping the harvest and consuming the produce: all are absorbed in the social relationships of the domestic economy. If there are too many mouths to feed, some go hungry, but they are not unemployed. The growth of the division of labour, of paid labour and the employment of workers, gives rise to a different constellation of needs: production and consumption are differentiated. In the expansion of labour activity through a market system men and women need jobs or employment, they become wage labour.

While human activity and work fulfil human needs, the Marxist notion of class structure modifies the ways that work is organized and labour is performed. Work as fulfilment of human needs, it is argued by many Marxists, is vitiated, even precluded by the capitalist class structure. The division of societies into classes gives rise to a dominant and an exploited class. The significance of this division is that the dominant class, as such, does not participate in labour activity, though the dominant class and its agents shape the social relationships in which work takes place. While the consumption needs of members of the dominant class are met, they do not make any contribution to fulfilling human needs. Class relations also have their impact on the activity and labour of the exploited class. Exploitation means that the workers' exchange with nature is not an expression of their will but is determined by the domination of the ruling class. The social relations in which paid work takes place are based on exploitation and involve conflict. Under capitalism, much (not all) work is instrumental, it is organized by the capitalist class for the realization of exchange-values and for the extraction of surplus though in the process use-value is produced.[3] Under such conditions the fulfilment of the workers' needs, it is argued, is made impossible. The worker becomes *alienated*.

## ALIENATION OR FULFILMENT IN EMPLOYMENT?

In the late 1960s and 1970s in western countries, alienation was the primary focus of concern of Marxists. Alienation is one of the most ambiguous words used in the social sciences. One may distinguish between three meanings of the term. First, alienation is used in a very general sense to describe a lack of correspondence between people (as individuals or groups) and society; it depicts a state of malaise in social relationships involving feelings of isolation, powerlessness, self-estrangement and normlessness. Secondly, Marxist writers particularly have focused on control of the product of labour. As ownership of the means of production is vested with the capitalist class, the worker's product is alien to him and, in a societal perspective, there arises a disjunction between production (for profit) and human needs. This approach sees the primary source of alienation (both at work and in society) to lie in ownership relationships. Thirdly, many writers (Marxist and non-Marxist) have found the essence of alienation to lie in the modern process of production; for this school, the nature of and context in which work is performed are alienative.

The thrust of most recent western scholarship has been on the third approach and has been inspired by Marx's *Economic and Philosophical Manuscripts*. Such writers have emphasized the fact that large-scale mass-production process manufacture leads to the fragmentation of production and to the extreme division of labour. The repetitiveness of jobs in mass production, the deskilling of manual and non-manual work, and the increasing domination of management over workers have led Marxists to deny that such employment fulfils human needs. Such critics are agreed that rather than developing a person's potential powers, 'capitalist labor consumes these powers without replenishing them, burns them up as if they were a fuel, and leaves the individual worker that much poorer. The qualities that mark him as a human being become progressively diminished.'[4] Writers such as Braverman[5] emphasize the deskilling process involved with the advance of capitalism. An individual becomes 'a living appendage of the machine'.[6]

It would be mistaken, however, to regard work, even under capitalism, as alien to people's needs. Needs are relative to the development of society and are socially defined. Under conditions of modern capitalism, wage labour is a means to meet the necessities of life: it is an instrumentality to fulfil the prime needs of reproduction (food, shelter). It is also valued in itself. To be gainfully occupied or employed is a mark of social recognition of one's contribution to society. The dominant class legitimates itself by claiming to contribute to wealth-creation—profit is a reward for risk-taking, and even Royalty performs the ceremonial aspect of government and is claimed to contribute to the 'tension-management function' of society. For Marxists, a distinction here is between the parasitical class which lives off labour and the productive class which creates value.

This line of reasoning, which posits employment as a major dynamic of modern society, has been questioned in recent years. Writers such as Claus Offe[7] have argued that in advanced western societies, work and employment no longer have such an important role. Following sociologists such as Dahrendorf and Bell, Offe argues that labour and wage dependency no longer play a major role as the focus of collective concern.[8] In their stead, as organizing principles, Offe suggests concepts such as 'way of life', post-industrial society, and the home.[9] Socialist writers, such as Gorz and Willis, have also opposed the oppressive ideology of work under capitalism and called for the positive use of free time.[10]

In the 1980s, the advent of high levels of unemployment in the West has led to a different emphasis on work and employment. The stress on the 'alienative' character of work current in the 1960s has been put to one side and replaced by a concern for the 'right to work'. There has developed a recognition of the severe deprivation which ensues if work is denied to a person and has eclipsed the writings of Bell and Offe and led to a reappraisal of employment. Contemporary writers analyse work in four dimensions: for the individual—the provision of income, the 'social recognition' of the worth of the employed person and his or her social status: an activity to occupy and structure the day; an environment in which social conviviality outside the family may be enjoyed; finally, work results in the provision of goods and services which other people may enjoy.[11] The moral and social values engendered by capitalism make work—and especially an occupation and employment—a human need. Unemployment is not only a potential cost to the economy in that labour is underutilized, but it is a cost to the unemployed individual and to society. Employment is the main means by which national income is distributed. The burden of unemployment is socially differentiated, the poorest groups with no or little capital bear the brunt of the costs and politically it may be socially divisive and destabilizing.

What is true about the critique of Dahrendorf, Bell and Offe is that, as incomes and consumption pass certain thresholds, the marginal utility of money falls. The 'motivation' effect of additional money has declined for social groups who have sought satisfaction outside the work role. Just where these consumption thresholds are located is a controversial matter and it seems likely that middle-class strata (earning, say, more than double the average wage) will have lower motivation for extra income than lower income groups. Financial incentives also vary between societies, being greater in market-type societies such as the USA and lower in welfare states such as pre-Thatcherite Britain. The system of pecuniary rewards is dominant in the contemporary United States, here retirement in old age may be considered as the postponed gratification of the earned efforts of labour. In welfare states, such as the USSR, security in old age and automatic pensions give rise to a need for greater satisfaction in work. However, the psychological effect of a *decrease* in income, as with unemployment, gives rise to dissatisfaction for all social groups in all societies.[12] In a nutshell, rises in money income do not make all people more satisfied but reductions in money income invariably lead to increases in frustration and dissatisfaction.

## WORK UNDER SOCIALISM

Marxists in socialist states have always adopted a positive attitude towards the need for people to work. With regard to labour, the ideology of Soviet Marxism may be called the 'Protestant ethic of socialism'.[13] Lenin's analysis of work recognizes its primacy for the building of socialist society. For Lenin, work was not only the fulfilment of man's 'species being' but was bound up with the development of productive forces. Capitalism (and its form of labour) was progressive compared with feudal society. Lenin stressed the economic and social advance of wage labour over serfdom. As he put it in *The Development of Capitalism in Russia*, 'Compared with the labour of the dependent or bonded peasant, the labour of the hired worker is a progressive phenomenon in all the branches of the economy.'[14]

Unlike advanced capitalist countries, where wage labour was taken for granted, the Soviet state set about creating conditions for the growth of a class of wage-labourers. In *The Immediate Tasks of Soviet Power*, Lenin considered that a major task of the Soviet government was 'to teach the people how to work'.[15] Large-scale factory production, then characteristic of capitalism, was regarded as being capable of fulfilling a higher level of human needs than artisan labour. The most advanced forms of labour organization had to be copied from the West. For Lenin, Taylorism (or scientific management) was 'the last word of capitalism' and 'its greatest scientific achievements [lie] in the field of analysing mechanical motions during work, in the elimination of superfluous and awkward motions, in the working out of correct methods of work, and in the introduction of the best system of accounting and control, etc'.[16] Taylorism has affinities with Leninism in that it subscribes to 'scientific principles' and hierarchical forms of organization and control. They share common values in seeking to improve efficiency through the rational organization of the work process and increasing the tempo of work. Taylorism has been adapted to the process of work in the USSR with important amendments.

In creating the conditions of a socialist attitude towards work, the Soviet political leadership was confronted not by workers who had become alienated by capitalist conditions of labour but by peasants used to the rhythm of traditional agricultural production and untouched by the protestant reformation. The cultural background to the Soviet industrialization process is a conditioning factor of immense importance. The 'Protestant ethic', contingent on the rise of capitalism in Western Europe, did not provide an analogous value-system on which the Soviet leaders could build. Hence Stalinism as an ideology had elements of the provision of a motivating work ethic. In the early period of Soviet power the Soviet leadership encouraged full employment primarily to bring about economic advance—to create the material basis of communism. Also a new type of labour process under socialism was thought to be possible. Work as salvation is a common element in the Puritan's and Stalin's world-view. 'Alienation' played little part in Soviet Marxist philosophy during the period before the death of Stalin. The major disjunction between producers and society was analysed in terms of the second approach to alienation defined above (p.9)—the separation of the product of labour from its maker.

During the 1950s even the discussion of the *Economic and Philosophical Manuscripts* did not lead to alienation being considered to lie in the work process.[17] The political conditions present in the USSR necessary for the abolition of alienation as a structural condition were held to be the public ownership of the means of production, the demise of the capitalist class, and the replacement of production for the market by planning (i.e. the creation of use instead of exchange values).

Under these conditions labour power (*rabochaya sila*) is not a commodity which is bought and sold under conditions of the competition of capitals. There is, however, a quasi-market for labour. Ownership is vested in the state which, representing the interests of society, manages the employment of labour through the planning organs. As a contemporary Soviet writer, Sorokina, has expressed it, in the USSR labour power has a dual character: it is the property of society, as the state is the major employer, and it is the property of the worker, who is paid wages for his work.[18] 'Material incentives' are given to compensate workers for effort and quality of labour. The market, however, is restricted; wages are not responsive to the direct interaction of supply and demand, and combinations of workers are not allowed to bargain for sectional interests. Differentials (at least until the advent of Gorbachev) are relatively modest. Social regulation through state planning of wage-scales coexists with individual negotiations between worker and management.

The emphasis on the duty to labour which has been made explicit in The Fundamental Laws or Constitutions of the Russian

Republic and of the USSR should be interpreted with this in mind. In distinction from capitalist states, the Constitutions have always defined work as a right and duty of citizens: the state therefore has an obligation to provide employment. In the twentieth century, western capitalist governments put their policy emphasis on consumption rather than work. Unemployment is mitigated by the provision of a minimum standard of living through unemployment or social welfare benefit. Full employment in socialist states is a vindication of the Marxist notion that labour is the source of value and that idleness is degenerate. It is also recognition that industrial development requires a different work ethic from the traditional peasant one.

The Bolsheviks in 1918 were conscious that they should define the essence of the socialist system. As Sverdlov put it: 'Just as in the days of the French bourgeois revolution . . . there was proclaimed a Declaration of Rights of Man and of the Citizen . . . so today our Russian Socialist Revolution should likewise make its declaration . . .'[19] The Declaration abolished private ownership of the means of production, ratified workers' control and, what is of our primary concern, 'in order to do away with the parasitic classes of society and [to] organize the economic life of the country, universal labour duty is introduced'. The first Constitution of the RSFSR, published on 3 July 1918, reiterated the obligation of all citizens to work, and proclaimed the freedom of citizens from economic exploitation. Constitutional rights were restricted to those who laboured, symbolically indicating the importance of labour in the new Republic. In the early years of the Revolution, labour (like military service) was an obligation—a *povinnost'* as it was described in the 1918 Constitution. Similar sentiments have been expressed in the 1936 and 1977 Constitutions. In 1936 it was declared that: 'Work in the USSR is a duty, a matter of honour for every able-bodied citizen—He who does not work shall not eat'. Citizens had the right to work and to 'guaranteed employment'. However, work was now regarded as a duty (*obyazannost'*) and was defined as such in these constitutions.[20]

In the development of the USSR up to around 1956, work was regarded as an essential component of building socialism. The emphasis was not on the content or form of labour so much as the socio-political necessity of work. Hence Marxism—Leninism, as it developed under Stalin in the USSR, became an ideology which was used to develop work attitudes necessary for industrial growth. These attitudes were transmitted to the peasantry, and to the newly arrived townspeople. Such ideological precepts were accompanied by many massive campaigns glorifying the factory and its work in general which sought to create a positive attitude to labour in an urban setting.

## CHANGING CONCEPTIONS OF WORK

The declarations of the 1936 and 1977 Constitutions of the USSR have witnessed a change in emphasis concerning the role of work. The earlier constitutional claims (and policy which derived from them) emphasized the social necessity of work in order to provide the necessities of life; work was a duty to create the conditions of the first stage of the communist mode of production. Work was seen as a human necessity and was counterposed to the idleness of a parasitical ruling class. In the 1977 Constitution (Article 60), the citizen is given a right to socially useful activity chosen by him or her; in practice, the choice of a trade or profession. This recognition signals a development in the Soviet conception of work under 'mature socialism'. Individual satisfaction in, and with, work is now of greater importance to policy-makers. As the late Leonid Brezhnev put it: 'Socialism as a social structure has within it great possibilities for the rational and human use of society's main productive force—human labour.'[21] Under socialism work should become 'a need and a pleasure'.[22] It is assumed that people should have work in keeping with their capabilities, education and professional training. In general, people are not directed to work in any particular geographical area, or in any branch or enterprise of the economy, and people cannot be sacked without the agreement of the local trade union or without following the due process of law.[23]

In 1984, Chernenko reiterated: 'the principle of socialism, which is sacred to us, is from each according to his ability, to each according to his work. This is the foundation of the social justice that our working class and our people, for the first time in history, have converted from dreams into living reality.'[24] In his speech to the Party Congress on 25 February 1986, Gorbachev also emphasized the fact that the essence of social justice of the Soviet system is 'from each according to his abilities, to each according to his work'.[25] The notion that people have a right and a duty to work is one of the most firmly bedded, 'taken for granted' assumptions made by citizens and policy-makers in the USSR. Aganbegyan echoes many people's sentiments when he says, 'I have always considered that the chief joy of life and the one that gives it meaning is work'.[26] In distinction from capitalist society, Kosalapov (then editor of *Kommunist*) described socialist society as a 'working society' not a 'consumer society' and S. Ivanov, writing in *Pravda* in March 1983, makes explicit that one of 'the fundamental duties of the government is to provide work for every citizen'.[27] The economic system, argues Ivanov, operates in such a way as to provide work—and a choice of work. The universality (*vseobshchnost'*) of labour distinguishes socialism from capitalism. These views are given wide publicity in the Soviet Union. For instance, a broadcast on Moscow Radio on 28 January 1985 contrasted 'USSR Employment with USA Unemployment'. Reporting on the USSR Central Statistical Agency's report of economic achievements for 1984 which stated that 'complete employment of the workforce was ensured in the country . . . [and] has become a way of life', it was concluded that: 'Complete employment under socialism and growing unemployment in capitalist countries are characteristic features of different social systems . . .'[28]

The Soviet ideology of labour provides greater constraints on the political leadership than is found under capitalism: not only is there an expectation that paid work will be provided for all but that such work is required to be 'satisfying'. Economic reformers and planners make explicit the goal of the provision of employment: 'In the system of socialist production relations, guaranteeing able-bodied people jobs is one of the most important independent tasks of the planned development of social production . . .'[29] E.R. Sarukhanov, in an authoritative review of labour under socialism, points out that 'socialism creates the possibility for the full use of the workforce because the development of social production is made subordinate to the task of satisfying the growing material and cultural demands of the members of society. . . . Socialist reproduction is an unlimited process, because in socialist society there is no limit to the growth of requirement for people. . . .

Labour is a need—a means of man's development, of realising his capabilities . . .'[30] As Gorbachev emphasized in his speech commemorating the 150th anniversary of Lenin's birth:

For the first time in history, the working man has become the master of his country, the maker of his own destiny. The guaranteed right to work and its remuneration, society's care for man from his birth to old age, the wide access to culture, the respect for the individual's dignity and rights, the steady expansion of the working people's participation in management—all these are eternal values and inseparable features of the socialist way of life. Herein lies the most important source of political stability, social optimism and confidence in the future.[31]

To abrogate the right to, and provisions of, employment would seriously undermine the ideology and legitimacy of the ruling groups in the USSR. In his speech to the 27th Party Congress, Ligachev stressed that: 'Socialism cannot allow and will not allow large groups of working people—and the count may well be in millions—to find themselves redundant in society as a result of scientific and technical progress, not prepared for work in the new conditions . . .'[32]

There are three functions to having an occupation (*zanyatost'*): (i) economic (promoting economic growth): (ii) income (participation in and creation of national income); and (iii) social (the realization of social needs through labour).[33] In framing social policy, the social, psychological and physiological aspects of employment are given greater emphasis than in capitalist societies.[34]

## PROBLEMS OF MOTIVATION FOR WORK

Offe and other critics of the work process under contemporary capitalism have pointed to the developing crisis of 'exchange-rationality' when market conditions do not act as 'effective and reliable' spurs to individual action.[35] A socialist society, however, anticipates this condition by stressing more the collective necessity (rather than merely the individual instrumentality) for work activity. The Soviet dictum of 'giving according to one's ability and receiving according to one's work' poses the contradiction between individuals' expressive needs for work and the instrumental returns from work. Needs cannot be met solely through an increase in pay. Zaslavskaya has pointed out that wage incentives are proving to be less effective: 'managers claim in recent years . . . that many workers have no serious interest in extra money.'[36] The increased material well-being of the country reduces the economic need to work intensively. She argues that workers' effort is not recompensed properly. The need to calculate proper norms and incentive payment has been taken up by the Gorbachev leadership.[37]

The other side of the contradiction, however, has to do with the development of individuals' interest in work—their possibilities of giving according to their abilities. Zaslavskaya points out that greater independence and initiative is necessary for working people to express their creativity.[38] The conditions of labour, access to education and social services, the allocation to work 'according to people's abilities' (rather than by privileged position), the creation of a management structure enabling workers to work efficiently, are also important considerations in a socialist system.[39] The provision of services to the non-working population (children, pensioners, and other groups such as the disabled) also has to be ensured to fulfil socialist criteria of social justice. If Habermas and Offe are correct in pointing to the limitations of 'market incentives' (including the reserve army of unemployed) as a motivating force for work, then orthodox Soviet economists and sociologists have a case in seeking to improve motivation for work outside the market nexus. A current danger in Soviet policy is to copy western market-type forms of incentives to the extent of undermining a socialist pattern of organization.

The low-pay/full-employment economy characteristic of the USSR creates its own problems. It is often argued that the desire for 'satisfying' work, the absence of a 'reserve army' of unemployed and ineffective wage incentives lead to a poorly motivated workforce and this in turn undermines another tenet in the Soviet concept of building socialism—the steady rise in material welfare. While such factors undoubtedly make increases in labour productivity difficult to obtain, one should not put all the fault on the policy of full employment: countries experiencing unemployment also have difficulties in raising labour productivity and, as noted above, in securing motivation for work. Even more fundamentally, the market as an institution has been faulted by some western commentators as a means to satisfy human wants.[40] (See discussion below, p.218.)

There is a tension in Soviet society between the economic requirements of the economy and the aspirations of many people. The provision of paid employment is a traditional social goal (both for the individual and the society of which he or she is part) and has to be reconciled with the aspirations for different types of work expressed by individuals. Soviet policy-makers therefore are constrained by policy objectives which have not been adopted by governments under capitalism: (a) the provision of employment for all the population, and (b) the requirement to give opportunities to people to find satisfaction in such work.

Other contradictions occur over the 'rational' use of labour (*ratsional'naya zanyatost'*) and people's individual preferences. The Soviet labour specialist, Kostakov, has pointed out that the needs of the population may not coincide with the needs of production; the necessity of activity in the workplace is not the same as human need under communism. In order to reconcile individual interests with production ones, differentials in respect of wages, pensions and holidays are established. Another example of a contradiction is the need of women to participate in employment to enhance their personal development and society's need for women to replenish the population stock.[41] (Working women have fewer children and some commentators, recognizing 'women's labour in housework' and in child-raising, have advocated a reduction in the level of women's employment.)[42] Conflicts of social and individual interests also occur over redundancies; this topic will be taken up later.

Under the conditions of socialist states we must distinguish between different types of alienation and disenchantment with work. Prior to the 1960s Soviet writers were mainly concerned with the structurally-induced types of disjunction under capitalism between the labourer and his product involving the production of exchange rather than use-values. In more recent times attention has focused on a type of dissatisfaction occurring when individual workers are unhappy with the conditions of their labour and with the jobs that they are required to do under conditions of modern technology. In this latter sense, 'alienation' has been developed by western writers such as Seeman and Blauner[43] (the third sense defined above, p.9). Such writers shift the emphasis away from structural factors associated with a mode of production, to the individual's perceptions of his or her labour which are shaped by the technology of modern production. 'In modern industrial employment, control, purpose, social integration and self-involvement are all problematic.'[44]

Many Soviet studies have pointed to the rise of such attitudes in the labour process in the USSR.[45] The expansion of consumerism in the USSR has led to a greater 'instrumentality' in the attitudes of workers towards work, and the rising levels of education have led to a growth in desire for interest and self-satisfaction in work.[46] The greater use of the market, of material incentives and of a consumerist mentality has led to more 'instrumentalism' in the attitudes of workers towards work. Despite condemnation of 'consumerism', the Leningrad study of young workers found that 'some young people are undergoing a so-called instrumentalization of their attitude towards work, that is, the basic values of labour are shifting from the sphere of its content to the area of working conditions and remuneration.'[47]

Soviet sociologists and other commentators have advocated greater participation in management in the enterprise and various schemes of team-work assembly to overcome monotonous work.[48] Lenin's ideas of Taylorism and the importation of western methods of the work process (particularly mass-production assembly) have been somewhat updated by the advocacy of the more humane face of contemporary western procedures and the modernization, as it were, of brigade and team methods, and various other types of 'socialist emulation'. These are not only, as invariably interpreted in the West, ways to increase labour productivity but are intended to develop a moral tone appropriate to a socialist form of work behaviour. Indeed, some Soviet sociologists (particularly Yadov and Zdravomyslov) have been at pains to argue that increasing 'satisfaction' with work will not necessarily increase labour productivity. Similarly, recent Soviet discussions on the election of managers and an enhanced role to the labour collective are also indications of ways in which a more 'socialistic' labour process may be created.[49] The imbalance between people's aspirations for jobs with the array of posts available is a problem which is to be resolved through the 'lowering of ambition' and a different form of school socialization—particularly the provision of vocational education.

In considering these disjunctions between aspirations for work and the kinds of jobs available, one must bear in mind that (unlike under capitalism) the dominant ideology requires not only that work for all has to be provided but that this work should give satisfaction to the worker. The relatively high proportion of real income derived from 'social consumption' (highly subsidized housing, travel, health, education, leisure) makes the use of material incentives less potent as an incentive to labour than under capitalism. There are therefore structurally-induced expectations which make the fit between aspiration and reality more difficult to achieve than in the West. Getting the 'right attitude' towards work is not just a way of increasing labour productivity but has 'a direct relationship to the moral state of the entire people, the entire society'.[50]

A major difference between socialist states and capitalist ones is that in the former there is less differentiation between 'the individual realm of work'[51] and the collectivized provision of welfare. The Soviet factory is the hub of the distribution of welfare benefits; leisure provision, recreation and housing are closely linked to the enterprise through the trade union and ancillary organisations.[52] This gives the workplace a greater role in the life of the individual than it does in the West. The high effective labour participation rate also precludes the development of counter-cultures, as in the West, where non-work and unemployment may be normal and legitimate. Measures initiated by Andropov and continued by Gorbachev against 'parasitism' (see below p.55) have to be seen against the backcloth of a value system emphasizing the social utility of labour.

REFERENCES

1. *The German Ideology* reprinted in T. B. Bottomore and M. Rubel, *Karl Marx: Selected Writings in Sociology and Social History* (London: Penguin, 1963), p. 75. Work is not only a fundamental category in Marxist approaches but is also a major component in the classic bourgeois sociologists' concept of an acquisitive society, such as found in Weber and Durkheim.
2. *Economic and Political Manuscripts, of 1844* (Moscow, 1959), p. 75.
3. See *Capital*, 'The Labour Process and the Process of Producing Surplus-Value', vol. 1 (Moscow: FLPM,1958), p. 177.

4. B. Ollman, *Alienation: Marx's Conception of Man in Capitalist Society* (Cambridge: Cambridge University Press, 1976), p.137.
5. *Labor and Monopoly Capitalism* (New York: Monthly Review Press, 1974).
6. *Capital*, vol.1, p. 484.
7. Claus Offe, 'Arbeit als sotsiologische schlusselkategorie', in *Krise der Arbeitsgesellschaft?* (Frankfurt, 1983).
8. Ibid., pp. 45, 50.
9. Ibid., p. 59.
10. A. Gorz, *Paths to Paradise: On the Liberation from Work* (London: Pluto Press, 1985); Paul Willis, *Learning to Labour* (Farnborough: Saxon House, 1977), p. 102.
11. The various functions of employment are discussed in M. Jahoda, *Employment and Unemployment: A Social-Psychological Analysis* (Cambridge University Press, 1982); C. Fraser, 'The Social Psychology of Unemployment', in M. Jeeves (ed.), *Psychology Survey*, no. 3 (London: Allen and Unwin, 1981). A. K. Sen, *Employment, Technology and Development* (Oxford: Oxford University Press, 1975). M. Ellman, 'Full Employment—Lessons from State Socialism', *De Economist*, 127, N.4, 1979. Soviet views will be discussed below.
12. Offe, *op.cit.*, p. 53.
13. D.Lane, 'Leninism as an Ideology of Soviet Development', in E. de Kadt and G. Williams (eds), *Sociology and Development* (London, Tavistock, 1974).
14. *Collected Works* (Moscow, 1960–70), vol. 3, p. 598.
15. Ibid., vol. 27, p. 259.
16. Ibid.
17. See the useful discussion of Soviet views by M. Yanowitch, 'Alienation and the Young Marx in Soviet Thought', *Slavic Review*, no. 1 (1967).
18. I.F. Sorokina, *Osobennosti vosproizvodstva rabochey sily v usloviyakh razvitogo sotsializma* (1979), p. 25.
19. 'The Opening of the Constituent Assembly' (18 January 1918). Report in James Bunyan and H.H. Fisher, *The Bolshevik Revolution 1917–18. Documents and Materials* (California: Stanford University Press, 1934), p. 372.
20. I am indebted to Steve Wheatcroft for pointing out this distinction between the usage in the 1918 and 1936 Constitution.
21. L.I. Brezhnev, *Leninskim kursom* (Moscow, 1982), vol. 9, p. 310.
22. *Leninskim kursom*, (Moscow, 1970), vol. 2, p. 270.
23. S. Ivanov, 'Pravo na trud i obyazannost' trudit'sya', *Pravda*, 18 March 1983, p. 2.
24. K.U. Chernenko, *Pravda*, 6 October, 1984. Translated in *CDSP*, vol. 36, no. 40 (31 October 1984), p. 5.
25. As transcribed in BBC *Summary of World Broadcasts* (SU/8193/C/18), 26 February 1986.
26. A. Aganbegyan, 'Sdelay vse, chto mozhesh', *Trud*, 17 October 1981.
27. R.I. Kosalapov, in *Pravda*, 4 March 1983; and Ivanov, 'Pravo na trud i obyazannost' trudit'sya', *Pravda*, 18 March 1983, p. 2.

28. B. Prokhorov, Moscow Radio, 28 January 1985. Reported in *USSR International Affairs*, United States and Canada, 29 January 1985.
29. A. Kotlyar, 'Polnaya zanyatost' i sbalansirovannost' faktorov sotsialisticheskogo proizvodstva', *Voprosy ekonomiki*, no. 7 (1983), p. 106. All Soviet economists and planners echo such sentiments: T. Sarkisyants, 'Pravo na trud: podlinnoe i mnimoe', *Trud*, 30 September 1982. The author emphasizes the constitutional provision for work, its role in Marxist thought and the success of the USSR in providing employment, in contrast to the USA.
30. E.R. Sarukhanov, in *Sotsial'no-ekonomicheskie problemy upravleniya rabochey siloy pri sotsializme* (Leningrad, 1981), p. 62.
31. M.Gorbachev, *Pravda*, 23 April 1985.
32. Speech to 27th Party Congress, *Pravda*, 26 February. (Reported in BBC *Summary of World Broadcasts*, SU/8196/C, p. 3)
33. M.I. Dolishni, *Formirovanie i ispol'zovanie trudovykh resursov*, (Moscow, 1978), p. 14.
34. Dolishni, p. 32 Yu. Lavrikov, S.M. Rusinov and V.I. Chumakov, *Integratsiya sotsialisticheskogo proizvodstva i upravlenie* (Moscow, 1976).
35. Offe, p. 55.
36. T.Zaslavskaya, *Sovetskaya Rossiya*, 7 January 1986, p. 1.
37. See below, Chapter 8.
38. Ibid.
39. T. Zaslavskaya, *Sovetskaya kultura*, 23 January 1986.
40. Robert E. Lane, 'Markets and the Satisfaction of Human Wants', *Journal of Economic Issues*, vol.12, no.4 (December 1978), pp. 799-827.
41. V.G. Kostakov, *Prognoz zanyatosti naseleniya* (Moscow, 1979), pp. 6-10.
42. A. Kolesnichenko, 'Trud, obschestvo, chelovek', *Pravda*, 19 May 1981, p. 2. Women now seek like men satisfaction in work. This is one of the findings of the replication of the Leningrad study, reported by Yadov in *Komsomol'skaya Pravda*, 9 February 1978.
43. M. Seeman, 'On the Meaning of Alienation', *American Sociological Review*, Vol. 24 (1959). R. Blauner, *Alienation and Freedom* (Chicago: Phoenix Books, 1967). Blauner's work has been well received in the USSR, see discussion in Yanowitch, p. 48.
44. Blauner, p. 15.
45. Particularly, A.G. Zdravomyslov *et al.*, *Man and His Work* (New York; IASP, 1967). On the increase of monotonous jobs, see discussion in *Znanie-sila*, no. 2. (1980). N.A. Aitov, *Sotsiologicheskie issledovaniya*, no. 3 (1979).
46. See N.F. Naumova, in V.I. Dobrynova (ed.), *Sovetski obraz zhizni segodniya i zavtra* (1976); V.A. Yadov and A.A. Kissel, *Sotsiologicheskie issledovaniya*, no. 1 (1974).
47. M. Levin, 'Molodezh' i trud', *EKO*, no. 8 (1983). Cited by E. Teague, *Labor Discipline and Legislation in the USSR: 1979–85* (Munich: RL Supplement 2/85), p. 7.
48. See A.G. Aganbegyan's account of 'Volvo-type' work teams and the importance of the 'social factor', 'Sdelay vse, chto mozhesh'. *Trud*, 17 October 1981. On Volvo, see also I.I Dakhno and M.N. Kapralova,

'Eksperiment 'Vol'vo' (iz Shvedskogo opyta)', *EKO* (1980) no. 4, pp. 172-84.
49. See Ya. S. Kapeliush, *Obshchestvennoe mnenie o vybornosti na proizvodstvo* (1969), translated in M. Yanowitch (ed.), *Soviet Work Attitudes* (New York, M.E. Sharpe, 1979), pp. 60-80. *Literaturnaya Gazeta*, 3 November 1976. O.I. Kosenko, in *Ekonomika i organizatsiya promyshlennogo proizvodstva*, no. 1 (1977), pp. 89-95. O.I. Kosenko, *Pravda*, 5 April (1983). On the changing expectations of young workers towards management, see V.A. Yadov, 'Molodezh' i trud: razmyshleniya sotsiologov i zhurnalista', *EKO* (1983), no. 8, pp. 117-25.
50. Zdravomyslov *et al.*, p. 146.
51. Offe, p. 54.
52. Enterprises vary in their ability to provide such services creating differences in the labour market. See below, chapter 4.

# 2 A Full-Employment Economy?

## THE EVOLUTION OF FULL EMPLOYMENT

In the period following the Revolution, the Soviet leadership was not only influenced by considerations concerning the building of 'communist man', but also by more pressing and immediate economic and political demands. In the early years of Soviet power, providing work (or reducing levels of unemployment) was not a priority.[1] It was not until 1930 or 1931 that one may say that mass unemployment came to an end in the USSR.[2] During the period of War Communism and the New Economic Policy, unemployment continued at levels comparable to those of Western European countries. The chief cause of unemployment was the movement of peasants to the town to seek work.[3] The draft of the first Five Year Plan, compiled in 1927, estimated that the unemployment level of 1.9 million of that year would rise to over 2.3 million in 1931–32.[4] The advent of the Five Year Plans, however, with their vast expansion programmes, led to an increase in employment opportunities not only in industry and building but also in the sphere of government services (e.g. health, education).

The Marxist ideology of work coincided with economic rationality. Soviet industrialization strategy was to maximize labour inputs, which were abundant and cheap whereas capital was scarce and expensive. Despite the growth of population of working age and the massive influx of peasants to the towns (1.6 million in 1928 and 2.63 million in 1930) the number of jobs increased to such an extent that mass unemployment was eliminated. The growth of the population of working age and the growth in the number of employed for the periods 1920–26,

1926–29, 1939–1959, 1959–1970, and 1970–1979 are shown in Figure 2.1. In the 1930s, a seven-hour day was introduced, labour was used 'around the clock' and the low-pay economy was instrumental in encouraging managers to maximize the recruitment of labour. Educational facilities and health services were expanded and these not only absorbed the unemployed but provided opportunities for the graduates of educational institutions. A massive increase in non-manual posts occurred providing work and opportunity for a middle class.

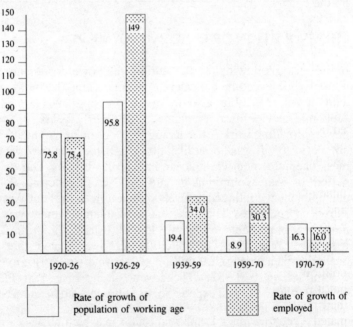

Rate of growth of population of working age

Rate of growth of employed

Source:   A. Kotlyar, 'Polnaya zanyatost' i sbalansirovannost' factorov sotsialisticheskogo proizvodstva', *Voprosy ekonomiki*, no. 7 (1983), p. 113.

*Figure 2.1: Growth of Population of Working Age and Growth of Employed Population*

The ending of *mass* unemployment, with its attendant low-pay economy, must be considered in the context of a developing society. The 'employed' population as a proportion of the able-bodied labour force was relatively low in the 1930s. A large share of the workforce was engaged in agriculture, either on individual plots or on collective farms, and there were administrative restrictions on their geographical and occupational mobility. Such groups of the population could not be considered to be 'employed' wage labour, and as such they were not part of the labour market. There was, as in many agricultural societies,'under employment' in the countryside in the sense that the peasants' time was either not usefully occupied with work or their marginal productivity was very low or even negative.

With the ending of mass unemployment, labour exchanges were closed and the matching of vacancies with labour demand took place mainly through a quasi-labour market. (The exchanges were reopened in 1967, see below pp.50−54). In the towns, workers were able to leave their jobs to work elsewhere: they were recruited by presenting themselves 'at the factory gate'. The government ended the payment of unemployment benefit from October 1930 and this encouraged mobility between jobs and areas and acted as a means to cajole the unemployed to work. The ending of mass unemployment helped to legitimate the Soviet government. It was, and still is, proclaimed as a success of Soviet power and considered to further the development of communist man. Since that time, it has become a 'sacred' element in Soviet policy.

It is mistaken to believe that ideology plays a constant role in political affairs. Ideology acts as a constraint on political leaders but it is within limits also capable of being adapted and suited to their political purposes. Marxism as an ideology of labour legitimated a regime under Lenin and Stalin in which all had a duty (*povinnost'*) to labour. The economic needs of Soviet Russia required not only a massive transfer of labour from village to town, but an ideology of work: Soviet Marxism provided it. The provision of full employment in contrast to the unemployment of capitalism became one of the Soviet Union's success stories. The leadership's claim to be building a 'socialist state' rested on the provision of employment for all. This in turn is a major constraint on economic policy. How far then is it true to say that the contemporary USSR provides full employment for the whole population?

## THE EMPLOYED LABOUR FORCE 1939 TO 1982

Before considering the actual rates of labour utilization and the extent to which different types of unemployment or underemployment continue, the definition of a number of relevant terms is necessary.

The *employed labour force* is usually understood to include persons above a specified age who are at work for pay (and in capitalist countries for profit) during a given period. This includes those who have a job but are temporarily absent for reasons of illness, injury, leave or industrial dispute. The self-employed are usually defined as 'employed' in the sense of being part of the economically active labour force, though from a social and occupational point of view (which does not concern us here) these two occupational statuses should not be confused. The *economically active population* includes members of the armed forces, but excludes unpaid domestic workers and full-time students.[5]

The term *unemployment*[6] is defined to include those people within a specified age range who are available for employment but whose work has been suspended or terminated, including those who have not had a job and are seeking employment. The essence of 'involuntary unemployment' is that the person must be of employable age, actively seeking work and unable to find it. There is also a minimum period of unsuccessful job search (usually three months, but often longer) which is necessary to qualify for the status of being 'unemployed' as far as the compilation of labour statistics in market economies is concerned. In the Soviet economy, unemployment statistics in this sense are not comprehensively collected.

Another distinction may be made in terms of *underemployment*. This has to do with the inadequacy of a person's employment, involving working involuntarily part of the time ('visible underemployment') or a 'misallocation of labour resources' such as underutilization of skill or low productivity ('invisible underemployment').[7] It is important to distinguish between underemployment (or overemployment) and unemployment as these situations are often confused and conflated. The *under*employed person (a) receives an income, (b) has an occupational status, and (c) has an activity to structure the day.

What is lacking, however, is (d) an effective contribution to production. The financial burden of the underemployed is borne by the employer and consumer. The social cost of being unemployed is borne largely by the unemployed person and welfare support as provided by the government (or in the West by charities). What is an inefficient labour policy for a firm or industry may not be so for society as a whole: taking account of social costs and political costs, it might be more beneficial to keep labour at work but underemployed than to have mass unemployment.

All studies of the Soviet labour force point to the fact that a very high proportion of the population is economically active. However, in comparative perspective, the legally sanctioned age of entry to paid labour is relatively high as a compulsory ten-year education (in some areas, eleven) gives a minimum age threshold of 17 years[8] and about 24 per cent of the population continues in full-time tertiary education to the age of 21 (or more).[9] The age of retirement is low—60 years for men and 55 years for women; and employees in certain industries (e.g. coalmining) are entitled to retire even earlier. Details about the exact proportion of the population in work, and the kind of work performed by people of various ages, have not been published by the Soviet government for the recent past. On the basis of the data available, however, one may make a number of estimates about the levels of employment.

*Table 2.1: Level of Employment for Social-Demographic Groups\**

|      | Youth (16−29) % | Middle-aged (30−49) % | Pre-pension age (50−55/60) % |
|------|------|------|------|
| 1959 | 78 | 80 | 70 |
| 1970 | 74 | 93 | 80 |
| 1979 | 76 | 96 | 84 |

\* Based on population census data.

*Source*: L. Chizhova, 'Kak luchshe ispol'zovat' trud razlichnykh sotsial'no-demograficheskikh grupp naseleniya', *Sotsialisticheski trud*, no. 8 (1984), p. 90.

Statistics on the labour force are published by the Central Statistical Administration in the annual statistical yearbook (*Narodnoe khozyaystvo SSSR*), these specify the number of persons employed in various industries and agricultural employment in terms of state farms (*sovkhozy*) and collective farms (*kolkhozy*). The censuses of the population (1959, 1970, 1979) define employment status (including pensioners in full-time work) and that of 1979 includes men and women occupied (as their main occupation) in private agricultural production. These official statistics have some deficiencies: the military and prison population are either ignored or included in other (non-specified) sources, part-time workers (such as children, students) and those working in the 'second economy' are excluded. People having more than one job may be counted twice in employment returns. Such deficiencies, of course, also apply to other countries' statistics. Table 2.1 shows employment levels on the basis of the census by age groups. These data show in summary form overall the high and rising participation rates. These figures, however, need to be further refined.

Table 2.2 shows data on various aspects of labour participation for various years from 1939 to 1982: the total population, that of 'working age', the full-time student population (over 17 years of age), the numbers of employed manual and non-manual workers, and those engaged in the 'social economy'[10] of collective farms. Study of the table brings out:

(a)   the growth, both relative and absolute since 1940, of the employed manuals and non-manuals (line 4),
(b)   the decline in the collective farm labour force (excluded here are those solely engaged on private plots) (line 5),
(c)   the increase of those in employment and study as a proportion of the population working age (line 6).

Compared to other countries, the USSR has a much larger economically active population. If one considers, as a crude statistic, the total number of economically active people, including collective farmers and those in private agriculture, divided by the total number of people in the economically active age groups (17−59 for men, 17−54 for women) one has a percentage in 1979 of 91.28 per cent. For the 16−59 and 16−54 cohorts the total is

Table 2.2: Labour Participation Rates in USSR 1939–82 (in millions)

| | | 1939 | 1959 | 1970 | 1975 | 1980 | 1982 |
|---|---|---|---|---|---|---|---|
| 1. | Total population | 190.678 | 208.827 | 241.720 | 253.261 | 264.5 | 268.8 |
| 2. | Population of 'working age' (16–59, 16–54) | | | | | | |
| | Official data (a) | 102.241 | 119.822 | 130.487 | 142.710 | 153.117§ | — |
| | US estimate (b) | — | — | (130.589) | (143.063) | 154.806 | 156.832 |
| 3. (a) | In compulsory education at day schools (over 15) (9–10 (11)$^{th}$ Classes). | (1940) 1.2 | (1960) 1.5 | 4.8 | 6.2 | 5.3 | 4.9 |
| (b) | Students in technical colleges (day courses) | (1940) 0.787 | (1960) 1.091 | 2.558 | 2.817 | 2.894 | 2.845 |
| (c) | Students in higher education (day courses) | (1940) .558 | (1960) 1.156 | 2.241 | 2.628 | 3.011 | 3.023 |
| 4. | Average number of manual and non-manual workers employed in national economy | (1940) 33.9 | (1960) 62.0 | 90.2 | 102.2 | 112.5 | 115.2 |
| 5. | Collective farmers employed in *obshchestvennom khozyaystve* | (1940) 29.0 | (1960) 21.8 | 17.0 | 15.4 | 13.1 | 12.7 |
| 6. | Lines 3 + 4 + line 2 (as %) | 35.6 | 54.87 | 76.48 | 79.7 | 80.79 | 80.3* |

Sources:  *Narodnoe khozyaystvo SSSR v 1974g.* (1975) p. 33
US Bureau of the Census, *Population Projections by Age and Sex for the Republics of the USSR 1970 to 2016* (May 1982 unpublished).
G. Baldwin, *Population Projections by Age and Sex: For Republics and Major Economic Regions of the USSR, 1970 to 2000* (Washington, D.C., 1979), p. 128.
*Narodnoe khozyaystvo SSSR v 1982g* (1983), pp. 287, 364–5, 454–5, 462.
*Narodnoe khozyaystvo SSSR v 1983g* (1984), p. 494.
*Vestnik statistiki*, no. 10 (1983), pp. 77–8.
*Vestnik statistiki*, no. 8 (1984), p. 75.

Notes:   * Line 2(b) used in calculations.
§ 1979 census. *Chislennost' i sostav naseleniya po dannym vsesoyuznoy perepisi naseleniya 1979g* (1984), p. 145.

88.38 per cent.[11] The Soviet rate for men aged 16−59 in 1979 was 88.46 per cent; the comparable figure (16−54) for women was 88.2 per cent. Comparative figures for West Germany (in 1980) are 86.3 per cent for men (15−59 year olds) and 54.7 per cent for women (15−54 year olds), and for France 82.7 and 53.9 per cent.[12] We must bear in mind that the Soviet Union has a higher participation rate in education and a younger retirement age and also that in market economies a large proportion (usually more than half) of employed women are working part-time. The higher participation of women becomes clearer when we consider age-specific rates.

*Table 2.3: Estimates and Projections of Labour Force Participation Rates in the USSR (by sex and age: 1959, 1970, 1980)*

| Sex and Age | 1959 | 1970 | 1980 |
|---|---|---|---|
| Male | | | |
| 16 to 19 years | 69.4 | 53.3 | 48.4 |
| 20 to 29 years | 91.0 | 89.7 | 89.5 |
| 30 to 39 years | 95.0 | 97.6 | 97.6 |
| 40 to 49 years | 93.0 | 95.9 | 95.9 |
| 50 to 54 years | 90.1 | 90.0 | 90.0 |
| 55 to 59 years | 83.5 | 79.9 | 79.9 |
| 60 years and over | 52.5 | 49.0 | 50.0 |
| | | | |
| Female | | | |
| 16 to 19 years | 71.0 | 47.8 | 40.8 |
| 20 to 29 years | 80.4 | 86.3 | 86.1 |
| 30 to 39 years | 77.7 | 92.7 | 92.7 |
| 40 to 49 years | 75.4 | 90.6 | 90.6 |
| 50 to 54 years | 67.7 | 77.3 | 77.3 |
| 55 to 59 years | 48.5 | 44.4 | 45.4 |
| 60 years and over | 33.8 | 25.0 | 26.0 |

*Source*: S. Rapawy, *Estimates and Projections of the Labor Force and Civilian Employment in the USSR, 1950−1990*, Foreign Economic Report no. 10 (Washington: US Department of Commerce, 1976), p. 15.

Unlike the practice in other countries,[13] the USSR does not release statistics on age cohort levels of employment. The United

States Foreign Demographic Analysis Division has calculated participation rates by age and sex and these are reliable estimates.[14] Some key figures are shown on Table 2.3. Here we observe for men in the 20–54 age bracket participation rates of over 90 per cent, rising to a maximum of 97.6 per cent in the 30–39 year age bracket. The fall-off at either end is due on the one hand to participation in higher education, and on the other hand to early retirements (retirement for men normally takes place at 55 and at 50 years for certain industries). Women also have a high participation rate, though lower than that of men. Of women in the 30–39 year age cohort, 93 per cent are in employment. The reduction at each end is due once again to full-time study and retirement. Differences in proportions in employment between men and women in the 20–50 age groups only come to from 3 to 5 per cent: during childbirth and associated leave women are recorded as being employed (in accordance with the 'temporarily absent' stipulation mentioned above).

The significance of these data is brought out in comparative perspective. In Table 2.4 are reproduced the economic participation rates for France, West Germany and Hungary for 1981. While for males, the Soviet participation rate is only a few points higher in the 30–50 age groups, the disparity becomes much greater when one studies the female population. The difference between the Soviet and Western European female labour force participation rates is from 20 to 40 percentage points greater. Moreover, Soviet women are employed on a full-time basis (some studies show that they are at paid work only one hour per week less than men), whereas a high proportion (usually more than half) of employed women in Western Europe are part-timers.

## 'UNDEROCCUPIED' SOCIAL GROUPS

Despite the ideological emphasis on work as a human need and the comprehensive provision by the economy of paid occupations there remain various forms of under- and unemployment in the USSR. The amount of 'involuntary' unemployment (in the sense of people actively seeking work but unable to find any) is low, and Soviet policy is intent on utilizing to the maximum its labour resources. Since the late 1970s, this task has been tackled with some urgency as the growth of numbers in the cohorts of employable age is

*Table 2.4: Economic Participation Rates for France, Germany and Hungary by Sex and Age, 1981*

| Age | Total Activity Rate | Male Activity Rate | Female Activity Rate |
|---|---|---|---|
| **FRANCE** | | | |
| 15–19 | 19.5 | 23.7 | 15.1 |
| 20–24 | 73.1 | 78.6 | 67.4 |
| 25–29 | 81.5 | 94.3 | 68.4 |
| 30–44 | 79.5 | 96.9 | 60.9 |
| 45–49 | 74.8 | 95.6 | 53.7 |
| 50–54 | 71.9 | 91.4 | 52.6 |
| 55–59 | 61.3 | 78.7 | 45.1 |
| 60–64 | 32.2 | 42.2 | 23.3 |
| 65+ | 3.7 | 5.3 | 2.6 |
| **WEST GERMANY** | | | |
| 15–19 | 43.5 | 46.4 | 40.4 |
| 20–24 | 76.4 | 81.4 | 71.0 |
| 25–29 | 76.8 | 89.4 | 63.8 |
| 30–44 | 77.6 | 97.7 | 56.7 |
| 45–49 | 75.4 | 96.5 | 53.2 |
| 50–54 | 70.5 | 93.1 | 48.2 |
| 55–59 | 57.0 | 81.9 | 39.0 |
| 60–64 | 26.0 | 44.4 | 13.3 |
| 65+ | 4.3 | 7.0 | 2.8 |
| **HUNGARY** | | | |
| 0–14 | 0.1 | 0.1 | 0.2 |
| 15–19 | 43.0 | 45.5 | 40.4 |
| 20–24 | 76.2 | 91.9 | 59.9 |
| 25–29 | 84.2 | 98.2 | 69.8 |
| 30–44 | 90.5 | 98.1 | 83.0 |
| 45–49 | 87.1 | 94.4 | 80.2 |
| 50–54 | 76.4 | 86.2 | 67.4 |
| 55–59 | 43.3 | 72.2 | 18.8 |
| 60–64 | 10.7 | 13.2 | 8.7 |
| 65+ | 3.5 | 3.9 | 3.2 |

*Sources*:   *1982 Yearbook of Labour Statistics* (Geneva: ILO, 1982), p. 29.

falling and the burden of the maintenance of the older population (which is rising) becomes heavier. There are three main social groups which Soviet analysts regard as being 'underoccupied': these are older school pupils and students, women and old age pensioners. The amount of part-time work is very small: ignoring participation in the second economy, it has been estimated that as a proportion of all workers, part-timers came to 0.32 per cent in 1974, 0.41 per cent in 1976[15] and 0.41 per cent in 1979. In 1978, out of a total of some half million part-time workers, women with children constituted 120,000: in industry were 28,000, state farms 8,000, building 4,600, other branches 82,000.[16] Education accounts for many of the residual: in 1974, 1.02 per cent of employees were part-timers. The urbanized Russian republic (RSFSR) employs more than the other republics: in 1975 about 2 per cent of the workforce there were part-time.

### Students

Many school pupils in rural areas work part-time in agriculture. In some areas of the country, as many as a third of all schoolchildren work in agriculture for more than six months of the year (see below, p.81). In the early 1980s, school-leavers entering the labour market have a gap of from three to six months[17] between leaving school and starting work. Students in university education numbered 5.3 million in 1982/83, of whom 60 per cent were full-time; another 4.5 million were in technical institutes (*tekhnikums*) with roughly the same proportion in full-time study.[18] Of those in full-time study, about half do not have a grant[19] and thus there is an available pool of labour with some spare time and a financial incentive to work. The extent of student employment is not known precisely. Novitsky and Babkina[20] suggest that about half of all part-time workers are students. They mostly work in agriculture and construction in the summer months. As for school pupils, it has been reported that about 3 million work on farms for one month in the summer.[21] No records are kept of student 'drop-outs'. In the Russian republic (RSFSR), it has been estimated that 180,000 young people a year leave secondary and higher education early. Kotlyar calculates that this represents an annual unemployment loss of 15,000 full-time workers.[22]

### Women

We have noted earlier the very high labour participation rates of women. There are, however, some women who are not employed, and Soviet policy-makers are attempting to bring them into the workforce. The 1979 census showed significant inter-republic variations in terms of the labour participation rate for women. The USSR average yearly participation rate was 47.8 per cent of the total female population and the average level of dependency was 29.7 per cent (i.e. the proportion of non-employed to employed). In the Russian republic (RSFSR) the comparable figures were 49.8 per cent and 26.0 per cent. In Latvia, however, the participation rate was much higher at 51.3 per cent and that of dependence lower at 25.1 per cent. At the other end of the scale came Turkmeniya (38.4 and 50.2 per cent), Armenia (44.8 and 39.7 per cent) Tadzhikistan (37 and 51.5 per cent), Kirgiziya (39.5 and 45.1 per cent), Azerbaydzhan (41.1 and 45.1 per cent), Kazakhstan (43.4 and 40.6 per cent) and Uzbekistan (38.4 and 48.3 per cent). Only in Tadzhikistan did private agricultural work as a main activity take up more than one per cent of the female labour activity (1.1 per cent).[23]

Whether these figures represent 'underutilization' or, as some western writers maintain, an excessive use of female labour, is a complicated matter of interpretation and policy choice. On the one hand are arguments concerning the social and political importance of the employment of women. An absence of paid employment, it is argued, belittles the social role of women: a lack of jobs *per se* leads to an inferior social status and financial dependence on men. The economy needs more workers, especially due to negative demographic patterns.

On the other hand, is the argument that the present levels of employment exploit women's labour. Not only do women bear the burden of the upbringing of children and the major share of housework, but they also occupy the most unskilled jobs, their occupational advancement is restricted and their pay is, on average, 30–35 per cent lower than men's. The concentration of women in low-paid industries is a vicious circle perpetuating low pay.[24] In a study of wage differentials in the cellulose, paper and wood processing industry of the USSR, Blyakhman and Zlotnitskaya found that women gave less priority to pay than to favourable working conditions, the proximity between workplace and residence, and the services provided by the enterprise. Men were found to be three times as likely to be oriented towards wages which compensated for unfavourable working conditions. Even with the same job skills, men have higher expectations concerning wages.[25] Women find social and psychological satisfaction in employment: one study found that 70.5 per cent of women with less than seven years' education sought a job, even if they had no financial need. The figure rose to 93 per cent for women with specialist secondary education.[26]

Economic demand has coincided with social policy, and has led to the high female participation rate. Increases in women's participation have followed the expansion of industry (in the 1930s), the decline in the number of men available for labour (during and after the Second World War) and the demographic labour shortage (during the 1970s and 1980s). With economic development there has been a tendency for men to move into skilled jobs and for women to be recruited from domestic or agricultural labour to fill unskilled jobs vacated by men,[27] though the number and proportion of Soviet women in skilled manual and professional jobs greatly exceeds those in advanced capitalist countries. M.Ya. Sonin has calculated that, typically, 31 per cent of male workers will be in the highly skilled manual grades of work (grades V–VI) whereas only 4 per cent of women will be so, in the unskilled categories (I–II), will be found 19 per cent of male workers and 66 per cent of the female.[28]

The policy options concerning women's employment are brought to a head over the issue of part-time work. Excluding the collective farm sector, only 0.41 per cent of the workforce is part-time, half of whom are women.[29] Two-thirds of all part-time workers are in the service sector, accounting for one per cent of the employees.[30] Leaving aside regional and ethnic factors, the major reason for the lower participation of women in the workforce is their responsibility for children and housework. It has been estimated that 8 to 9 per cent of urban women of employable age are lost to the workforce because of their need to care for young children at home; several million of these are women under 30 years of age.[31] Family burdens, together with the need for extra family income, favourably dispose many women to part-time labour. In 1977, one survey found that of women without an occupation, 40 per cent expressed a wish to work part-time. Moskoff, in summarizing Soviet research, concludes that 90 per cent of those who want part-time work are women; 22 per cent of women not at work sought part-time labour and 10 per cent of those in work preferred part-time jobs.[32]

While the provision of part-time work would undoubtedly draw into the labour force women who are engaged at home or in subsidiary agriculture, it would also deploy many women from full-time into part-time work. As the economic loss from the latter would considerably outweigh the gain from the former, policy-makers are loath to advocate a widening of opportunities for part-timers. In addition, management is often psychologically unprepared for the introduction of part-timers believing that changes will disrupt production even though worker productivity may be higher. Policy advocated by Gorbachev at the 27th Party Congress in 1986 was to increase the provision of part-time jobs and to develop work at home. As most of the present demand for part-time work is from women, its introduction would have the effect of creating a secondary labour market, which would be to the long-term disadvantage of women compared to men. The latter would regard employment as a career while women part-time workers would conceive of their job instrumentally as an added source of family income ('pin money') and social satisfaction. The part-time nature of their employment would effectively exclude women from managerial posts and would be detrimental to their occupational mobility. Part-time work would exacerbate the present condition of inequality of women *vis-à-vis* men caused by industrial and occupational segregation, inequality in educational opportunity, social attitudes defining 'women's work', and the responsibility of women for the maintenance of the family and the home.[33]

## Pensioners

We have seen that the Soviet Union has very high labour participation rates for the 'economically active' population, rather higher than those of capitalist states. Such participation excludes people who have retired either through disablement or old age. The official age of retirement, introduced in the late 1920s, however, is much lower than in the West. The retention in the workforce of women over 55 years of age and men over 60 years is one of the main ways that the reduction in the number of young workers coming into the labour market can be offset. The total number of people on pensions in the USSR has increased as follows: 4 million in 1941 (0.2 million being old age), 21.9 million (5.4 million old age) in 1961, 41.3 million (24.9 million old age) in

1971 and 51.4 million (35.0 million old age) in 1982.[34] The employment of old age pensioners has risen in recent years. As a proportion of the total Soviet labour force, old age pensioners were 0.8 per cent in 1960, 2.8 per cent in 1970, 4.3 per cent in 1975 and 6.9 per cent in 1982.[35] Of old age pensioners in 1960, 11.7 per cent were in employment. By 1970, the proportion had risen to 19 per cent and by 1982 it was 32 per cent.[36] (The number of people of retirement age in *full-time* work as defined in the 1979 census, however, was only 11 per cent.)[37]

As to disabled persons, some 25 to 30 per cent are employed. The majority of those with grade 3 disabilities (mildly disabled) have jobs; of those in grade 2 (severely disabled but not requiring constant care), only 5 per cent are employed; in group 1, a negligible number are employed. Most of such employment is in urban areas where special workshops have been set up; others work at home.[38] To encourage the recruitment of disabled people, enterprises are allowed to keep an extra proportion of profits when they employ them.[39] Significantly more disabled people could be employed if conditions were improved.

Since the early 1970s, Soviet policy has been to encourage pensioners to continue at work. Surveys have found that many workers reaching pensionable age would prefer to stay on. In the late 1970s, for instance, one study found that 79.5 per cent of men and 61.3 per cent of women wished to continue at work, and over 80 per cent of these desired to continue in their old job at the same place of work.[40] Pensioners may receive their pension in addition to their wage, subject to the condition that they may not have more than a total of 300 roubles per month.(Average earnings in 1982 was 177 roubles per month.) Should the pensioner's combined wage and pension exceed 300 roubles, the wage is reduced by the difference. One exception to liability to this deduction is pensioners employed in mining, non-ferrous metals and certain other essential industries: in these industries there is no wage ceiling and of course the minimum retirement age here is 55 years for men. Since January 1980, pensioners have been able to forgo drawing their pension at retirement age and to rely on their wages; in these circumstances they are able to qualify for a pension at an enhanced rate when they do retire and the maximum pension payable rises from 120 roubles per month to 150 roubles.[41]

In terms of labour supply and effective utilization, the financial incentives outlined above already show a significant increase in labour participation. In the republic of Azerbaydzhan in 1984, it was reported that 44 per cent of pensioners were in work and of those qualifying for pensions between 1982 and 1984 more than 70 per cent chose to continue working.[42] It seems likely that the labour participation rate of the under 70 age group will be approximately 35 per cent in the mid-1980s and will compensate somewhat for the relative decline of new entrants to the labour force. It will also bring the USSR more into line with western capitalist states as far as the age of effective retirement is concerned. Social policy for increasing the level of pensioners' labour force participation derives from the economic need to maintain present levels of employment and to reduce the number of dependants on the employed population.

## SOME CONCLUSIONS

While one is hampered by the lack of comprehensive and detailed statistics on levels of employment, the empirical data assembled in this chapter enable us to come to a number of reliable conclusions concerning the rates of labour utilization. First, since 1959, on any comparable basis, the labour force participation rate in the USSR has been of a very high magnitude. Second, the participation of women has been at a quantitatively higher level than that of women in industrialized advanced western countries and that of men in the 30−45 age group is comparable to advanced western countries. Third, due to the incidence of an early retirement age, the period of full participation ceases at an earlier age than in the West. The retirement age of men (60 years) and women (55 years) is much lower than in Western European countries and the 60−65 (men) and 55−65 (women) cohorts could provide a source of labour as the age cohorts of retirement age grow in size. Finally, the Soviet economy may be defined as one of full employment. This does not imply that the economy is without forms of unemployment or underemployment, topics we shall return to in Chapter 4.

# REFERENCES

1. Most writers, including Soviet ones, make this point. Jan Adam, 'Similarities and Differences in the Treatment of Labour Shortages', in Jan Adam (ed.), *Employment Policies in the Soviet Union and Eastern Europe* (London: Macmillan, 1982), p. 126; R.W. Davies, 'The End of Mass Unemployment in the USSR', in D. Lane (ed.), *Employment and Labour in the USSR* (Brighton: Wheatsheaf, 1986), pp. 29-31.
2. Davies, op.cit., p.11. Most Soviet writers claim that it was eliminated in 1930: K.I. Suvorov, *Istoricheski opyt KPSS po likvidatsii bezrabotitsii (1917-1930)* (Moscow, 1968), p. 8; L.S. Rogachevskaya, *Likvidatsiya bezrabotitsy v SSSR 1917-1930 gg* (1973), pp. 261-84.
3. Suvorov, pp. 146-7.
4. Cited by Davies, p.25.
5. In the discussion which follows, I rely on the definitions suggested by the International Labour Office (ILO), *Labour Force, Employment and Underemployment* (Geneva: ILO, 1982).
6. Ibid., p. 45.
7. Ibid., p. 12. No comparative statistics are available measuring such underemployment: *International Comparisons of Unemployment* (US Department of Labor, Bureau of Labor Statistics Bulletin, 1979) p. 3.
8. Until 1970, the compulsory length of schooling was nine years. The present 10-year schooling is universal, but some republics (Baltic and Caucasian) have an eleven-year obligatory schooling to compensate for the task of learning the Russian language in addition to the vernacular.
9. In 1982, there were 3.023 million full-time students in higher education and 2.845 million in technical colleges. The total number of 17−20 year olds was 24.75 million: *Narodnoe khozyaystvo v 1983g* (hereafter abbreviated to *Narkhoz v 1983g*) (1984), p. 494.
10. *Obshchestvennoe khozyaystvo*, i.e. working in collective agriculture rather than on individual plots producing for the free market.
11. Age cohorts calculated on the basis of US Bureau of the Census (see note 14 below), employed population: *Vestnik statistiki* no. 10 (1983), pp. 77-9. Murray Feshbach estimates the total labour force (16−54/59 years) participation rate in 1979 to be 88.1 per cent. This he derives by dividing the labour force (134,860,000) by the population of able-bodied ages (153,078,000): 'Population and Labor Force', in Abram Bergson and Herbert S. Levine, *The Soviet Economy: Toward the Year 2000* (London: Allen and Unwin, 1983), p. 99. My figures include 573,000 in private agriculture. The 1970 census reported the labour participation rate for males (20−59) as 93 per cent and for female (20−59) as 89 per cent. *Itogi vsesoyuznoy perepisi 1970g*, vol. 2, (1972), pp. 12-13; vol. 5, (1975), pp. 162-3.
12. These data may not be strictly comparable due to differences in bases but they indicate order of comparison. Figures for West Germany and France, *1981 Yearbook of Labour Statistics* (Geneva: ILO, 1981) p. 26 (data for 1980).

13. The International Labour Office publishes yearly statistics on the economically active population, divided by sex and age group, including data on Hungary and Poland. See *1982 Yearbook of Labour Statistics* (Geneva: ILO, 1982).

14. See particularly US Department of Commerce, Bureau of the Census, Godfrey S. Baldwin, *Population Projections by Sex and Age for the Republics of the USSR, 1970 to 2000.* International Population Reports, series, no. 26. (Washington, D.C.: 1979), p. 91. *Estimates and Projections by Labor Force and Civilian Employment in the USSR 1950 to 1990*, by S. Rapawy, Foreign Economic Report, no. 10 (Washington, D.C.: 1976). *Narodnoe khozyaystvo 1974g* (1975), p. 33 included a breakdown by the age of the population, and a total of the economically active age groups. Further unpublished estimates have been made by the US Bureau of the Census in 1982: my thanks to Stephen Rapawy for giving access to these data. There are no comprehensive statistics on part-time working.

15. Figures refer to employment in the 'national economy' and exclude collective farmers. Cited by W. Moskoff, 'Part-time Employment in the Soviet Union', *Soviet Studies*, vol. 34, no. 2 (1982), p. 272. The principal source he uses is T. Skal'berg, E. Tartirosyan and L. Kuleshova, 'Rabota s nepolnym rabochim dnem—vazhnoe sredstvo privlecheniya trudovykh resursov', *Sotsialisticheski trud*, no. 2 (1977). See also N. Rogovski, 'Effektivnost' truda v odinnatsatoy pyatiletke', *Voprosy ekonomiki*, no. 1 (1982).

16. Figure for 1979 from L. Kuleshova, 'Rezhim nepolnogo-rabochego vremeni pri organizatsii truda zhenshchin', *Planovoe khozyaystvo*, no. 12 (1978), p. 63. Data for 1978, Rogovski, p.6.

17. The latter figure given by E.L. Manevich, 'Ratsional'noe ispolzovanie . . .', *Voprosy ekonomiki*, no. 9 (1981), p. 63.

18. *Narkhoz SSSR v 1982g* (1983) pp. 465, 468.

19. Moskoff, p. 281.

20. A. Novitsky and M. Babkina, 'Part-time work and employment', translated in *Problems of Economics*, vol. 16, no. 9 (1974), pp. 45-6, cited by Moskoff, p. 282.

21. Yu. Viktorov, 'Treti semestr studentov', *Trud*, 23 July 1971, p. 1, cited by Moskoff, p. 281.

22. A. Kotlyar, *Pravda*, 13 May 1984.

23. *Chislennost' i sostav naseleniya SSSR* (1984), pp. 151-4.

24. For a review see *Women, Work and Family in the Soviet Union*, ed. G.W. Lapidus (New York: M.E. Sharpe, 1982), especially articles by Lapidus, Sonin, Kostakov and Kotliar and Turchaninova. On pay, see G. Lapidus's 'Introduction', pp.xx-xxii. The concentration of women in low-paying industries is greater in the USSR than in the West: a 'coefficient of determination' gave a figure of 0.7−0.8 in the USSR compared to 0.6 in Germany and Britain (data for late 1970s): Christopher Saunders and David Marsden, *Pay Inequalities in the European Community* (London: Butterworth 1981) pp. 230-1.

25. L.S. Blyakhman and T.S. Zlotnitskaya, 'Differentsiatsiya zarabotnoy platy

kak faktor stimulirovaniya truda', *Sotsiologicheskie issledovaniya* (1984), no. 1, p. 43. In this study the average pay for men was 262 roubles and for women 182 roubles—44 per cent lower (ibid).

26. Data cited by I. Bagrova, *Nedelya*, no. 32 (August 1977). Abstract in *CDSP*, vol. 29, no. 32 (August 1977), p. 6.

27. V.G. Kostakov, *Trudovye resursy: sotsial'no ekonomicheski analiz* (1976), part 5. Translation, 'Features of the Development of Female Employment', in G.W. Lapidus, *Women, Work and Family in the Soviet Union* (New York: M.E. Sharpe, 1982), pp. 41-2.

28. M.Ya. Sonin, 'Aktualnye sotsialno-ekonomicheskie problemy zanyatosti zhenshchin', in A.Z. Maikov, *Problemy ratsional'nogo ispol'zovaniya trudovykh resursov*, (1973), cited in D. Lane, *Soviet Economy and Society* (Oxford: Blackwell: 1985), p. 175. Women students made up 30 per cent of the complement in trade schools; Lane, *op.cit.*, p. 174.

29. L. Kuleshova, 'Rezhim nepolnogo rabochego vremeni pri organizatsii truda zhenshchin', *Planovoe khozyaystvo*, no. 12 (1978), p. 63.

30. A. Kurski *et al.*, 'Novye formy organizatsii rabochego vremeni', *Sots. trud*, no. 6 (June 1984), p. 76.

31. I. Bagrova, *Nedelya*, no.32. (August 1977). Abstract in *CDSP*, vol. 29, no. 32 (7 September 1977), pp. 5-6.

32. Kuleshova, p. 61; and Moskoff, p. 275; data cited from N. Shishkan, 'The Participation of Women in Social Production', *Problems of Economics*, vol. 20, no.3 (July 1977), p.29.

33. See discussion in Alastair McAuley, *Women's Work and Wages in the Soviet Union* (London: Allen and Unwin, 1981), pp. 120-6.

34. *Narkhoz SSSR 1922–1982* (1982), p. 453.

35. 1982: based on 8 million working pensioners given by L.A. Kostin, *Pravda* (4 January 1983), p. 3. Other data cited by Moskoff, p. 277.

36. M.S. Lantsev, *Sotsial'noe obespechenie v SSSR* (Moscow, 1976); L.A. Kostin, *Pravda* (4 January 1983), p. 3. E.L. Manevich has estimated that in 1980, 25 per cent of the 34.3 million old age pensioners were employed, 35 per cent of whom he considers on the basis of a sample survey could be employed full-time, *Voprosy ekonomiki*, no. 9 (1981). An interesting study of pensioners going beyond the topic of employment is V.D. Shapiro, 'Life After Retirement', *Soviet Sociology*, vol. 22, nos. 1-2 (1983).

37. L. Chizhova, 'Kak luchshe ispol'zovat' trud razlichnykh sotsial'no-demograficheskikh grupp naseleniya', *Sotsialisticheski trud*, no. 8 (1984), p. 90.

38. A.A. Dyskin, A.V. Sharapanovski and I.A. Starodvorski, 'On Home Employment for Disabled Persons in Cities and Rural Localities', translation from *Zdravookhranenie Rossiyskoy Federatsii* (1981), no. 1 (17-21), *Soviet Sociology*, vol. 20, no. 3 (1982), pp. 79-87.

39. A. Novitsky, *Trud* (29 January 1982).

40. S. Slavina and V. Kogan, 'Pensioner prishel na proizvodstvo. Kakie usloviya nado emu sozdat', *Sotsialisticheski trud*, no. 10 (1978), p. 136.

41. L. Kostin, *Pravda* (4 January 1983), p. 3.

42. M. Kaziev, *Pravda* (27 June 1984), p. 3.

# 3 Planned and Market Labour Mobility

Soviet spokespersons regard the ending of unemployment in the 1930s as being coterminous with the abolition of the 'reserve army' of unemployed labour and the ending of the labour market in the USSR. This is a half-truth. Compared to capitalist market societies, it is the case that wages were not effective in regulating the supply of labour, and the absence of a pool of unemployed made dismissal less effective as a means to discipline labour. The other part of the story is that the 'planning' of labour was only partial. At most, about a quarter of entrants to the labour force came from *Orgnabor* (the department concerned with labour supply)[1] and these did not necessarily stay in their first jobs. The vast majority of workers were recruited through informal channels and in practice moved from one job to another. Enterprises attempted to optimize their labour force by persuading valued workers to stay and to attract others from outside. In this more limited sense, a labour market existed and continues to the present day. Imperfections in labour markets and in the planning of labour lead to various types of unemployment which will be discussed after considering how the labour force is placed in jobs.

There are now six types of 'planned' mobility of labour (planned in the sense that there is some form of administrative recruitment and direction) in the USSR: (i) *Orgnabor*; (ii) 'transfers' of skilled workers within a branch of industry; (iii) 'social appeals' involving the mobilization of youth in new building projects; (iv) resettlement of families, usually from areas of rural labour surplus to areas of deficit; (v) labour exchanges which are not 'directive' in character; and (vi) the placement of graduates of various educational and training institutes under various Ministries.[2]

*Table 3.1: Sources of Workforce Recruitment*

|  | RSFSR 1980 % | Ukraine 1975 % | L'vov 1975 % |
|---|---|---|---|
| Organized worker recruitment | 0.7 | 5.3 | 3.3 |
| Agricultural resettlement | 0.2 | — | — |
| Youth job placement | 2.8 | — | — |
| Allocation of trade school graduates (PTUs) | 9.3 | 6.7 | 8.9 |
| Personnel allocation of graduates of institutions of higher education (VUZy) | 1.9 | — | — |
| Personnel allocation of graduates of secondary specialist education institutions (SSUZy) | 3.0 | — | — |
| Transfers from other enterprises | 3.8 | 3.5 | 2.7 |
| Social appeals | 0.5 | — | — |
| Hiring by enterprises themselves | 77.8 | 84.5 | 85.1 |
| including job placement channels | 9.7 | — | — |
| Total | 100.0 | 100.0 | 100.0 |

*Source*: For RSFSR, Kotlyar, 'Sistema...' (see reference 22 below), p. 53, data refer to all branches of the economy; for Ukraine and L'vov, M.I. Dolishni, *Formirovanie i ispol'zovanie trudovykh resursov* (1978), p. 202, figures for industry only.

The respective weights of the various forms of recruitment including the market are shown on Table 3.1 for the Ukraine (1975), L'vov province (1975) and the Russian republic (RSFSR) in 1980. It can be seen that organized or administrative channels of labour placement control no more than 15 per cent of labour movements; labour bureaux only deal with some 10 per cent of total recruitment, when all forms of recruitment are taken into account. Enterprises directly hire most hands, and in various *oblasts* of the USSR between 60 and 80 per cent of those taken on will have left other jobs.[3] While the job placement bureaux account only for 10 per cent of job recruitment, in recent times their role has increased, the proportion of placements by them rising nearly two and half times between 1970 and 1980. Comparative statistics for 1975 and 1980 for the Russian republic are shown on Table 3.2. Recruitment by enterprises themselves fell by some 14 per cent. The administrative allocation of labour must be considered in the context of the 'market' continuing to be the main way in which labour is recruited—though the 'market' for labour does not adjust its price (wages) as freely as in market systems. This has led to the rise of a second economy and various forms of self-employment.

*Table 3.2: Dynamics of the Organizational forms of Manpower Allocation in the RSFSR for 1970–80 (in per cent; 1970 = 100)*

|  | 1975 | 1980 |
|---|---|---|
| Organized recruitment | 99.6 | 98.0 |
| Agricultural resettlement | 93.3 | 87.1 |
| Youth job placement | 83.0 | 53.1 |
| Allocation of trade school graduates | 123.6 | 140.6 |
| Individual allocation of higher educational institution graduates | 127.8 | 149.0 |
| Individual allocation of secondary vocational education institution graduates | 126.5 | 136.3 |
| Transfer | 84.2 | 79.2 |
| Hiring by the enterprises themselves (industry) | 91.2 | 86.2 |
| including job placement service | 191.3 | 245.9 |

*Source*:   Kotlyar, *loc. cit.*

## ORGNABOR

When it was introduced in 1931, *Orgnabor's* principal task was to recruit labour from collective farms to urban industry. In practice, collective farms were required to provide industrial enterprises with labour. The collective farmer was denied individual mobility. In such a way 'transitional unemployment' was eliminated and Soviet Russia, bad though urban housing was, did not experience the shanty town and mass poverty conditions of many developing societies. Also, forced labour projects organized by the security services used prisoners to make up deficits in labour supply. In the 1930s, 2-3 million prisoners (about 15 per cent of the workforce) might have been engaged in building, mining and lumber,[4] (this includes the bulk of the criminal population who are required to work). No data are currently available on the extent of this practice; one estimate in 1982 is that 3 million people work in camps felling timber, building gas pipelines and other construction projects,[5] (total employment in 1982 was 127.9 million).

By 1953 the agencies of *Orgnabor* directed mainly urban workers from areas of labour surplus to those of deficit. Since 1967 the agencies of *Orgnabor* have been subordinate to the Republican State Committees on the Use of Labour Resources. The plans for labour procurement are made in the Republican Gosplans after considering requests from Ministries and other production organizations. Gosplan USSR coordinates the flow of such workers between branches of the economy and different republics. In the pre-war period urban workers numbered some 15 per cent of *Orgnabor*'s total; by 1971/74 they came to 73.7 per cent. *Orgnabor* now helps relocate workers in the far north, Kazakhstan, the Urals, Siberia and the far east. In the 1951−69 period, a third of transferred workers in the RSFSR went to Siberia and the far east; by 1974 this had risen to 49 per cent. For some industries, most of the workers were sent to Siberia and the east: in the Ministry of Communications the proportion was 89.4 per cent; industrial and construction materials, 87 per cent; transport construction, 75 per cent; and timber, 79 per cent. Of the total number of workers taken on in industry by enterprises in 1974, 4.7 per cent came through *Orgnabor*—in fishing the proportion was 12.4 per cent, and in timber-felling, 11.8 per cent.[6]Most workers coming under *Orgnabor* are unskilled, over 25 years of age and unmarried (only 2.4 per cent took their families). They sign on for short contracts—under six months, or from one to three years. In 1974, three-quarters of workers recruited through *Orgnabor* were on at least yearly contracts.

In 1984 some 400,000 persons a year were being channelled through *Orgnabor* to work in labour-deficient areas: 85 per cent were under 40 years of age and 70 per cent had a trade. Since 1984, workers who sign up for a fixed minimum term period are to have greater payments, better travel conditions, and the amount of baggage carried has been doubled. An allowance is made for travelling time and special loans are available for setting up home.[7]Workers are bound by their contracts and can only leave without penalty if the administration fails to honour their contract. If they leave for any other reason, it is considered as absenteeism and the worker loses his uninterrupted work record, he may also be fined and have to pay his own fare home. Research has shown that conditions (housing, catering, leisure) are often poor and that many workers leave before their contract is fulfilled.[8]

## TRANSFERS WITHIN INDUSTRIAL MINISTRIES

The most obvious form of direction takes place within enterprises or industrial conglomerates. The larger the industrial unit, the greater the internal mobility—and the lower the rate of labour turnover as measured by workers handing in their notice at the plant. In the early 1970s, one study showed that about 8 per cent of the workforce changed jobs internally. Those who move to other enterprises by agreement with the heads of enterprises averaged 3-4 per cent of the workforce per annum between 1967 and 1974.[9]

Planned movement within branches of industry is usually associated with the transfer of workers to new enterprises. For instance, the new Volga car factory built between 1970 and 1972 recruited 8000 skilled workers from other car plants. When various forms of internal reorganization take place either through closing down plants or through managerial initiatives, workers who change jobs are benefited in the following ways: they keep their uninterrupted work record (this also applies to a spouse who also decides to move); they receive payment when moving and retraining; they have priority in housing and childcare: they receive expenses for moving and a lump-sum displacement based on their average salary; and their dependants also receive an allowance.[10] Such mobility, sponsored within industrial branches, is relatively underdeveloped. Maslova calls for the following improvements and changes in organization: transfers and their associated rights should be extended to enterprises outside the branch of industry; a uniform statute should be enacted standardizing and applying the conditions of internal transfers to all displaced workers; where retraining for jobs in short supply takes place, workers should be able to receive their previous level of wages.[11]

## SOCIAL APPEALS

A peculiarly Soviet form of meeting labour shortages is the device known as 'social appeals' (*obshchestvennye prizyvy*). This form of recruiting labour was first organized by the Young Communist League (Komsomol) in 1956. It involves participation in permanent employment, chiefly in construction and in enterprises in the northern and eastern areas of the country. Young people leaving school or college figure largely in this group. In 1971, three-quarters of the Moscow Komsomol's appeal included young people between 18 and 25 years of age; 83 per cent were Komsomol members. The height of this movement was in the 1956−65 period when 1,800,000 young people volunteered for work: of these 1,100,000 enrolled on seven-year contracts.[12]

Another form of 'social appeal' is that of the summer student detachments who normally work for a short period on building projects. In 1967, 100,000 students participated on such schemes, a figure which rose to 619,000 in 1974.[13] These volunteer short-term workers provide labour for building projects such as the trans-Siberian railway. Usually such workers do not have relevant skills and 75 per cent have to be trained on the job.[14]

## RESETTLEMENT OF FAMILIES

This form of labour movement enables agricultural areas with labour shortages to be populated. Such resettlement was especially important in the early 1950s. Since that time the numbers participating have fallen. Taking 100 as the average movement between 1951−1955, the index fell to 59.1 in 1961−65 and 40.2 in 1971-74.[15] Since 1974, the following benefits are payable to families wishing to move voluntarily to rural localities where labour is needed. Travel and transportation of personal goods are paid for, and there are allowances of 200 roubles for the head of the family and 75 roubles for each member; quarters are provided for resettlers; and on state farms new settlers are excused paying rent for two years after moving.[16] Though the majority of families stay permanently, many move back from the Urals, Western Siberia and the Volga regions. Of settlers in the RSFSR in the period 1951–70, 13.6 per cent left after one year and 24 per cent after two years; by 1970–74 the rate had fallen to 6.9 per cent for first-year leavers.[17] Major dissatisfaction lay with living and working conditions. Despite improvements, discontent with conditions in rural areas continues. Most migration in the 1980s was of this form, accounting for 80 per cent of moves; only 20 per cent came under 'organized' schemes noted above.[18]

## EMPLOYMENT BUREAUX

In 1967, employment bureaux were reopened in the USSR. Such offices were organized under the Councils of Ministries of the Republics. They provided information about jobs and also gave advice to potential job takers. They also had the functions of assisting the state planning agencies with measures for retraining and transferring labour and with formulating proposals for the planning and national utilization of labour. The state planning agencies (Gosplans) coordinated the work of the bureaux. The bureaux not only deal with enquiries from workers seeking jobs but also are linked to special commissions for certain categories of labour: youth, juvenile offenders, invalids and demobilized officers, and ex-convicts. These commissions need not be described in detail here. It should be noted, however, that the authorities set up such specialist bureaux in order to maximize the recruitment of all types of labour. People defined as invalids or handicapped are the responsibility of the social security offices. The organs of the Ministry of Internal Affairs find jobs for ex-convicts through job placement bureaux.

Youth Placement Commissions (*Kommissii po trudoustroistvu molodezhi*) are agencies of the local soviets.[19] Enterprises are supposed to reserve a certain proportion of jobs for school-leavers (around 5 per cent). School-leavers from ordinary schools are not obliged to use the Commissions: in 1979, 35 per cent of leavers in Moscow did not do so and a similar proportion was reported for

Orel in 1976.[20] As far as vocational schools (PTUs and SPTUs) are concerned, these are invariably linked to 'base enterprises' or industries (such as the railways) which absorb graduates who are subject to initial placement in jobs. The same is the case with graduates of specialized secondary and higher educational institutions. Gosplan and the Ministry of Higher and Secondary Specialized Education, in conjunction with the 'consuming' Ministries, draw up assignments for graduates who are allocated to jobs, normally for a three-year period. This is a form of direct labour recruitment and by-passes intermediary bureaux.

The placement of school and college graduates is one area in which Soviet planners can meet deficits and shortages. This system, however, has some inefficiencies. Many students 'drop out'—in the RSFSR, 180,000 students per annum prematurely leave educational institutions. 'No records are kept on these people and no purposeful work is being done to place them in jobs.'[21] Kotlyar has also pointed out that administrative placement often breaks down. He cites a report in *Pravda* (12 July 1981) to the effect that in 1981 in the Russian republic, enterprises and institutions refused to take 1,000 physicists, more than 1,100 chemists, and 750 biologists from universities.[22] Graduates also with impunity fail to turn up at their assigned jobs.[23]

By 1974 the employment bureaux covered nearly all towns with populations of between 100,000 and 400,000, and in some republics they were also located in medium-sized towns of 50,000 to 100,000.[24] Of workers recruited to industry, 8.7 per cent in 1971 came from the bureaux and 14.1 per cent in 1974 (data for USSR). In some republics the proportions were higher: in 1974, in Armenia, it was 40.7 per cent, and in Uzbekistan, 22.8 per cent were so recruited.[25] In the 1980s greater use of labour exchanges on a nationwide scale has been advocated to fill vacant jobs. In June 1980, it was decreed that all towns with populations over 20,000 should have bureaux. By 1982, 830 towns had employment bureaux; in the course of the tenth Five Year Plan (1976–80), 13 million people were placed through them, and in 1982 and 1983, 6 million.[26] However, as noted above, the recruitment of most labour still takes place 'at the factory gate' rather than through offices. A study in 1980 of 156 production units showed that only 31 per cent of labour requirements were filled through administrative channels and of these 19 per cent were school graduates.[27] By 1982, 25−30 per cent of *new* job seekers used the job placement services.[28] In Perm, it has been reported that 85 per cent of workers already have jobs before they leave their own factories and labour placement officers often fail to fulfil their placement assignments.[29]

The role of the bureaux is as an intermediary. Neither worker nor enterprise need take the job or the worker on offer. In 1973, of the total number of enquiries by workers, 86.9 per cent were sent to jobs by the exchanges; 64.6 per cent actually took them up,[30] that is, a third of the offers were turned down. Most of those seeking and accepting jobs through the exchanges were younger workers with lower levels of education (primary or incomplete secondary).

The bureaux are financed by the enterprises using them, though many calls have been made in the Soviet press for a transfer of funds to the local soviets for support of job placement bureaux.[31] Fees vary as they are fixed by the republican price committees. Enterprises make an initial payment in accordance with their size. In addition, payment is also made for each worker taken on (e.g. 2 roubles in the Russian republic; 3 roubles in the Ukraine, 4 roubles in the far north). In some republics the enterprise only pays a fixed fee. Kotlyar has pointed out that the system of enterprises paying for job placements encourages a high turnover by the job placement bureaux. Their dependence on enterprises 'impedes the performance of their functions of supervising the utilization of manpower, the observation of work-force ceilings etc.'[32] A study of bureau users in 1971 found that only 10 per cent were seeking their first job. Of the remainder, dissatisfaction with existing jobs was as follows: 35 per cent were dissatisfied with wages and conditions of work, 15.5 per cent wanted better housing or childcare facilities or to live closer to their work, 6.2 per cent had been sacked for disciplinary offences, and 4 per cent had been laid off or their contracts had come to an end.[33] In the RSFSR, 88 per cent of moves were within given localities (*rayons*), and only 2.7 per cent were to other republics.[34]

The main difference from *Orgnabor* is that the worker comes to the bureaux after having left his job on his own initiative. His labour contract is an individual matter between him and the enterprise and the potential recruit does not receive any financial incentives to take up the post. The bureaux have reduced the amount of time between jobs by from five to fifteen days depending on the locality.[35] An advantage of the bureaux is that through them, workers have a greater choice of job—in Leningrad in 1974, every applicant was offered two to three vacancies.[36] The most frequent use of exchanges is made by industry and construction.

The bureaux do not have a comprehensive or compulsory coverage, though in some areas those dismissed for disciplinary offences have to be channelled through such offices. Some enterprises do not bother with the offices and rely on word-of-mouth communication and recruit 'at the gate'. Some even 'intercept' job seekers outside the labour exchange offices.[37] As a result the bureaux do not have a full picture of vacancies and become less useful to job seekers. They are often short of staff and are unable to deal with requests for jobs outside their areas.[38] Also enterprises do not send in all vacancies and sometimes they ask for more labour than they really need. In 1984, for the RSFSR, it was reported that about 40 per cent of vacancies for manual workers were reported to the labour bureaux, 17 per cent for engineers and technicians, and 14 per cent for office workers. The position is similar in other republics.[39]Maslova points out that if workers made redundant ('freed') by an enterprise refuse the jobs offered by their employer, they lose their rights concerning the type of job they are entitled to and also they may lose their uninterrupted service record.[40] Such a procedure could be extended if the labour bureaux were made the intermediaries in the job search; workers made redundant through technical advance or reorganization would be placed according to their qualifications without loss of earnings.[41]

Kotlyar[42] is among the professionals who advocate that the responsibility for placing discharged workers in jobs should be transferred from Ministries, Departments and enterprises to the organs of the USSR (and Republican) State Committees on Labour and Social Problems. He points out that the 1970 resolution, 'On the Procedure for Strengthening the Interest of Workers in Increased Production Output, the Rising of Labour Productivity and the Reduction of Employed Personnel', gives Ministries, Departments and enterprises the obligation to find work for displaced workers: 'This frequently places the administration in serious difficulties and impedes the disengagement of workers who are awaited in other divisions of the national economy.'[43] However, Kotlyar also notes that workers who change jobs, and even those fired for violating labour discipline, often receive higher salaries at their new place of work. A selective study (no details are given) found this to be the case in 30 per cent of the cases, moreover wage rises were as much as 30 per cent.[44] This would seem to indicate that such moves were often to the worker's advantage. Only 12 per cent of job changers in the RSFSR return to their original workplaces.[45] However, Kotlyar has estimated that some 40 per cent 'of the overall total of job movements do not correspond to the interests of citizens, labour collectives or society as a whole' and entail unnecessary costs.[46] Job changers also regularly take up different trades: this occurred in 30 per cent of all cases studied in the RSFSR, and of those hired at 'the gate', 52 per cent.[47] Despite Kotlyar's specious arguments, this is not necessarily a bad thing, as the labour force is responding to industrial requirements.


## THE UFA-KALUGA EXPERIMENT

The imperfections in the market operating through the labour bureaux led in 1970 to the so-called Ufa-Kaluga experiment.[48] This system extended the rights of the employment bureaux in that area over most vacancies which had to be filled through the bureaux. The exceptions were leading cadres (directors, chief engineers), professors and teachers, scientists, specialists in health and education, senior government employees, young specialists and youths finishing school and graduates of trade schools.[49] In all other cases enterprises had to make known their vacancies to the labour bureaux. Enterprises retained the right whether or not to hire workers sent to them by the bureau. A payment of 3 roubles was made by the enterprise for each person sent by the bureau and subsequently employed.[50]

   This system had some advantages. The authorities had a better idea of the labour shortages and could identify enterprises with excessive demands. This enables resources to be channelled to the training of labour.[51] In Ufa-Kaluga, job changing when people took new posts was reduced by 5 per cent in Kaluga and 12 per cent in Ufa. Registered labour shortages in enterprises in Ufa dropped

2.2 times in 1970–72; in Kaluga the number of enterprises with employees in excess of planned targets was reduced from 40 to 17. The bureaux exercised an effective control over enterprises' labour recruitment. From 1970 to 1984, personnel turnover in Kaluga dropped from 17.8 to 11.6 per cent.[52]

The mandatory scheme however has not been adopted in other areas where enterprises have been allowed to continue hiring workers independently. This is probably a result of pressure from the industrial enterprises and Ministries who objected to control over the labour supply by the bureaux; such control made production more difficult by depriving enterprises of labour reserves. Individual workers also objected to the scheme as it deprived them of choice. Hence 'planning' of labour comes into conflict with powerful enterprises and skilled workers who have a short-term interest in a labour market in conditions of labour scarcity.[53]

## THE VOLUNTARILY UNEMPLOYED AND SELF-EMPLOYED SUB-CULTURES

The absence of planning over the labour force has led to a sub-culture of the unemployed, or 'parasites' and to the formation of gangs of self-employed labourers (*shabashniki*). These are relatively small groups of people outside the formal labour market.

The prevalence of voluntary unemployed people in the USSR has been the concern of some commentators since the early 1970s though our knowledge of 'drop-outs' from employment is fragmentary.[54] Some evidence exists of a growing sub-culture of 'non-workers'. In the first half of the 1980s, many letters were published in the press concerning the prevalence of parasites. In May 1983, *Pravda* reported that officials of the USSR People's Control Committee investigated several cities in the Ukraine, Chelyabinsk, Novosibirsk and other areas, and it was found that the non-working 'parasitic' population was equal to from three-quarters to the whole of the reported labour shortage in these areas.[55] Many people were found to be permanently idle—that is, not working for a whole year. The Soviet Procurator-General, A.M.Rekunkov deplored the fact that 'the law enforcement organs annually expose tens of thousands of citizens who have not worked anywhere for a long time . . ., one crime in four or five is committed by those who are not working or studying.'[56] The government newspaper *Izvestiya* (5 April 1985) published an article by Professor I. Karpets, the Director of the Institute for Studying the Causes of and Elaborating Measures to Combat Crime in the USSR. He pointed out that: 'In many regions there has been a noticeable increase in the number of persons not engaged in the sphere of social production and leading a parasitical life. . . . The parasite becomes a real violator of the fundamental principle of our society (the principle of social justice). . . . In certain circumstances attempts to live at other people's expense are directly classified as criminal and such persons are forced to work in line with the court's sentence.'

The 'voluntarily unemployed' however, also includes those who are 'self-employed'. This activity involves the provision of services 'on the side', such as motor repairs, and painting and decorating. Brigades of 'migratory workers' (*shabashniki*) do building work at high prices. Karpets concedes that such people are not strictly parasites, but as they often obtain materials and equipment illegally they engage in 'parasitic activity'. 'Parasites' in the sense of people who do not labour and enjoy publicly provided services, often form part of a criminal sub-culture. In Latvia a study showed that one quarter of offenders were unemployed at the time of the offence, and that of these, two-thirds had 'led a parasitic way of life' for three years.[57] Another study in the Chuvash autonomous republic showed that 50 per cent of those convicted for leading a parasitic way of life had previous convictions, and 82 per cent were ordered by the court to undergo treatment for alcoholism.[58] An estimate of 500,000 'parasites' living in the USSR has been leaked to the western press, allegedly originating from the First Deputy Procurator of the USSR.[59] Karpets reports that the 'number of people who lead a parasitic way of life is quite noticeable in a number of regions'.[60]

In late 1982 and early 1983, in an attempt to tighten up on labour discipline and to draw as great a number of the working population as possible into the workforce, the authorities enforced the law on 'parasites'. This law (Article 209 of the RSFSR criminal code) states that a person (usually a man, because of the many exemptions for women) who has been living off others for four months can be charged with parasitism, as long as he or she has been given warning after three months to find a job. The sanctions are a maximum of two years' imprisonment for a first conviction and a minimum of one year and maximum of three years' imprisonment for a subsequent conviction for the same offence.[61] In his address to the 27th Party Congress Gorbachev deprecated the persistence of parasites and others who misappropriate socialist property. He promised 'additional measures' against them in the near future.[62]

These draconian administrative measures should not detract from the responsibility of government to provide work. Fifteen days after a request has been received, the executive committees of local soviets are obliged to provide work and accommodation for idlers. Karpets emphasizes the fact that the 'instructions of Soviet executive committees are binding on enterprises, institutions and organizations'.[63] Rekunkov points out that it is obligatory for directors of enterprises and other establishments to employ people found idle, and sent to them by the police. Having been sent to a job, however, the authorities find it cumbersome to check whether the individual has continued in it satisfactorily.[64] In practice the law is difficult to enforce. Other commentators point out that such parasites often contrive to get themselves sacked. 'Assignment and treatment' centres for parasites find it difficult to obtain work for them. When they do so, vagrants often do not turn up for work but remain in the centre.[65]

Employers also dislike taking on such employees and there is some evidence to show that the employers make life hard for them by giving them more (compulsory) overtime, and send them to help out in other enterprises and in agriculture.[66] A report by the Deputy Chief of the Omsk Ministry of Internal Affairs Administration has pointed out that many enterprises, 'on various pretexts . . . "purposefully" rid themselves of indisciplined people and attract reliable, skilled cadres to replace them.'[67] He goes on to point out that dismissals and transfers have a bad effect on the morale of such workers who become sources of public disorder. 'The more people who are dismissed for negative reasons, the higher the overall level of crime'. Maintaining people in jobs has social benefits and a more stringent policy of labour efficiency leading to sackings would have social costs, borne by society at large. One may surmise quite confidently that the security services favour full employment and administrative, rather than market, methods to achieve it.

## SHABASHNIKI

Despite the gloomy picture of crime and drunkenness given above, many so-called 'parasites' do useful work. Groups of people, typically men aged 25–40, group together into brigades of labourers. They take on jobs in agriculture and building on a piece-rate basis for a given price. Such workers are called *shabashniki*. Their wages range from twice to eight times the regular rate for a job.[68] The 'economic mechanism' of such employment has been described as follows: 'The migrant labourer is given complete independence in setting his goal and in choosing the means of achieving it. The book-keeping is simple: my money for your work. If there are no materials, find them. If there's no machinery, get some. There's no oversight, no supervision.'[69]

The parasitical nature of *shabashniki* is derived not from not working but from its entrepreneurial activity and from a tendency of such groups to obtain their materials illicitly.[70] Detractors regard them as having inflated or 'unearned' incomes. From the point of view of the utilization of labour resources, which is our concern here, *shabashniki* should increase the number of people at work though they are not employed by an enterprise for a wage. Though they may work for only part of the year (six to eight months), in 1984 Fedorchuk reported that thousands of brigades head for areas of labour shortage and that in some rural areas 50 per cent of building work was completed by them. A survey conducted in Armenia found that of seasonal workers going outside the republic, 55 per cent had previously not been employed, 20 per cent had had part-time jobs, and 25 per cent had jobs they did not like. The main incentive to work outside Armenia was the very high level of wages as most of the Armenians were poorly paid peasants.[71] In the RSFSR, the Republican Goskomtrud found that 10–15,000 people participate for from six to eight months per year in *shabashniki* activity. In Armenia the figure is 25,000.[72] Their numbers in total have been estimated at about 400,000.[73] In the mid-1980s, opinion turned somewhat in their favour, and an article in *Izvestiya* pointed to their higher productivity and to the fact that they fulfilled the Leninist criterion of payment 'according to one's work'.[74] Such workers are also geared to working for 'end-results'. Fedorchuk, in the same interview, conceded that penal measures alone could not overcome the illegal activities associated with *shabashniki*: 'the main thing here is to improve the economic mechanism'. An article in *Izvestiya* has further pointed out that readers' letters indicate that employees of 'monitoring agencies' (i.e. those concerned with allocating and controlling labour) are opposed to *shabashniki*, whereas 'everybody else—economic executives, officials, workers, agronomists—is to one degree or another "in favour"'. The largest number of letters in favour originate from researchers and engineers.[75]

## CONTROL OF THE LABOUR MARKET

Current practice has moved away from compulsory registration and direction of labour because it limits freedom of choice by employees and employers. But influential writers such as Maslova[76] and Kotlyar argue for a comprehensive system of job placement organizations. Even by the middle of 1984, only 15 per cent of job moves came under the control of local agencies. In 1984, Kotlyar pointed out that labour moved from 'labour-deficit regions to labour-surplus [ones], from enterprises whose staffs were below strength to enterprises with above-plan numbers of employees.'[77] Such a system would enable more efficient intra- and inter-branch mobility to take place and would facilitate greater geographical mobility. Giving an institution such as the State Committee on Labour responsibility for job moves would also 'relieve enterprises of the obligation to find jobs for the employees they released'.[78] The more 'spontaneous' job recruitment ('at the factory gate') would become redundant. Such proposals, including the setting-up of uniform allocation procedures, administrative sanctions and fines on uncooperative officials have been widely canvassed in the USSR, but have not been taken up.[79]

The organizing principles of labour placement are the market ('recruitment at the factory gate') which has been and is currently dominant in the USSR and administrative direction (the 'Kaluga-Ufa experiment'). A greater emphasis on planning and discipline will encourage the Soviet authorities to move towards the weakening of rights of enterprises to recruit labour, to strengthen the placement of workers through labour exchanges and to exert sanctions as suggested above. Labour experts like Kotlyar argue pursuasively that recruitment of labour by enterprises (i.e. the 'free market') differs significantly from the organizational forms ('planning') of the socialist state. Clearly, enhanced administrative control of labour would entail giving more powers to labour placement agencies; this is an example of the 'strengthening of labour discipline' which has been emphasized under the Andropov−Chernenko−Gorbachev leadership.[80] The higher rates of labour mobility required by more intensive forms of production will probably lead to the introduction of severance pay, extended periods of retraining on full pay,[81] and the transfer of responsibility for re-employment from enterprises to labour exchanges. Such measures will reduce the number of 'parasites' and *shabashniki*. But more flexible payment of wages at enterprises as reward for 'end-products' is more likely to undermine the opportunity for self-employment.

## REFERENCES

1. John Barber, 'The Development of Soviet Employment and Labour Policy 1930−1941', in D. Lane (ed.), *Labour and Employment in the USSR* (Brighton: Harvester Press 1986), pp. 55-6.
2. Social security institutions are also involved with placing invalids, the Ministry of Internal Affairs settles released prisoners and 'parasites'. The military authorities also help servicemen transferred to the reserves. These forms of placement are discussed by A. Kotlyar, 'Sistema trudoustroystva v SSSR', *Ekonomicheskie nauki*, no. 3 (March 1984), pp. 50-60.
3. Ibid.
4. Barber, p. 59.
5. D. Satter, *Wall St Journal*, 24 June 1982.
6. I.S. Maslova, *Ekonomicheskie voprosy pereraspredeleniya rabochey sily pri sotsializme* (1976), p. 153. No total numbers are given in this source. Most of the following section is based on information given by Maslova.
7. Tass statement, 2 October 1984. Reported in *FBIS: USSR National Affairs*, 12 October 1984.
8. Maslova, pp. 165-6.
9. Data cited in I.S. Maslova, *Elconomicheskie voprosy pereraspredeleniya rabochey sily pri sotsializme* (1976), pp. 95-6. Extractive industries had

higher rates: the oil industry 8.5 per cent, coal 7.6 per cent, building materials 8.0 per cent: ibid., p. 97.

10. Maslova, pp. 101-2.
11. Ibid., pp. 104-5.
12. Ibid., p. 106.
13. Ibid., p. 108.
14. Ibid., p. 110.
15. Ibid., p. 128. No indication of the total number of families moved is given.
16. Moscow Home Service, 11 December 1976. Reported by BBC *World Broadcasts* SU/5404/B/6 (5 June 1977).
17. Maslova, p. 130.
18. On the Baikal–Amur railway construction (BAM) 50 per cent of the migrants came under some organized scheme. V.P. Chichkanov, *Izvestiya*, 11 December 1984; *CDSP*, vol. 35, no. 50, p. 8.
19. See M. Matthews, *Education in the Soviet Union* (London: Allen and Unwin, 1982), pp. 58-61.
20. E.R. Sarukhanov, *Sotsial'ekonomicheskie problemy upravleniya rabochey siloy pri sotsializme* (1981) p. 87; A. E. Kotlyar (ed.), *Dvizhenie rabochey sily v krupnom gorode* (1982), p.141, cited by A. Helgeson, *Finding Work in the Soviet Economy: Employment Agencies for First-Time Job Seekers* (NASEES Annual Conference, 1984), p. 3. For an account of a local labour bureau's work with school-leavers, see V. Orlov, *Turkmenskaya Iskra*, 23 March 1982, p. 2.
21. A. Kotlyar, *Pravda*, 13 May 1984; *CDSP*, vol. 36 (1984), no. 19, p. 9.
22. A. Kotlyar, 'Sistema trudoustroystva v SSSR', *Ekonomicheskie nauki*, no. 3 (March 1984), p. 56.
23. See Helgeson, p. 6.
24. Maslova, p. 170.
25. Ibid., p. 171.
26. L.A. Kostin, 'Reservy . . .' (1984), p. 37.
27. L.A. Kostin, *Trudovye resursy v odinnadtsatoy pyatiletke'* (1981), p. 29.
28. V. Yaborov, *Pravda*, 25 March 1982; CDSP, vol. 34, no. 12 (1982), p. 12.
29. Yaborov, *op.cit.*
30. Maslova, p. 175.
31. Yaborov, *op.cit.*; *CDSP*, *op.cit.*
32. A. Kotlyar, *Pravda*, 13 May 1984.
33. Data based on survey in 13 towns in RSFSR. Chernichenko notes that in Kaluga the payment from enterprises per hire was three roubles in 1984: *Izvestiya*, 2 August 1984.
34. Maslova, p. 181.
35. For details, see Maslova, p.182. In Perm, it has been reported that on average it takes 24 days for a person on his own to find another job, with the help of a 'city personnel department', the maximum time taken is 10 days. Yaborov, *op.cit.*; *CDSP*, *op.cit.*
36. Maslova, p. 181.
37. Yaborov *op.cit.*
38. D. Mazitov (head of a bureau in Bashkir), *Pravda*, 25 May 1983; *CDSP*, vol.

35 (1983), no. 21, p. 20. Mazitov calls for greater powers for the job bureaux.
39.  Based on sample surveys by USSR Committee on Labour and Social
     Affairs. Cited by A. Chernichenko, *Izvestiya*, 2 August 1984; *CDSP*, vol.
     36, no. 31, p. 14. A hiring fee of 3 roubles is given here. In the Ukraine and
     Latvia an attempt was made to have a system of contracts between
     enterprises and bureaux, presumably with a lump-sum payment.
     Chernichenko advocates extension of the Kaluga system.
40.  Maslova, p. 194.
41.  Ibid., p. 195.
42.  A. Kotlyar, 'Sistema trudoustroystva v SSSR', *Ekonomicheskie nauki*, no. 3,
     March 1984.
43.  *Loc.cit.*, p. 57.
44.  Ibid., p. 58. There may be an element of special pleading here as 70 per cent
     would have had presumably lower or equal wages.
45.  Ibid.
46.  *Pravda*, 13 May 1984; *CDSP*, vol. 36, no. 19, p. 9. Here he repeats an
     argument advanced earlier in his book: A. Kotlyar (ed.), *Dvizhenie
     rabochey sily v krupnom gorode: Problemy regulirovaniya* (1982), pp.
     119-22.
47.  Ibid.
48.  A bureau was formed in Ufa in 1968. For an early account, see G.
     Kudryashev in *Izvestiya*, 10 February 1971, p. 3.
49.  Maslova, p. 195.
50.  A. Chernichenko, *Izvestiya*, 2 August 1984.
51.  Maslova.
52.  Chernichenko, *op.cit.*
53.  Positive references, however, are often made in the Soviet press.
     Chernichenko advocated the extension of the experiment to reduce labour
     turnover (ibid.).
54.  Ya. Dzenitis, 'Bor'ba s tuneyadstvom—put' real'nogo sokrashcheniya
     prestupnosti', *Sotsialisticheskaya zakonnost'*, no. 10 (1984), p. 5.
55.  V. Nekrasov (assistant head of department of USSR People's Control
     Committee), *Pravda*, 19 May 1983, p. 3. On 27 March 1984, *Pravda* ran
     another article citing examples of youths hanging around with no work to do.
56.  Moscow broadcast, 17 December 1984. Reported in *FBIS: USSR National
     Affairs* and *Political and Social Development*, 18 December 1984, p. 2.
57.  Ya. Dzenitis, p. 3.
58.  N. Filippov. 'Sovershenstvovat' praktiku bor'by tuneyadstvom', *Sovetskaya
     yustitsiya*. No. 10, May 1984.
59.  *Le Monde*, 20 October 1984. There were also 11.7 million summonses a year
     for drunkenness.
60.  *Izvestiya*, 5 April 1985.
61.  I. Portnov and V. Fokin, 'Deyatel'nost' suda po presecheniyu
     paraziticheskogo obraza zhizhi', *Sovetskaya yustitsiya* no.4, February 1984,
     pp. 21-3. For an overview of labour laws, see S. Karpinski, 'Razvitie
     trudovogo zakonodatel'stva v usloviyakh zrelogo sotsialisticheskogo
     obshchestva', *Sotsialisticheski trud*, no. 9 (1981), pp. 3-10.

62. M. Gorbachev, *Pravda*, 26 February 1986.
63. Karpinski, ibid.
64. Moscow broadcast, 17 December 1984.
65. See account of a reception and assignment centre by a correspondent in Khabarovsk, *Izvestiya*, 4 February 1985.
66. Portnov and Fokin, p.22.
67. *Pravda*, 3 May 1980, p. 2. In Omsk, he points out that 25,000 people per year leave work of their own volition and 3000 are dismissed by the administration. Managers respond 'very unwillingly' to the militia's requests to take people from the register of 'temporarily unemployed'.
68. For a full account, see Patrick Murphy, 'Soviet *Shabashniki*: Material Incentives at Work', *Problems of Communism*, vol. 35 (1985), p. 51.
69. N. Kvizhinadze and Yu. Mikhailov, *Komsomolskaya pravda*, 3 November 1982. English translation in *CDSP*, vol. 34, no. 46, p. 10.
70. Murphy, pp. 52, 54-5.
71. Interview with Fedorchuk in *Literaturnaya gazeta*, 29 August 1984. English translation, *CDSP*, vol. 36, no. 34, p. 5. On Armenia see discussion between I. Kruglyanskaya and S.A. Karapetyan, *Izvestiya*, 15 April 1986, English summary in *CDSP*, vol. 38, no. 16 (1986), pp. 6, 24.
72. Kh. Bokov, 'Shabashnik ili udarnik', *Trud*, 16 December 1983. Many others, of course, participate in summer harvesting and are released by enterprises to do so. In Leningrad 6000 people commute daily in summer to work in the fields: *Izvestiya*, 3 July 1983. Cited by A. Tenson, RL 269/83, p. 2. On Armenia, see Kruglyanskaya and S.A. Karapetyan, *op.cit.*, p. 6.
73. In the Ivan Franko province of the Ukraine, 15,000 seasonal workers depart annually to other regions. N. Kvizhinadze and Yu. Mikhailov, *Komsomol'skaya pravda*, 2 November 1982. English translation in *CDSP*, vol. 34, no. 46, p. 9.
74. I. Kruglyanskaya, *Izvestiya*, 30 July 1985. English version in *CDSP*, vol. 37, no. 30 (1985), pp. 5-6.
75. I. Kruglyanskaya, *Izvestiya*, 14 December 1985. English summary *CDSP*, vol. 37, no. 50 (1985) pp. 28-9.
76. See, Maslova, p. 197.
77. A. Kotlyar, *Pravda*, 13 May 1984.
78. Ibid.
79. Yaborov, *Pravda*, 25 March 1982. Kotlyar and Chernichenko are examples of a long line of proposals. M.Ya. Sonin made similar suggestions in 1959: *Vosproizvodstvo rabochey sily v SSSR i balansy truda* (1959).
80. Kotlyar cites in support of his position the resolution 'On Supplementary Measures to Strengthen Work Discipline', *Pravda*, 7 August 1983, cited in *Economicheskie nauki*, no. 3 (March 1984), note 7.
81. The reduction in the numbers employed in administration following the merging of five Union Republican Ministries into one agro-industrial complex in 1985, led to displaced staff being paid full salary for three months. Cited by A. Trehub, 'Unemployment in the Soviet Union', RL 412/85 p. 1.

# 4 Types of Involuntary Unemployment

While mass structural unemployment is not a characteristic of the USSR, one must consider the presence of other forms of unemployment and underemployment, the most important types of which are 'structural', 'seasonal' and 'frictional'. Structural unemployment is an absence of jobs in a particular labour market. This usually occurs on a regional basis. Population grows in a given area at a faster rate than the supply of jobs. In addition, certain districts might be predominantly concerned with a particular industry having a relatively narrow and specialized pattern of skills: for instance, the mining industry recruits few women workers, in textiles men are a minority and agriculture (at least in the USSR) has a preponderance of unskilled manual workers. 'Seasonal' unemployment is linked to the cyclical nature of production or of demand. In the Soviet Union, due to the inclement winter weather, this is particularly the case with agriculture, fishing, open-cast mining and building. 'Frictional' unemployment occurs when workers are idle between jobs or statuses. School-leavers or demobilized military may not wish, or may be unable, to find suitable work immediately. If workers are hierarchically or geographically mobile there may be periods of idleness between the time that workers leave one job and take up another.

## FRICTIONAL UNEMPLOYMENT

In any modern economy, however perfectly organized, there are likely to be periods of 'friction' when school-leavers come onto the market or when employees voluntarily change jobs. Instantaneous individual adjustments which would be necessary to equilibrate supply of (and demand for) labour even in a perfectly free market are impossible to achieve: in any labour market there are always some jobs vacant and some people seeking work. This is illustrated in Figure 4.1. At wage W, ONi is demanded, but only ON is employed. The frictional level of unemployment is N-Ni.[1]

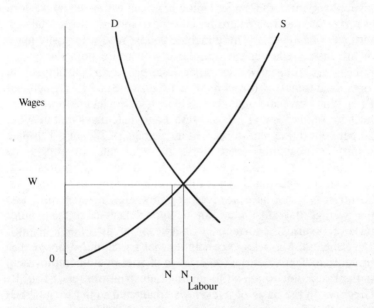

*Figure 4.1: Frictional unemployment*

In market economies, it is usually reckoned that even with full employment, 2–3 per cent of the workforce will remain 'frictionally' unemployed. 'Frictional' unemployment is not usually counted in market economies as giving a person an unemployed status. The length of the period recognized as being 'between jobs', or actively seeking work, makes a great deal of difference to unemployment statistics. People unsuccessfully seeking work for less than four weeks are usually excluded, and in some countries, such as Sweden, the qualifying period is as much as 60 days.[2]

## MEASUREMENT OF TURNOVER

Frictional unemployment is the major source on which the rate of unemployment in the Soviet Union has been estimated by western experts. Such estimates are based on extrapolation from data on turnover (*tekuchest'*). These include people who voluntarily leave or are dismissed, but exclude those who retire, join the armed forces, are transferred to other enterprises or participate in 'organized transfers' (*orgnabor*). On such a basis, Mesa-Lago and Peter Wiles have attempted to calculate total Soviet unemployment rates for the 1950s and 1960s. Mesa-Lago[3] calculates that in 1960, 20 per cent of the workforce lost an average of 27 work days as a result of changing jobs: this gives a rate of 'aggregate unemployment' at 3.3 per cent. As Mesa-Lago points out, however, the statistical basis for these calculations has some flaws. Turnover may not have involved any time-lags in some cases and the average days lost may not be representative of the whole: turnover varies enormously between areas[4] (see below). Nevertheless, Mesa-Lago concludes that a rate of 2-3 per cent is 'roughly indicative of the importance of frictional unemployment in the USSR due to job shifts among industrial workers'.[5] Paul R. Gregory, on the basis of interviews conducted in the early 1980s with 2,800 Soviet emigrés living in the United States, estimates that the level of unemployment is 2½ to 3 per cent.[6] Peter Wiles, basing his estimate on a 30 calendar day average idleness for a job-changer in Krasnoyarsk city, calculates a 1.3 per cent frictional unemployment rate for the USSR.[7] In the Soviet journal *Trud* in 1974, it was reported that in the RSFSR 3.5 million people in industry and building changed jobs: it was further calculated that this represented a loss of 400,000 person work years. If one expresses this as a proportion of total employment in industry and building one may calculate an annual rate of frictional employment of 1.5 per cent.[8] In the Belorussian Republic in

1976/77, it has been calculated that the equivalent of 10-11,000 people were lost to production in industry and building as a result of turnover.[9] This represents a loss of under one per cent per year.[10]

Turnover varies between regions and between industries. In 1967, it averaged 22.1 per cent in the USSR, with a range of from 18.6 per cent in Belorussia to 39.8 per cent in Tadzhikistan.[11] In the USSR, turnover fell in industry from 22.1 per cent in 1967 to 19.8 per cent in 1972.[12] Teckenberg cites the following rates for the RSFSR for the late 1960s—in the coal industry: 17.1 per cent, metal: 14.8 per cent, chemicals: 18.8 per cent, machinery: 18.1 per cent, light industry: 20.8 per cent, construction materials: 34.4 per cent, the food industry: 35.7 per cent.[13] A study by Borisov in Minsk province found the following rates of turnover—in all industry in 1975: 16.9 per cent (20.1 in 1970), in machine tools and metalworking: 18.2 per cent (22.4 in 1970), woodworking and cellulose and paper industries: 11.3 per cent (17.6 in 1970), chemicals and petrochemicals: 21 per cent (25.4), light industry: 14.5 per cent (13.7), food: 26.6 per cent (30.4), glass: 10.5 per cent (17.5). This represents an average turnover of 16.6 per cent in 1975 and 20.1 per cent in 1970.[14] M.I. Dolishni provides some interesting data on turnover in the Ukraine. In the eighth Five Year Plan (1966–70), turnover totalled 19 per cent of the industrial workforce per annum (about 1 million workers changed their place of work), by 1970–75 the average total had fallen to 700,000, representing a total loss of 1.5 per cent of industrial production.[15] In the early 1980s, 20 million workers changed jobs or retired each year; a third of these represented 'natural' transfers—joining the army or higher education, going on retirement or invalidity pensions—giving a net rate of job changers of 14 per cent of the employed workforce.[16]

To conclude, though levels of turnover declined in the late 1970s[17] and early 1980s, one might estimate a range of 1.3–1.5 per cent of the work force being frictionally unemployed at any time in the USSR. Labour turnover is not necessarily an economic cost and from a macroeconomic point of view it may have some benefits. But Soviet enterprises regard turnover as a cost: it disrupts the work process, new workers require training, and they are initially less efficient. Enterprises anticipate and attempt to minimize the disruptive effects of turnover by 'overfulfilling' the plan for labour: in 1975, Gosplan USSR planned 101.6 million jobs, and actual employment totalled 104.1 million.[18] The movement (*peremeshchenie*) of individuals between regions, industries and trades is a necessary response to the changing requirements of industrial needs. From the point of view of the individual, turnover through dissatisfaction with one job may lead in another to greater satisfaction and better conditions.[19]

## COMPARATIVE STUDY OF TURNOVER

Though labour turnover has been stressed as a cause of unemployment in the USSR, it is not a phenomenon stemming from the socialist organization of work. The level of turnover in comparative perspective, despite the protestations of some Soviet managers and economists, is not particularly high. The data we have considered above give turnover rates of around 20 per cent for Soviet industrial production.[20] In an authoritative survey of the literature, James L. Price shows that the median reported level of the annual turnover in western (mainly American) goods-producing industry was 50 per cent, with a range around the median of 39 per cent; in manufacturing industry the median was 54 per cent (range, 21 per cent) and mining 38 per cent (range, 13 per cent).[21] The latter figures are aggregated averages and some studies include separations due to retirement and death. Even so, rates of turnover under capitalism are very much higher than in the USSR; and American rates may be double the Soviet figures. (Rates in capitalist countries, however, may fall in periods of high unemployment.)

Labour turnover in the Soviet Union is a phenomenon which has many features in common with that of western industrial societies. Studies of turnover usually attempt to distinguish between rates for men and women, manual and non-manual workers, younger and older workers and poorly qualified and educated workers.[22] A study carried out in Belorussia in 1974 of 1634 people at job placement bureaux found that 53.5 per cent of those who had given up their jobs were under 30 years of age; of these 67.6 per cent had primary or incomplete secondary education.[23] They also had

*Table 4.1: Motives of employees of very large industrial enterprises in Novosibirsk and the Altai Kray who left work voluntarily*

| Reasons for Leaving | Altai Kray 1977–78 % | Novosibirsk 1964 % | Novosibirsk 1970 % |
|---|---|---|---|
| *Job Skills* | 12.1 | 14.0 | 11.7 |
| Work does not fit training or qualifications | 3.9 | 4.0 | 3.8 |
| Dissatisfaction with job | 7.2 | 8.9 | 7.2 |
| Lack of promotion prospects | 1.0 | 0.8 | 0.7 |
| Monotonous character of work | — | 0.3 | — |
| *The Organization of Labour* | 8.6 | 2.1 | 3.8 |
| Unrythmical work | 3.9 | 1.0 | 0.5 |
| 3 - Shift system of work | 4.7 | 1.1 | 3.3 |
| *Work Conditions* | 8.2 | 3.2 | 4.6 |
| Physically taxing work | 3.0 | 2.0 | 2.1 |
| Dirty work | 3.1 | 0.3 | 0.7 |
| Harmful Work Conditions | 1.8 | 0.9 | 1.8 |
| Lack of changing/showering facilities | 0.3 | — | — |
| *Personal Motives* | 35.8 | 38.0 | 42.7 |
| State of health | 6.5 | 5.7 | 4.0 |
| Change of residence | 16.4 | 26.9 | 21.9 |
| Marriage and childbirth | 8.2 | 4.9 | 2.7 |
| Lack of opportunity for study | 4.7 | 0.5 | 14.1 |
| *Standard of Living* | 28.8 | 35.1 | 31.2 |
| Unsatisfactory pay | 11.5 | 13.0 | 12.5 |
| Lack or absence of housing | 11.3 | 9.2 | 10.0 |
| Distance between home and work | 3.3 | 6.2 | 6.5 |
| Lack of child-care provision | 2.7 | 6.7 | 2.2 |
| *Relations within the Workplace* | 2.2 | 1.1 | 1.8 |
| Relations with administration | 1.8 | 0.9 | 1.7 |
| Disliked colleagues | 0.4 | 0.2 | 0.1 |
| Other motives | 4.2 | 5.7 | 4.2 |

Source: *Formirovanie i stabilizatsiya kvalifitsirovannykh kadrov promyshlennosti i stroitel'stva* (Novosibirsk, 1982), p. 216.

short service records: some 80 per cent of voluntary leavers had less than three years' service and 53.4 per cent had less than one year.[24] Another study found that turnover among 16–29 year olds was four times greater than among 30–39 year olds and 10–11 times greater than among those over 50 years old.[25] Reasons for leaving work in industrial enterprises in Lvov in 1976[26] were as follows: 1.7 per cent because work was not available in their own trades, 6.6 per cent were dissatisfied with the nature of work, 6.1 per cent were discontented with the organization (*rezhim*) of work, 13.2 per cent disliked the distance from work, 12 per cent wanted higher wages, 2.2 per cent felt children's pre-school facilities to be inadequate, 6.9 per cent changed their residence, and 35.2 per cent left for other reasons. Another study of voluntary leavers from enterprises in the Altai district and Novosibirsk in Siberia found that 'personal motives' closely followed by 'standard of living' accounted for the highest proportion of those who left. The 'organization of labour' accounted for relatively few moves. The details are shown in Table 4.1.

Following Price's analysis of the western literature, we may concur that workers with long service have lower rates of leaving than those with short service, younger workers have higher rates of turnover than older ones, lower skilled manuals experience more turnover than the skilled, non-manuals have lower rates than manuals, and women have higher rates than men.[27]

The conclusion that levels of turnover are significantly lower than in the West may be advanced confidently despite the ambiguities in statistical reporting. This is a surprising conclusion. One would expect that the higher the rate of labour utilization (i.e. in the West, the lower the rate of unemployment) the greater the level of turnover.[28] As March and Simon have expressed it: 'Under nearly all conditions, the most accurate single predictor of labor turnover is the state of the economy.'[29] Price points out that 'No evidence could be located which contradicts the hypothesised relationship between level of employment and turnover.'[30] In the Soviet Union, however, the growing *shortage* of labour would appear to be associated with a *decline* in turnover rates.


## LIMITATIONS ON LABOUR TURNOVER

There are a number of institutional variables which may explain why Soviet rates are lower than western ones. People seek to leave their jobs if on balance their dissatisfaction is greater than their

*Table 4.2: Pay Differences by Grade and Trade at Various Enterprises*

| Job | Grade | Wage by Factory (Roubles) | | | | |
|---|---|---|---|---|---|---|
| | | Proletarski molot | Tooling factory | Avtogidrousilitel | A.T.E. | A.P.Z. |
| Turning-machine setter | 6th | 193.19 | — | 179.82 | 175.34 | — |
| | 5th | 159.11 | 127.31 | 154.61 | 149.82 | — |
| | 4th | — | 109.75 | 133.28 | 129.10 | — |
| Repairer | 3rd | 88.89 | — | 100.09 | 112.49 | 89.20 |
| | 4th | 111.87 | 116.93 | 114.87 | 129.10 | 102.36 |
| | 5th | 130.23 | 136.13 | 133.28 | 149.82 | 119.18 |
| | 6th | 151.31 | 155.88 | 155.09 | 174.34 | 138.46 |
| Electrician-fitter | 3rd | 85.70 | 95.60 | 100.09 | 112.49 | — |
| | 4th | 102.36 | — | 114.87 | 129.10 | — |
| | 5th | 119.18 | 124.83 | 133.28 | 149.82 | — |
| | 6th | 138.46 | — | 155.09 | 174.34 | — |
| Plumber | 3rd | — | — | 114.63 | 112.49 | 102.36 |
| | 4th | — | — | 131.59 | 128.76 | 117.56 |
| | 5th | — | 148.18 | 152.92 | 149.41 | 137.42 |
| | 6th | — | — | 177.88 | 173.86 | 158.88 |
| Fitter/Toolmaker | 4th | — | 108.49 | 114.87 | 124.66 | 102.36 |
| | 5th | — | 126.70 | 133.28 | 160.15 | 119.18 |

*Source: Z. Skarupo, 'Sokrashchenie tekuchesti i uluchshenie ispol'zovaniya rabochey sily', Planovoe khozyaystvo, no. 6 (1977), p. 122.*

satisfaction. 'Satisfaction' is linked to a number of variables. In the West level of pay plays an important though by no means the only part in an individual's satisfaction with work. Low pay, other things being equal, leads to dissatisfaction and labour mobility.[31] Pay, however, does not respond to shortage in the USSR in the same way as in the West and wage differentials are much lower. Nevertheless, while wage-scales are laid down by national and local bodies of Goskomtrud, there is in practice considerable responsiveness of earnings to local conditions and relative labour shortage. Pay responds to shortage, but not to the same extent as in western capitalist labour markets. This can be illustrated by the data collected in Belorussia (Table 4.2) where workers of an identical skill working in various factories are shown to receive different levels of wages. Policy, however, is to reduce these differences which are put down to inadequate 'norming' policy.

Generally speaking, workers of a given skill grade should receive an identical wage for identical work, unlike under capitalism where wages should be linked to what particular labour markets can pay. As noted above, dissatisfaction with pay figures prominently as a subjective cause for leaving—21.4 per cent in industry, 29.6 per cent in the public service sector, 23.4 per cent in transport and communications.[32] Turnover is also linked to wage levels: workers earning under 120 roubles had a 22.5 per cent turnover rate, those earning 120—30 roubles 20.3 per cent, and for those earning 130—40 roubles it fell to 17.9 per cent.[33] These figures again may be related to skill level and length of service. Of crucial significance is that in the USSR a given pay rate does not, through inflation, decline in real income terms to the same extent as it has done in the West. Satisfaction is only marginally increased with a pay rise, though dissatisfaction more than proportionally rises with a *fall* in pay.

The 'level of integration' of the worker has been found to be a significant determinant of turnover in the West: it is inversely related to turnover. Where workers have high levels of participation in primary group relations then integration is high and turnover low. The Soviet factory attempts to create positive identification on the part of the workforce. The relatively high levels of participation in social, economic and political organizations at the workplace, particularly in large and successful enterprises, have led me to conclude that the Soviet worker has a high level of identification with his/her work groups.[34] The provision of social services and housing through the factory collective distinguishes the Soviet factory from that in the West. The lack of housing in the vicinity of a potential new employer[35] is an effective deterrent for workers to stay put— though they do not lose their factory housing should they change jobs.

The other most important determinant of labour mobility is opportunity. In the West, full employment gives rise to opportunity. Though the labour market is imperfect, knowledge is relatively widespread and workers are able by changing jobs to better their conditions, pay and status. Fewer women have full-time employment and the need for two or more members of a family unit concurrently to find suitable jobs does not happen as often as in the USSR where full-time employment for married women inhibits their geographical mobility. In the West, mobility is also enhanced by a free market for housing in the private sector: here again is a structural difference with the USSR, where the private urban housing market is small. Outside of local networks, knowledge of available jobs is low in the USSR. There is no national labour market. Job-placement bureaux are of limited and local utility. The media is not developed as a source of job recruitment, and competitive recruitment is not practised. Hence in the Soviet Union knowledge of job opportunity is low and this deters turnover, even though people are not administratively prevented from moving to new jobs.

One other caveat should be borne in mind when comparing Soviet with capitalist market-type societies. Transfers and displacement occur in the Soviet Union within enterprises and administrative units, such as industrial ministries. Charged with the responsibility of finding work for displaced workers and having a shortage of labour, enterprises are usually large enough to transfer excess labour from one plant to another. As in western societies, large-scale employers produce low levels of turnover[36] as displacements may be absorbed in the organization which has many of the characteristics of primary rather than secondary markets, providing careers and not just jobs for employees. The variation in turnover by size of factory in the USSR is shown on Table 4.3: part (a) is drawn from a study in Belorussia, and part (b) from the Ministry of Machinery for Light Industry and the Food

Table 4.3: Level of Turnover by Size of Enterprise

| (a) | Enterprises by size of labour force | Number of enterprises in the group | Coefficient of turnover |
|---|---|---|---|
| | 200 | 8 | 37.0 |
| | 201-500 | 10 | 23.3 |
| | 501-1000 | 6 | 20.2 |
| | 1000+ | 5 | 12.4 |
| | | 29 | 16.7 |

| (b) | Enterprises by size of workforce | Average turnover of workers 1973–75 (%) | Services provided for workforce (range) |
|---|---|---|---|
| | less than 250 | 40.2 | 1 – 2 |
| | 251 – 500 | 26.9 | 2 – 3 |
| | 501 – 1000 | 21.7 | 3 – 5 |
| | 1001 – 2000 | 20.9 | 4 – 7 |
| | 2001 – 5000 | 17.4 | 6 – 8 |
| | 5001 – 10,000 | 13.7 | 9 – 12 |
| | 10,000+ | 7.9 | 12 – 15 |

Sources:    (a) Skarupo (1977), p. 118.
(b) A. Gal'tsov, 'Ukreplenie predpriyatiy - vazhny faktor snizheniya tekuchesti kadrov,' Sots.trud, no.1 (1977), p. 34.

Industry. Turnover at the smallest factories (under 200 workers) is three times as great as at the largest (over 1000). The large enterprises have great advantages in providing varied and constant work and resources to finance a wide range of social activities and welfare services (factory shops, holiday provision, kindergartens, health services and housing). As shown in part (b), very large factories provide 7–15 times the services for the workforce compared to very small enterprises. At present, Soviet enterprises have a responsibility to find alternative work for workers displaced by new technology or reorganization and this stimulates within-factory mobility. Western firms, however, have no responsibility for finding work for their redundant employees and the onus falls on the employee and is facilitated by the government through the labour exchange and welfare maintenance policies. The economic system in the USSR ensures not only full employment, but also job security.


## STRUCTURAL UNEMPLOYMENT

Structural unemployment is defined as a lack of demand for certain types of labour caused either by a reduction in demand for particular products or as a result of an increase in the supply of workers. In advanced western market economies shifts in demand for products lead to regional imbalances in the labour market: for instance, a reduction in primary industrial output causes unemployment in mining and agricultural areas. In western countries in recent years, the increased numbers of women seeking work is another source of structural unemployment. An economy may solve such imbalances either by moving workers from areas of labour surplus to labour scarcity or by creating jobs in areas of labour surplus. An excess of labour in peasant-type agriculture is not strictly 'structural unemployment' for reasons discussed above; it is, however, a waste of labour resources.

Demographic changes in population affect labour supply independently of the existing location of industry. The 'labour supply' in any country has to be seen in a geographical perspective because workers are members of families and localities and local networks tend to inhibit mobility. Industrial development and population reproduction are never perfectly symmetrical. In the USSR, the major potential mismatch between population supply and labour demand is to be found in the growth of the labour supply in the Central Asian areas of the country among the agricultural indigenous population whereas the major industrial developments are occurring in the Siberian areas and the traditional European zones. The chief structural change in demand is likely to be for labour associated with intensive growth in the tertiary sector. Before considering Soviet policy on population migration and industrial location, the magnitude of the problem may be indicated by study of the changes in labour supply.

Table 4.4:   Total Population and Average Annual Change, for the USSR and Republics 1950–1980*

| Republic | 1950 | 1960 | 1970 | 1980 | Average annual percent change | | | | Percent distribution | | | |
|---|---|---|---|---|---|---|---|---|---|---|---|---|
| | | | | | 1950–60 | 1960–70 | 1970–80 | 1950–80 | 1950 | 1960 | 1970 | 1980 |
| USSR | 178,547 | 212,372 | 241,640 | 264,486 | 1.7 | 1.3 | 0.9 | 1.3 | 100.0 | 100.0 | 100.0 | 100.0 |
| Baltic Republics | 5,614 | 6,078 | 6,846 | 7,423 | 0.8 | 1.2 | 0.8 | 0.9 | 31 | 2.9 | 2.8 | 2.8 |
| Lithuania | 2,573 | 2,756 | 3,127 | 3,420 | 0.7 | 1.3 | 0.9 | 0.9 | 1.4 | 1.3 | 1.3 | 1.3 |
| Latvia | 1,944 | 2,113 | 2,363 | 2,529 | 0.8 | 1.1 | 0.7 | 0.9 | 1.1 | 1.0 | 1.0 | 1.0 |
| Estonia | 1,097 | 1,209 | 1,356 | 1,474 | 1.0 | 1.1 | 0.8 | 1.0 | 0.6 | 0.6 | 0.6 | 0.6 |
| Slavic Republics | 145,735 | 169,662 | 186,146 | 197,929 | 1.5 | 0.9 | 0.6 | 1.0 | 81.6 | 79.9 | 77.0 | 74.8 |
| RSFSR | 101,438 | 119,046 | 130,036 | 138,365 | 1.6 | 0.9 | 0.6 | 1.0 | 56.8 | 56.1 | 53.4 | 52.3 |
| Ukraine | 36,588 | 42,469 | 47,111 | 49,953 | 1.5 | 1.0 | 0.6 | 1.0 | 20.5 | 20.0 | 19.5 | 18.9 |
| Belorussia | 7,709 | 8,147 | 8,999 | 9,611 | 0.6 | 1.0 | 0.7 | 0.7 | 4.3 | 3.8 | 3.7 | 3.6 |
| Moldavia | 2,290 | 2,968 | 3,568 | 3,968 | 2.6 | 1.8 | 1.1 | 1.8 | 1.3 | 1.4 | 1.5 | 1.5 |
| Transcaucasian Republics | 7,700 | 9,774 | 12,291 | 14,227 | 2.4 | 2.3 | 1.5 | 2.0 | 4.3 | 4.6 | 5.1 | 5.4 |
| Georgia | 3,494 | 4,129 | 4,685 | 5,041 | 1.7 | 1.3 | 0.7 | 1.2 | 2.0 | 1.9 | 1.9 | 1.9 |
| Azerbaydzhan | 2,859 | 3,816 | 5,115 | 6,112 | 2.9 | 2.9 | 1.8 | 2.5 | 1.6 | 1.8 | 2.1 | 2.3 |
| Armenia | 1,347 | 1,829 | 2,491 | 3,074 | 3.1 | 3.1 | 2.1 | 2.8 | 0.8 | 0.9 | 1.0 | 1.2 |
| Kazakhstan | 6,592 | 9,755 | 13,004 | 14,858 | 3.9 | 2.9 | 1.3 | 2.7 | 3.7 | 4.6 | 5.4 | 5.6 |
| Central Asian Republics | 10,616 | 14,135 | 19,785 | 26,081 | 2.9 | 3.4 | 2.8 | 3.0 | 5.9 | 6.7 | 8.2 | 9.9 |
| Uzbekistan | 6,194 | 8,395 | 11,796 | 15,765 | 3.0 | 3.4 | 2.9 | 3.1 | 3.5 | 4.0 | 4.9 | 6.0 |
| Kirgiziya | 1,716 | 2,131 | 2,932 | 3,588 | 2.2 | 3.2 | 2.0 | 2.5 | 1.0 | 1.0 | 1.2 | 1.4 |
| Tadzhikistan | 1,509 | 2,045 | 2,899 | 3,901 | 3.0 | 3.5 | 3.0 | 3.2 | 0.8 | 1.0 | 1.2 | 1.5 |
| Turkmenia | 1,197 | 1,564 | 2,158 | 2,827 | 2.7 | 3.2 | 2.7 | 2.9 | 0.7 | 0.7 | 0.9 | 1.1 |

Sources:   Data for 1950 to 1970 from US Bureau of the Census. 'Population Projections by Age and Sex for the Republics and Major Economic Regions of the USSR 1970 to 2000; Series P.91. no. 26 (Washington DC: 1979), p. 3. And for 1980 from TsSu. 'Narodne khozyaystvo SSSR v 1979: statisticheski ezhegodnik (Moscow: Statistika. 1980), p. 10. Cited in G. Baldwin, 'Demographic Trends in the Soviet Union: 1950–2000', Soviet Economy in the 1980s, part 2, p. 267.

* Population in thousands at 1 January. Figures may not add to totals due to rounding.

*Table 4.5: Crude Birth Rates, Death Rates and Natural Increase of the Population of Union Republics**

| | 1940 | | | 1960 | | | 1970 | | | 1980 | | | 1984 | | |
|---|---|---|---|---|---|---|---|---|---|---|---|---|---|---|---|
| | Births | Deaths | Natural Increase | Births | Deaths | Natural Increase | Births | Deaths | Natural Increase | Births | Deaths | Natural Increase | Births | Deaths | Natural Increase |
| USSR | 31.2 | 18.0 | 13.2 | 24.9 | 7.1 | 17.8 | 17.4 | 8.2 | 9.2 | 18.3 | 10.3 | 8.0 | 19.6 | 10.8 | 8.8 |
| RSFSR | 33.0 | 20.6 | 12.4 | 23.2 | 7.4 | 15.8 | 14.6 | 8.7 | 5.9 | 15.9 | 11.0 | 4.9 | 16.9 | 11.6 | 5.3 |
| Ukraine | 27.3 | 14.3 | 13.0 | 20.5 | 6.9 | 13.6 | 15.2 | 8.8 | 6.4 | 14.8 | 11.4 | 3.4 | 15.6 | 12.0 | 3.6 |
| Belorussia | 26.8 | 13.1 | 13.7 | 24.4 | 6.6 | 17.8 | 16.2 | 7.6 | 8.6 | 16.0 | 9.9 | 6.1 | 16.5 | 10.5 | 6.0 |
| Uzbekistan | 33.8 | 13.2 | 20.6 | 39.8 | 6.0 | 33.8 | 33.6 | 5.5 | 28.1 | 33.8 | 7.4 | 26.4 | 36.2 | 7.4 | 28.8 |
| Kazakhstan | 40.8 | 21.4 | 19.4 | 37.2 | 6.6 | 30.6 | 23.4 | 6.0 | 17.4 | 23.8 | 8.0 | 15.8 | 25.4 | 8.2 | 17.2 |
| Georgia | 27.4 | 8.8 | 18.6 | 24.7 | 6.5 | 18.2 | 19.2 | 7.3 | 11.9 | 17.7 | 8.6 | 9.1 | 18.5 | 8.8 | 9.7 |
| Azerbaydzhan | 29.4 | 14.7 | 14.7 | 42.6 | 6.7 | 35.9 | 29.2 | 6.7 | 22.5 | 25.2 | 7.0 | 18.2 | 26.6 | 6.8 | 19.8 |
| Lithuania | 23.0 | 13.0 | 10.0 | 22.5 | 7.8 | 14.7 | 17.6 | 8.9 | 8.7 | 15.1 | 10.5 | 4.6 | 16.2 | 10.9 | 5.3 |
| Moldavia | 26.6 | 16.9 | 9.7 | 29.3 | 6.4 | 22.9 | 19.4 | 7.4 | 12.0 | 20.0 | 10.2 | 9.8 | 21.9 | 11.1 | 10.8 |
| Latvia | 19.3 | 15.7 | 3.6 | 16.7 | 10.0 | 6.7 | 14.5 | 11.2 | 3.3 | 14.0 | 12.7 | 1.3 | 15.7 | 12.9 | 2.8 |
| Kirgiziya | 33.0 | 16.3 | 16.7 | 36.9 | 6.1 | 30.8 | 30.5 | 7.4 | 23.1 | 29.6 | 8.4 | 21.2 | 32.1 | 8.3 | 23.8 |
| Tadzhikistan | 30.6 | 14.1 | 16.5 | 33.5 | 5.1 | 28.4 | 34.8 | 6.4 | 28.4 | 37.0 | 8.0 | 29.0 | 39.8 | 7.4 | 32.4 |
| Armenia | 41.2 | 13.8 | 27.4 | 40.1 | 6.8 | 33.3 | 22.1 | 5.1 | 17.0 | 22.7 | 5.5 | 17.2 | 24.2 | 5.8 | 18.4 |
| Turkmenia | 36.9 | 19.5 | 17.4 | 42.4 | 6.5 | 35.9 | 35.2 | 6.6 | 28.6 | 34.3 | 8.3 | 26.0 | 35.2 | 8.2 | 27.0 |
| Estonia | 16.1 | 17.0 | -0.9 | 16.6 | 10.5 | 6.1 | 15.8 | 11.1 | 4.7 | 15.0 | 12.3 | 2.7 | 15.9 | 12.5 | 3.4 |

* Per thousand of population
Source: *Narkhoz SSSR v 1984g* (1985), pp. 34–5.

## DEMOGRAPHIC CHANGE

The major sources of, and shifts in, population in the various republics of the USSR are illustrated on Table 4.4. This table shows population growth for the USSR from 1950 to 1980, broken down into the various republics. While each republic shows an increase in population from 1950 to 1980, the relative share of the Slavic republics (RSFSR, Ukraine and Belorussia) fell from 81.6 per cent in 1950 to 74.8 per cent in 1980. The annual percentage increase in the Central Asian republics (Uzbekistan, Kirgiziya, Tadzhikistan and Turkmenia) was 3 per cent between 1950 and 1980, and for Kazakhstan was 2.7 per cent. These figures, of course, reflect the ageing of the population and do not directly indicate the proportions in the various age groups.

The birthrates by republics are shown on Table 4.5. Compared with the national average of 17.4 in 1970 and 18.9 in 1982, the Central Asian republics ranged from 30.5 to 35.2, and from 31.2 to 38.7 on the two dates respectively. These figures again confirm the rapid growth of population in Central Asia, Kazakhstan and the Caucasus and the almost static birthrate of the European, and especially the Baltic, republics.

These data may be further refined between urban and rural populations and between the various nationalities. Table 4.6 depicts the proportion of rural population by republics. This shows the preponderance of village-dwellers in Central Asia in 1979: Uzbekistan 59 per cent, Kirgiziya 61 per cent, Tadzhikistan 65 per cent and Turkmenia 52 per cent. The number of collective farmers is again highest in Central Asia: compared with an All-Union average of 14.9 per cent it is 24.7 per cent in Uzbekistan, 20.3 per cent in Kirgiziya, 26.3 per cent in Tadzhikistan, and 33.4 per cent in Turkmeniya.

The eponymous nationalities in the Central Asian republics are clustered in collective farms in the rural areas. The rural locations of the Central Asian nationalities are shown on Table 4.7. Only 25.6 per cent of Russians were rural in 1979—34.4 per cent in the RSFSR. Of the Central Asian nationalities, however, 67.7—80.4 per cent were rural in 1979—an average of 76.5 per cent of Central Asians within their titular republics. Study of the figures over time shows a much greater rural decline for Russians than for the Central Asian nationalities.

*Table 4.6: Republican Population of USSR, by Level of Urbanization and Social Groups (1979 Census) (% of total population)*

|  | Manual workers | Non-manuals | Collective farmers | % Rural |
|---|---|---|---|---|
| USSR | 60.0 | 25.1 | 14.9 | 38 |
| RSFSR | 63.0 | 26.9 | 10.0 | 31 |
| Ukraine | 54.8 | 22.2 | 23.0 | 39 |
| Belorussia | 55.8 | 22.8 | 21.3 | 45 |
| Uzbekistan | 52.9 | 22.3 | 24.7 | 59 |
| Kazakhstan | 68.0 | 25.5 | 6.5 | 46 |
| Georgia | 55.6 | 26.5 | 17.8 | 48 |
| Azerbaydzhan | 59.6 | 23.6 | 16.7 | 47 |
| Lithuania | 56.8 | 23.1 | 20.0 | 39 |
| Moldavia | 52.6 | 17.5 | 29.8 | 61 |
| Latvia | 58.6 | 27.8 | 13.5 | 32 |
| Kirgiziya | 57.8 | 21.9 | 20.3 | 61 |
| Tadzhikistan | 53.0 | 20.6 | 26.3 | 65 |
| Armenia | 64.2 | 26.1 | 9.7 | 34 |
| Turkmeniya | 44.2 | 22.2 | 33.4 | 52 |
| Estonia | 60.9 | 28.8 | 10.2 | 30 |

*Source*: *Chislennost' i sostav naseleniya SSSR* (1984), pp. 1955.

*Table 4.7: Rural Population by Nationality, RSFSR and Central Asia*

| Republic | Nationality | Rural population as % of total republican population | | Nationality as % rural | | Nationality as % rural within titular republic | |
|---|---|---|---|---|---|---|---|
|  |  | 1970 | 1979 | 1970 | 1979 | 1959 | 1979 |
| USSR | — | 43.7 | 37.7 | 43.7 | 37.7 |  |  |
| RSFSR | Russians | 37.7 | 30.7 | 32.0 | 25.6 | 45.1 | 34.4 |
| Kazakhstan | Kazakhs | 49.7 | 46.1 | 73.3 | 68.4 | 75.7 | 73.7 |
| Central Asia | Central Asians | 61.9 | 59.3 | 75.3 | NA | 80.2 | 76.5 |
| Kirgizia | Kirgiz | 62.6 | 61.3 | 85.4 | 80.4 | 89.0 | 85.5 |
| Tadzhikistan | Tadzhiks | 62.9 | 65.1 | 74.0 | 71.9 | 80.4 | 74.5 |
| Turkmeniya | Turkmen | 52.1 | 52.0 | 69.0 | 67.7 | 73.7 | 68.3 |
| Uzbekistan | Uzbeks | 63.4 | 58.8 | 75.1 | 70.8 | 79.8 | 77.0 |

*Source*: Adapted from M. Feshback, 'Trends in the Soviet Muslim Population—Demographic Aspects', *Soviet Economy in the 1980's*, Part 2 (1982), p. 316. See also V.I. Kozlov, *Natsional'nosti SSSR* (1982), pp. 80, 100.

On the basis of these data one may conclude that increases in the workforce will occur in the Central Asian areas of the country, and principally among the eponymous population. Such increases will take place among the rural population.

Earlier we discussed the labour force participation rate for the population of the USSR. Our present task is to define it in the various republics. As previously pointed out, there is no direct Soviet statistic available on this topic. One can, however, express the total numbers of manual and non-manual workers for a given year as a proportion of the economically active age groups 16−54/59. These are calculated on Table 4.8. The crude employed labour participation rate has been calculated by dividing the total number of manual and non-manual workers (column 4) by the economically active population age groups (16−54/59) (column 3). This statistic has some imperfections; column 4 includes pensioners working full-time, and column 3 includes students and members of the armed forces. It also excludes from the employed population collective farmers and those in private agriculture. For our purposes, however, column 5 does indicate variations in the regional levels of labour utilization. Set against an average participation rate for the USSR of 72.6 per cent, the Central Asian republics have low scores ranging from 50.3 per cent (Tadzhikistan) to 58.7 per cent (Kirgiziya). These low participation rates reflect the low level of urbanization and the large collective farm work force.

The Soviet census of 1979 defined the economically active population[37] (*zanyatoe*) and those in private agriculture. Table 4.9 shows the republican breakdown, with figures for men and women. One cannot directly extrapolate from the data shown to levels of underemployment. The numbers reflect the age distribution of the population—a population with many children will obviously have a lower level of employment than one with a preponderance of young adults. As the populations of the Central Asian republics have a large number of young dependants, one might expect the proportion of 'employed' to be lower than that of the European republics. This is indeed the case—the Central Asian republics have a range of 41.5−45.5 per cent for men compared to the USSR average of 55.7 per cent, and 37.0−39.5 per cent for women compared to an All-Union average of 47.8 per cent. With the ageing of the populations, many more Central Asian

*Table 4.8: Labour Participation Rates by Manual and Non-Manual Workers in Republics of USSR, 1980*

|  | 1980 total population | 1980 economically active age groups | | 1980 Average number of employed manuals and non-manuals | Crude labour participation rate % |
|  |  | 16—54/59 year | | | |
|  |  | % | N | | 5 |
|  | 1 | 2 | 3 | 4 | (4 ÷ 3) |
| USSR | 262,486 | 58.9 | 154,806 | 112,498 | 72.6 |
| Lithuania | 3,420 | 57.4 | 1,965 | 1,461 | 74.3 |
| Latvia | 2,529 | 57.3 | 1,451 | 1,202 | 82.8 |
| Estonia | 1,474 | 56.5 | 834 | 700 | 83.9 |
| RSFSR | 138,365 | 60.5 | 83,781 | 65,612 | 78.3 |
| Ukraine | 49,953 | 58.6 | 29,289 | 20,042 | 68.4 |
| Belorussia | 9,611 | 59.5 | 5,727 | 4,046 | 70.6 |
| Moldavia | 3,968 | 58.5 | 2,323 | 1,511 | 65.0 |
| Georgia | 5,041 | 59.4 | 2,997 | 1,978 | 65.9 |
| Azerbaydzhan | 6,112 | 54.0 | 3,305 | 1,802 | 54.5 |
| Armenia | 3,074 | 57.7 | 1,776 | 1,192 | 67.1 |
| Kazakhstan | 14,858 | 58.3 | 8,664 | 6,043 | 69.7 |
| Uzbekistan | 15,765 | 48.0 | 7,571 | 4,169 | 55.0 |
| Kirgiziya | 3,588 | 52.2 | 1,876 | 1,102 | 58.7 |
| Tadzhikistan | 3,901 | 47.2 | 1,842 | 927 | 50.3 |
| Turkmenia | 2,827 | 49.3 | 1,394 | 711 | 51.0 |

*Source*: *Narkhoz v 1982g* (1983) p. 367. Cols. 2 & 3 estimates derived from 1970 census calculated by US Bureau of the Census. Cited in G. Baldwin, *Population Projections by Age and Sex: For the Republics and Major Economic Regions of the USSR* (Washington D.C.: US Department of Commerce, 1979), p. 128.

nationalities will come into the labour market. Labour participation rates are particularly low in the Central Asian villages, and here is a reservoir of labour supply. In addition, the traditional use of children in the fields increases the number of workers available: a sociological study of mobility in the Uzbek and Turkmen republics found that over a third of school-age children worked in the fields for six or more months a year.[38]

*Table 4.9: Republican Economically Active Population and in Private Agriculture\**

| Urban and rural | | Economically active % | Private agriculture % | Pensioners % |
|---|---|---|---|---|
| USSR | Men | 55.7 | 0.0 | 10.3 |
| | Women | 47.8 | 0.4 | 19.6 |
| RSFSR | Men | 59.0 | 0.0 | 10.7 |
| | Women | 49.8 | 0.3 | 21.3 |
| Ukraine | Men | 56.6 | 0.1 | 12.9 |
| | Women | 48.3 | 0.5 | 23.0 |
| Belorussia | Men | 56.3 | 0.1 | 11.3 |
| | Women | 48.7 | 0.5 | 21.3 |
| Uzbekistan | Men | 42.2 | 0.0 | 6.5 |
| | Women | 38.4 | 0.2 | 10.9 |
| Kazakhstan | Men | 50.7 | 0.0 | 7.6 |
| | Women | 43.4 | 0.5 | 12.9 |
| Georgia | Men | 53.9 | 0.1 | 9.5 |
| | Women | 47.4 | 0.4 | 16.6 |
| Azerbaydzhan | Men | 46.5 | 0.0 | 5.7 |
| | Women | 41.1 | 0.3 | 11.0 |
| Lithuania | Men | 55.1 | 0.1 | 11.6 |
| | Women | 48.4 | 0.7 | 18.6 |
| Moldavia | Men | 54.9 | 0.1 | 10.2 |
| | Women | 49.7 | 0.5 | 16.9 |
| Latvia | Men | 58.9 | 0.1 | 12.7 |
| | Women | 51.3 | 0.4 | 21.0 |
| Kirgiziya | Men | 45.5 | 0.0 | 7.4 |
| | Women | 39.5 | 0.4 | 12.7 |
| Tadzhikistan | Men | 41.5 | 0.0 | 6.0 |
| | Women | 37.0 | 0.1 | 9.1 |
| Armenia | Men | 50.2 | 0.1 | 6.1 |
| | Women | 44.8 | 0.5 | 11.0 |
| Turkmenia | Men | 44.1 | 0.0 | 5.5 |
| | Women | 38.4 | 0.6 | 9.4 |
| Estonia | Men | 58.7 | 0.1 | 12.0 |
| | Women | 50.9 | 0.3 | 20.8 |

*Table 4.9 continued*

| Urban and rural | | Economically active % | Private agriculture % | Pensioners % |
|---|---|---|---|---|
| Rural population | | | | |
| USSR | Men | 50.8 | 0.1 | 11.6 |
| | Women | 41.2 | 0.8 | 24.2 |
| Kazakhstan | Men | 45.6 | 0.0 | 7.4 |
| | Women | 38.1 | 0.8 | 13.2 |
| Uzbekistan | Men | 38.9 | 0.0 | 6.2 |
| | Women | 36.5 | 0.2 | 10.6 |
| Kirgiziya | Men | 40.9 | 0.1 | 6.9 |
| | Women | 36.3 | 0.4 | 12.7 |
| Tadzhikistan | Men | 38.4 | 0.1 | 5.8 |
| | Women | 35.3 | 1.5 | 8.9 |
| Turkmenia | Men | 40.0 | 0.0 | 5.4 |
| | Women | 37.1 | 0.5 | 9.7 |

\* Main occupation including full-time pensioners.
*Source*: *Chislennost' i sostav naseleniya SSSR* (1984).

We may summarize our discussion so far as follows. The Central Asian republics have a rapidly growing population which is located among the eponymous nationalities which are predominantly rural. The European nationalities have a stable population profile; the proportion of old age dependants is likely to rise significantly. Two main sources of increased labour supply may be identified: first, the post 55/59 age groups on pensions, predominantly in the European areas; and, second, the Central Asian nationalities. The former are in areas with existing job vacancies and have appropriate skills. The latter nationalities are in rural areas lacking employment opportunities at present, and young people there have insufficient industrial and commercial skills.


MIGRATION

Demand for labour in the 1980s is in the industrialized European areas of the country and in the developing parts of West Siberia.

However, Soviet writers recognize that in western Siberia, the Urals, the Volga and the Central Black Earth areas, more people leave than arrive. In some of the European mining areas, the exhaustion of supplies leaves a surplus of workers to be redeployed and the development of the oil and gas complex in such areas as Tyumen led to labour shortages in western Siberia for industry and agriculture. Despite wage differentials, population has also moved away from western Siberia.[39] Migration to these areas has been largely of European rural populations; the rural Central Asian nationalities have remained in the collective farms in the countryside. Between the censuses of 1970 and 1979, the rural population of Kirgiziya rose by 18 per cent, Uzbekistan by 21 per cent, and Turkmeniya by 28 per cent.[40] Here population is grouped in the traditional large, extended family. In 1979, the average size of Russian ethnic families was 3.2—for Uzbeks it was 6.2, for Kazakhs 5.5, Kirgiz 5.7, Tadzhiks 6.5 and Turkmens 6.3.[41] The pattern of migration between the Central Asian and European parts of the country differs: in the former, males leave the villages for work in the cities and women stay in the villages. Central Asian rural women not only remain unemployed but also maintain the traditional way of life.

As noted above, the republics of the Caucasus and Central Asia have lower levels of employment than elsewhere. The journal *Zarya Vostoka* has pointed out that the republic of Georgia has a much lower index of participation of people in social production than the national average. During the ninth Five Year Plan, 'the development rates of industry and construction were insufficient to produce a substantial rise in the employment level of the able-bodied population.'[42] A correspondent of *Pravda*, discussing the malutilization of labour resources in the Tadzhik republic pointed out that 'The number of unemployed women increases each year, and the main reason is that they have no opportunity to learn a vocation. . . . the Tadzhik Republic State Planning Committee excludes mothers with several children from the manpower resources and thereby creates the illusion of high employment.' It has also been pointed out that mechanization of agriculture leads to job losses.[43] In Kirghizia, it has been reported that a third of those employed in domestic work and private plots could be employed in paid labour if there were the jobs available.[44] Similarly, in Turkmenia in 1979, two writers from the Turkmen

Labour Research Institute mentioned the need to increase the level of employment, given the rise in the able-bodied population. They recommended the provision of light industry and the production of more local consumer goods.[45] The needs of the growing population have also been noted by Geydar Aliev, when First Secretary of the Azerbaydzhan Party organization. In 1976, he pointed to the 'considerable number' of employable people without jobs and the need for further new building.[46]

Unemployment has also been reported in the RSFSR to be greater in small and medium towns and in the rural areas, whereas in large towns there is a deficit of labour.[47] An exceptional view has been attributed to A. G. Aganbegyan who, in 1965, was reported as saying that in small and medium towns, 25 to 30 per cent of the population 'able to work' were unable to find work, and the comparable figure in large towns was 8 per cent.[48] These figures are not qualified in the reported speech—we do not know whether they refer to the total population (including pensioners) or to those coming onto the labour market; we also lack information about the duration of such unemployment and whether the reference is to the lack of jobs available, or to the absence of acceptable jobs on offer. Such a statement interpreted literally is contrary to all other evidence on the scale of unemployment.

The Soviet demographer Perevedentsev has summed up the position on structural employment as follows: areas of labour surplus are located in Central Asia, south Kazakhstan, Transcaucasia, the north Caucasus, Moldavia and the western Ukraine. There is an acute shortage of agricultural labour in the Non-Black-Earth zone, the Urals, Siberia and the far east. He proposes a population shift, with the urban population of the Non-Black-Earth region going back to the countryside and urban people from the southern areas moving to the urban areas of Europe. A further move is recommended of rural people from the southern regions to the southern urban areas. This scenario involves a movement of European peoples out of the southern areas.[49]

## RURAL UNDEREMPLOYMENT IN CENTRAL ASIA

The tendency towards low geographical mobility and insularity of the eponymous nationalities is explained by their religious and ethnic background and their poor command of the Russian language. The standard of living in areas of labour shortage outside of Central Asia is not sufficiently higher to compensate for the harsher climate: the cost of living in Central Asia is 10 per cent lower than in the central Russian regions and collective farmers' earnings are higher: outward mobility would lead to a 'worsening of [the inhabitants'] material conditions'.[50] Different *folkways* or ways of life would be experienced by immigrants from the Asian sun belt. Urban dwellings have been built for smaller families and this creates an obstacle to mobility.[51] Private agricultural production in Central Asia is very profitable and a move to another area might well entail a fall in income.[52] The large families leave many women outside employment; in the early 1980s, in the urban areas of Tashkent, Andizhansk and Bukhara, 30 per cent of the population was not employed. Women constituted 92 per cent of the non-working able-bodied population 80 per cent of whom had children.[53]

In Tadzhikistan, employment bureaux have been set up and the resettlement of some of the population outside the republic has been planned.[54] Without migration to urban areas it seems likely that considerable underemployment will be absorbed in the collective farms of Central Asia and policy has been to develop industrial enterprises in small and medium settlements there. Many enterprises have been built in the countryside in the 1970s and, as a result, the proportion of manual and non-manual workers in rural areas rose from 7.4 per cent in 1960 to 13.3 per cent in 1977.[55]

However, the labour reserves in the countryside have not been absorbed by such developments. As an Uzbek economist has pointed out, mechanization of agriculture has occurred more quickly in cotton farming than new jobs have been created. In 1970 the State Committee on Labour of Uzbekistan estimated that 29 per cent of collective farmers had been made surplus to requirements. Since then the proportion has risen even more.[56] This has led to a 'forced retention' of workers in agriculture.[57] A review of the situation in Tadzhikistan by A. Gelischanow points to the inadequate level of jobs in the rural areas. The journal *Kommunist Tadzhikistana* reported a meeting between representatives of a village and government administrators in which it was pointed out that the population of Surkh was outstripping the availability of jobs: 'There is no work. The single . . . vegetable growing *sovkhoz* cannot provide jobs for all. There is too little land and too little water.'[58]

Another report in *Pravda* pointed to the rural labour surplus in Tadzhikistan and the inadequate level of industrialization. The labour surplus in agriculture does not promote 'the mechanization of agricultural work and the transition to progressive forms of labor organization and remuneration . . .'[59] Policy is to maintain jobs at the expense of low levels of income. Farms in the European areas of the USSR, in contrast, have witnessed a flight of young people to the towns, leaving an increasingly old and feminized workforce.

## URBAN LABOUR DEFICITS

There is no evidence for structural *urban* unemployment in Central Asia up to the mid-1980s. Most commentators conclude that despite its population growth, 'Central Asia has been experiencing a labour shortage'.[60] As inferred by the discussion above, the rural areas have population reserves, whereas the towns have a labour shortage. Rural unemployment in Central Asia may be estimated at around 4 per cent.[61] This position is summed up by Kh. Saidmuradov, Chairman of the Council for the Study of Productive Forces of the Tadzhik Academy of Sciences: 'A paradoxical situation arises: on the one hand, there is an acute shortfall in labor resources; on the other hand, an undoubted surplus.'[62] In Uzbekistan in 1978, R. A. Ubaydullayeva reported 'an acute shortage in labor resources' in the developing region.[63] The Deputy Chairman of the Uzbek State Committee for Labour Resources Utilization complained of the low rate of emigration from rural areas and noted: 'Finding work for young people in the countryside is an especially complicated problem.'[64] Rural overpopulation and underemployment would appear to be occurring. With mechanization, productivity in the countryside has been rising, thus reducing the number of jobs.[65] As Davlatov has pointed out: 'there is a contradiction between introducing brigade methods in agriculture [which will enhance labour efficiency] and the need to provide permanent work.'[66]

Labour shortage in the towns has been met by the immigration of workers from the European areas of the country and by a greater participation in the workforce by the indigenous population. In industry the share of the workforce by Uzbeks was 31.2 per cent in 1967 rising to 38.2 per cent in 1977; in building the corresponding figures were 34.8 and 35.6 per cent; in transport 41.2 and 44.4 per cent; in the massive Tashkent textile mills, the proportion of local nationalities employed rose from 17.1 per cent in 1966 to 40.3 per cent in 1979.[67] However, such developments have not been sufficient to meet the urban need for labour and to relieve the overpopulation in the countryside. As the Soviet economist Manevich has pointed out, in the central areas of Russia a quarter to a third of the rural population moves to the towns, whereas in Central Asia only 5 per cent does so. 'The indigenous peoples of the Transcaucasian republics move to the cities of their own republics but very rarely to other regions of the country, and the Central Asian indigenous peoples resettle unwillingly even in the cities of their own republics.'[68] In 1981, in Uzbekistan, 61.4 per cent of school-leavers who went to work found jobs in agriculture (12 per cent in industry and 6.8 per cent in building); of rural school-leavers a much higher proportion stayed in agriculture, and only 6 per cent worked in industry. 'The population mass remained in the village while industry remained with insufficient workers.'[69] G. A. Shister has complained that textile factories built in Andizhan and Namegan have been working at under-capacity because of labour shortage.[70] Outmigration from the cities of skilled workers has also taken place with a movement of the non-indigenous population to the European areas of the country and this has exacerbated the labour shortage in the towns of Central Asia.[71]

## LOCATION OF INDUSTRY

Soviet policy appears to favour the location of labour-intensive industries in small towns in Central Asia. An order of Gosplan in 1977 required that investment plans should reflect labour supply and that, therefore, new construction should take place in Central Asia. Bromley and Shkaratan point out that it is often suggested that traditional industries such as food-processing and light industry should be developed, rather than metal-working which the local nationalities find uncongenial.[72] An obvious strategy would be to bring cotton manufacture to Central Asia from the RSFSR where labour is in short supply.[73] The labour force participation rate in Central Asia could then be increased. However, in 1983, cotton procurement prices were raised, leading to increased incomes in the rural areas of Uzbekistan. As Sheehy points out, internal stability is probably more important than using unemployment and poverty as a stimulus to outward population movement.[74]

Many measures to stimulate the movement of population have been suggested. Kostin, for example, suggests improving urban housing and living conditions and raising wage incentives. He rejects specific policies aimed at different nationalities and advocates the better management of existing labour resources and attracting pensioners.[75] Bromley and Shkaratan recommend that the local lifestyles of the people be taken into account in industrial policy.[76] However, these recommendations have still to be translated into policy options. The traditional textile manufacturing areas of Ivanovo were extensively refurbished in the late 1970s and early 1980s, and mechanization of agriculture in Central Asia has been curtailed to allow surplus labour to be employed.[77] Kh. Saidmuradov, in discussing the movement of industry to small towns and settlements in Tadzhikistan, complains that Ministries are unwilling to site affiliates of major enterprises of the central industrial region in Tadzhikistan.[78] By 1982, however, some branches had been set up, particularly in the silk industry. These new factories experienced difficulties in recruiting skilled labour in the localities and productivity was only some 30 per cent of the parent enterprise.[79]

The provision of paid employment is the policy of the Soviet government. But the provision of paid work requires the location of industrial enterprises in areas of population surplus or the movement of such surplus to new places of work. In western societies, market stimulation—the carrot of a higher standard of living and the stick of rural poverty—impels labour to move. Such migrants, often drawn from underprivileged ethnic groups, form the basis of a secondary labour market performing unskilled low-paid jobs with no chance of advance and promotion. In the Soviet Union there is a lack of economic 'push': rural residents are shielded from poverty by relatively adequate remuneration. The evidence suggests that the contentment of the Central Asian nationalities is regarded as a prime matter of policy and the social cost of underemployment is carried by society as a whole. The absorption of labour into the rural community is partly a consequence of government procurement policy in providing sufficient resources to maintain life in the countryside thereby enhancing ethnic harmony and political stability. It is also partly due to the lack of 'pull' by the towns over the rural ethnic community. This in turn relates to the social barriers dividing ethnic groups and also to the absence at present of a consumer society qualitatively superior to traditional village life.

## REFERENCES

1. See J. Creedy (ed.), *The Economics of Unemployment in Britain* (London: Butterworth, 1981), pp. 101-2.
2. *International Comparisons of Unemployment*, U S Department of Labor, Bureau of Statistics Bulletin (1979), pp. 6-10.
3. C. Mesa-Lago, *Unemployment in Socialist Countries: Soviet Union, East Europe, China and Cuba* (Ph.D. Cornell University, 1968) pp. 126-7.
4. Kupriyanova reported a survey of industrial enterprises, conducted in 1981, which found that over half of those who changed jobs took longer than a month to find work; the average length of time taken was 53 days. Even those using employment bureaux took more than two months. Z.V. Kupriyanova, 'Tekuchest' kadrov: perelomit' nezhelatel'nye tendentsii', *EKO*, no. 5 (1981), p. 23. In the late 1970s Kotlyar and Talalai report a range of 25–30 days, 'Puti sokrashcheniya tekuchesti kadrov, *Voprosy ekonomiki* (1981), no. 5, p. 37. M. I. Dolishni cites another survey which reports that every worker on average loses 23 days' work on changing place of work: *Formirovanie i ispol'zovanie trudovykh resursov* (1978), p. 211. David E. Powell has noted a number of Soviet reports on numbers of days lost when changing jobs: in industry and construction in the RSFSR in 1971–72, it was 26 working days, in Armenia 73 days, and Moscow 25 days: 'Labor Turnover in the Soviet Union', *Slavic Review*, vol. 36, no. 2 (1977), p. 272. M. Feshbach estimates that on average 20 days were lost between jobs in 1962–63: *New Directions in the Soviet Economy* (Washington, D.C.: 1966), p. 734.
5. Ibid., p. 128.
6. UPI press report, 19 February 1985.
7. P. Wiles, 'A Note on Soviet Unemployment by U.S. Definitions', *Soviet Studies*, vol. 23 (1972), p. 628. Using a more complicated method he comes up also with a figure of 1.3 per cent and a range of 1.0 to 1.8 per cent, pp. 625-66.

8. Interview with K.A. Novikov, 'Rabochie ruki strany', *Trud*, 11 May 1974, p. 2; and *Narodnoe Khozyaystvo RSFSR v 1973g* (1974), p. 365.

9. Z. Skarupo, 'Sokrashchenie tekuchesti i uluchshenie ispol'zovaniya rabochei sily', *Planovoe khozyaystvo*, no. 6 (1977), p. 118.

10. The total of workers in industry and building was approximately 1.3 million, hence 11,000 would approximate 0.893 per cent of the total workforce. *Statisticheski ezhegodnik Belorusskoy SSR* (Minsk, 1974), p. 149, *Narodnoe khozyaystvo Belorusskoy SSR*, (Minsk, 1978), p. 169.

11. L. M. Danilov, *Dvizhenie rabochikh kadrov v promyshlennosti* (1973), p. 128. Cited by David E. Powell, 'Labor Turnover in the Soviet Union', *Slavic Review*, vol. 36, no. 2 (1977), p. 271.

12. Z. Skarupo, 'Sokrashchenie tekuchesti i uluchshenie ispol'zovanie rabochey sily', *Planovoe khozyaystvo*, no. 6 (1977), p. 118.

13. E.S. Rusanov, *Raspredelenie i ispol'zovanie trudovykh resursov SSSR*, (1971), p. 111. Cited by W. Teckenberg, 'Labour Turnover and Job Satisfaction', *Soviet Studies*, vol. 30, no. 2 (April 1978), p. 195.

14. Skarupo (1977), p. 119.

15. M.I. Dolishni, *Formirovanie i ispol'zovanie trudovykh resursov* (1978), p. 212.

16. A. Kotlyar and M. Talalay, 'Puti sokrashcheniya tekuchesti kadrov', *Voprosy ekonomiki*, no. 5 (May 1981).

17. See Dolishni, pp. 211-13.

18. Ibid., p. 203.

19. E.I. Ruzavina, *Zanyatost' v usloviyakh intensifikatsii proizvodsta* (1975), p. 37. A study cited by Ruzavina showed that on average a worker took part in regional migration every 12 to 15 years; the average period of work in one branch (*otrasl'*) of industry was 5.6 years and the time at one factory 3.3 years.

20. This figure is accepted by other western writers: A. J. Pietsch estimates 21 per cent, Working Paper no. 19 (Munich: Osteuropa-Institut, 1976), pp. 31-3; and Teckenberg, 22 per cent: W. Teckenberg, 'Correspondence', *Soviet Studies*, vol. 33, no. 3 (July 1981), p. 484.

21. James L. Price, *The Study of Turnover* (Iowa: Iowa State University, 1977), p. 63.

22. Dolishni, pp. 214-223.

23. Skarupo (1977), p. 120.

24. Ibid.

25. A.E. Kotlyar and M.I. Talalai, 'Kak zakrepit' molodye kadry', *EKO*, no. 4 (1977), p. 27.

26. A study based on 161 industrial enterprises cited in Dolishni, p. 217.

27. On western literature, see Price, Chapter 3.

28. See ibid., pp. 29-31.

29. J. G. March and H. A. Simon, *Organisations* (New York: Wiley, 1958), p. 100. Cited by Price, p. 31.

30. Ibid.

31. See ibid., p. 82.

32. Skarupo (1977), p. 124.

33. Ibid., p. 122.
34. See D. Lane and F. O'Dell, *The Soviet Industrial Worker* (Oxford: Martin Robertson, 1978), Chapters 2 and 3.
35. To provide work for men in a town with employment for women, a new metal manufacturing factory was planned. The absence of housing and the inadequate housing budget for the area precluded its completion. See account in *Pravda*, 20 April 1977; *CDSP*, vol. 29, no. 16 (1977), p. 24.
36. See empirical findings in Price, pp. 89-90.
37. This figure also included people of pensionable age with a full-time occupation (i.e. not drawing a pension). ˙
38. D. I. Zyuzin, 'Prichiny nizkoy mobil'nosti korennogo naseleniya respublik srednei Azii', *Sotsiologicheskie issledovaniya*, no. 1 (1983), p. 112.
39. E. Kostin, *Trudovye resursy SSSR* (1979) pp. 107-8. A. Sozykin (Chairman *Goskomtrud*), 'Trudovoy potentsial Rossii', *Planovoe khozyaystvo*, no. 12 (1978), p. 29. On Siberia, see also A. Sozykin, 'Kadry dlya Sibiri: potrebnost', i rezervy', *EKO*, no. 5 (1980).
40. *Naseleniya SSSR* (1980), p. 3. See discussion in G. A. Shister, 'Istochniki popolneniya rabochego klassa Uzbekistana na etape razvitogo sotsializma', *Istoriya SSSR*, no. 6 (November 1981), pp. 28-9.
41. *Chislennost' i sostav naseleniya SSSR* (1984), pp. 284-5.
42. *Zarya Vostoka* (12 January 1979), p. 2. Translation in *CDSP*, vol. 31, no. 4, (1979), p. 6.
43. O. Latifi, *Pravda*, (20 April 1977), p. 2. Abstract in *CDSP*, vol. 29, no. 16 (1977), p. 25.
44. S. Begaliev, *Planovoe khozyaystvo*, no. 6 (June 1983), pp. 31-8.
45. *Turkmenskaya Iskra*, 21 December 1979. Summarized in BBC *Summary of World Broadcasts*, SU/W1072/A/2, 29 February 1980.
46. *Bakinskiy rabochi*, 20 October 1976. Listed in *Radio Liberty Research*, RL 499/76, 15 December 1976.
47. I. F. Sorokina, *Osobennosti vosproizvodstva rabochey sily v usloviyakh razvitogo sotsializma'* (1979), p. 114.
48. *Bandiera Rossa* (Rome, July 1965). Reprinted in The Association for the Study of Soviet-Type Economies, *The Asti Bulletin*, vol. 7, no. 2 (Summer 1965), p. 2.
49. V.I. Perevedentsev, 'Migratsiya naseleniya i razvitie sel'skokhozyayst-vennogo proizvodstva', *Sotsiologicheskie issledovaniya* no. 1, (January–March 1983), pp. 57-61.
50. D.I. Zyuzin, 'Prichiny nizkoy mobil'nosti korennogo naseleniya respublic sredney Azii', *Sotsiologicheskie issledovaniya*, no. 1 (1983), p. 115. It would be incorrect, however, to conclude that average living standards are higher in the villages of Central Asia; one has to take account also of the large number of family dependants which brings down average incomes.
51. Kh. Saidmuradov, 'Sovershenstvovat' mekhanizm khozyaystvovaniya: potentsial trudovykh resursov', *Sotsialisticheskaya industriya*, 25 November 1978. O. Latifi and V. Usanov, *Pravda*, 18 June 1984: English version in *CDSP*, vol. 36, no. 24, pp. 1-5.
52. See Zyuzin, p. 115.

53. G.A. Shister,'Istochniki popolneniya rabochego klassa Uzbekistana na etape razvitogo sotsializma', *Istoriya SSSR*, no. 6 (1981), p. 38.
54. A correspondent noted that Tadzhikistan has sufficient labour reserves for itself and that Gosplan USSR had asked for an organized supply of workers for buildings in the RSFSR and Kazakhstan: *Kommunist Tadzhikistana*, 7 January and 13 October 1977.
55. Shister (1981), p. 32.
56. G. Shister, 'Vazhny faktor rosta i sovershenstvovaniya struktury rabochego klassa Uzbekistana', *Kommunist Uzbekistana* (1983), no. 2, p. 36. U. Kurbanov (First Secretary of the Matcha District Committee), writing in *Pravda*, 1 September 1980, also draws attention to the lack of jobs in Tadzhikistan consequent on mechanization of the cotton-growing industry.
57. T. Mirzayev, 'Problemy vysvobozhdeniya rabochey sily iz sel'skogo khozyaystva Uzbekistana', *Ekonomika sel'skogo khozyaystva*, no. 5 (May 1981), pp. 83-7.
58. *Kommunist Tadzhikistana*, 8 July 1979. Cited by A. Gelischanow, *The Employment Situation in Tajikistan*, RL 482/83. (Munich), p. 2.
59. O. Latifi and V. Usanov, *Pravda*, 18 June 1984; *CDSP*, vol. 36, no. 24 (1984), p. 1. They point out that a quarter of the rural population is engaged in domestic and private farming.
60. See the detailed examination by M. Feshbach, 'Prospects for Outmigration from Central Asia and Kazakhstan in the Next Decade', US Congress, Joint Economic Committee, *Soviet Economy in a Time of Change*, (Washington, D.C.: 1979), vol. 2, pp. 660-3.
61. For basis of calculation, see A.-J. Pietsch, 'Shortage of Labour and Motivation Problems of Soviet Workers', in D. Lane (ed.), *Labour and Employment in the USSR* (1986), p. 185.
62. Kh. Saidmuradov, *Sotsialisticheskaya industriya*, 25 November 1978. Cited by Feshbach, p. 661.
63. R. A. Ubaydullayeva, *Obshchestvennye nauki v Uzbekistane*, no. 2 (28 February 1978). Cited by Feshbach, p. 663.
64. *Pravda vostoka* (7 August 1976), p. 3. Cited by Feshbach, pp. 662-3.
65. M. Daniya-Khodzhaev, *Pravda vostoka* (7 August 1976), pp. 2-3. Cited in *Radio Liberty Report*, no. 424/76 (29 September 1976).
66. I. Davlatov, 'Mezhregional'naya integratsiya—vazhny faktor intensifikatsii proizvodstva', *Ekonomicheskie nauki*, no. 9 (1984), p. 49.
67. Shister (1981) pp. 35-6.
68. E. Manevich, 'Vosproizvodstvo naseleniya i ispol'zovanie trudovykh resursov', *Voprosy ekonomiki*, no. 8 (August 1978), p. 39. Cited by Feshbach, p. 670, n. 80.
69. Shister (1983), p. 39.
70. G.A. Shister, *Istoriya SSSR*, no. 6 (1981), p. 32.
71. D.I. Zyuzin, 'Prichiny nizkoy mobil'nosti korennogo naseleniya respubliki sredney Azii', *Sotsiologicheskie issledovaniya*, no. 1 (January 1983), p. 115.
72. Yu. Bromley, O. Shkaratan, 'Natsional'nye traditsii v sotsialisticheskoy ekonomike', *Voprosy ekonomiki*, no. 4 (1983), pp. 40, 42-3.
73. Kostin, Chapter 7.

74. Sheehy, pp. 8-9.
75. Kostin, Chapter 7.
76. 'Natsional'nye trudovye traditsii-vazhny faktor intensifikatsii proizvodsta', *Sotsiologicheskie issledovaniya*, no. 2 (1983), p. 47.
77. Oral report.
78. Kh. Saidmuradov, as cited by Feshbach, *loc.cit.*, *Sotsialisticheskaya industriya*, 25 November 1978.
79. S. Ezhkov, *Pravda*, 2 November 1982.

# 5 Labour Productivity

Whilst Soviet leaders and commentators, as well as those in the West, agree that 'productivity' and especially 'labour productivity' are currently the key to economic advance, what these terms entail and how they are to be achieved are matters of ambiguity and dispute. Discussions of 'productivity' involve the whole gamut of features of economic life. As Salter has put it, in 'the interpretation of even the simplest measures of productivity arises a host of very complex problems. For behind productivity lie all the dynamic forces of economic life: technical progress, [capital] accumulation, enterprise, and the institutional pattern of society.'[1]

We may define productivity as the relationship between the aggregate of factor inputs (labour and capital) and the aggregate of outputs. Labour productivity is the contribution of labour to output. From the viewpoint of the economy, labour input has three main aspects: the quantity of labour employed, its quality and organization. We have discussed the 'quantity' of labour earlier, in terms of the rate of labour utilization. 'Quality' and organization are our concern in this chapter. In making comparisons between societies and over time, it is important to bear in mind that labour is utilized with capital: the age, quantity and quality of the capital stock should also be taken into account in a comprehensive study of productivity. The quality of labour has to do with its effectiveness and efficiency. Experience, effort and educational level influence the ability of employees to perform their tasks efficiently.

Labour productivity, expressed as output per employee in a given period, may rise because the composition of capital has changed or because materials used have improved. Hence measures of 'labour' productivity may reflect changes in other factor inputs. Productivity may also be distinguished from efficiency. Low productivity says nothing about efficiency, because the latter is concerned with the effective utilization of inputs. Output produced may be such that no other organization of the given factors could increase it. Measures of economic efficiency must compare parallel situations, taking account of variations in capital stock, scale of production, quantity and quality of labour. If capital and materials are scarce in relation to labour inputs, then labour productivity will be low, though it may not be inefficiently used. The distinction between 'intensive' and extensive labour productivity hinges on changes in the content or quality of labour rather than on increasing the amount of labour employed.

## THE LEVEL OF LABOUR PRODUCTIVITY

Labour productivity in the USSR is known to be much lower than in advanced western economies. Bergson, in an authoritative comparative study, estimated that in 1960 gross material product per employed worker in the USSR was only 31 per cent of that of the USA. It ranked lower than other West European countries in this respect: Italy's comparable output was 34 per cent, the United Kingdom's 49 per cent, Germany and France 51 per cent.[2] One of the major concerns of Soviet planners in the 1980s is to improve labour productivity: this has been a constant theme of recent Soviet leaders. This is associated with the movement of the economy from an 'extensive' form of development to an 'intensive' one.

'In terms of historical scale, significance and implications, the regearing of our national economy along the lines of intensive development may rightly be placed alongside such a very profound change as socialist industrialisation which radically altered the face of the country.'[3] Soviet writers on the economy constantly refer to the need to 'maximize' and 'to improve the efficiency' of factors of production. Tikhonov in the same speech referred to improvements in labour productivity as being 'the principal factor' in economic growth under the eleventh Five Year Plan (1981–85). It was planned that productivity of labour should rise between 17 and 20 per cent, and such increases were planned to account for 85–90 per cent of the growth of the national income.

'Pace, quality, thrift and organization [*tempy, kachestvo, berezhlivost', organizovannost'*] these are the main slogans of the day. . .'[4] In these words Gorbachev epitomizes once more the goal of increasing productivity. The priorities of policy are 'to raise labour productivity, improve the quality of production, economise on resources'.[5] The 'acceleration of economic growth' is crucial to the party programme and to the success of the twelfth Five Year Plan (1986–90). In his discussion of the revision of the Party Programme, Gorbachev emphasized the switch to the 'intensive tracks of development' and 'the attainment of a superior level of organization and efficiency for the Soviet economy.'[6] The draft *Basic Guidelines for the Economic and Social Development of the USSR in 1986-1990 and in the Period up to the year 2000* calls for '*a shift [in] production to a primarily intensive path of development, to achieve a cardinal increase in the productivity of social labour, and to accelerate the rates of economic growth on that basis*'.[7] The increase in national income in the twelfth Five Year Plan (1986–90) is to be achieved 'wholly through increasing labour productivity'.[8] The goal of the present Soviet leadership is to attain 'the highest level of labour productivity in the world'.[9]

As Gorbachev stated in his speech in October 1985 when making his report on the introduction of the new version of the Third Programme of the CPSU: 'in the new Five Year Plan, the increase in national income and in the output of all branches of material production will, for the first time, be obtained wholly through increasing labour productivity.'[10] There will be an increased rate of retirement of fixed assets, an increase in the rate of capital investment by 80–100 per cent and selectivity in investment; machine tools are to be favoured.[11] In the next Five Year Plan labour productivity is to rise 130 to 150 per cent.[12] The essence of Gorbachev's policy is that improved productivity is the key to the acceleration of economic change, and the movement to the 'intensive track' of development.[13] In his election address, reported in *Pravda* on 21 February 1985, Gorbachev claimed that by 'using the same machine tools, the same equipment and the same land, it is possible to produce more output and of better quality, with fewer outlays. . . . It is important . . . again and again, to study all of the factors, all of the components, that ensure highly productive labour and enhance the mechanism for the dissemination of advanced experiences.' Thrift and business efficiency are the psychological attitudes to be fostered by management.

To achieve these rates of increase, the work process has to be more effectively organized, workers have to be more efficient: either more must be produced with the same levels of manning or a given level or production must be achieved with fewer workers. Soviet experts on labour suggest many ways that labour may be more productively used. Kostin[14] is indicative of current thinking when he advocates eight major ways to utilize more effectively and efficiently labour resources: (1) the modernization of equipment; (2) more investment in re-equipment rather than construction of new units; (3) greater flexibility in labour utilization, with multiple machine operation; (4) specialization of production and repairs; (5) greater use of scientific work organization (i.e. time and motion study); (6) the improvement of 'moral and material incentives' at work and 'socialist competition'; (7) the reduction of loss of working time and better labour discipline and (8) limiting the number of employees.

In fact, however, the rate of productivity growth had suffered a long-run decline, much to the concern of Soviet economists[15] and political leaders. Table 5.1 shows the growth of productivity of labour for the eighth (1966–70), ninth, (1971–75), tenth (1976–80), eleventh (1981–85) and the projected increase for the twelfth (1986–90) Five Year Plans. This table shows the decline in the *rate* of increase up to 1980. Tables 5.2 and 5.3 bring out, however, the fact that productivity in absolute terms has continued to rise steadily since 1940. There are important variations in the sectors shown in the table: machine tools and metal-working had the highest growth of labour productivity, light industry and food have had much lower rates. From 1980 to 1983, the fuel industry had a negative growth rate, falling to 99.6 in the latter year.[16]

Annual national income for manual and non-manual employees has risen from 1292 roubles in 1960 to 3120 in 1984,[17] but the return on capital assets has declined. The rates of growth of capital (*fondovooruzhennost'*) per worker employed in industry rose by 246 per cent between 1970 and 1984, and the average level of productivity in industry increased by 176 per cent (see table 5.4). The return on capital therefore has declined. Also the 'shift' index

*Table 5.1:* Growth of Productivity of Labour in the Eighth, Ninth, Tenth, Eleventh, and Twelfth Five Year Plans (percentage growth for the Five Year Plan)

| | 8th 1966–1970 Achieved % | 9th 1971–1975 Achieved % | 10th 1976–1980 Achieved % | 11th 1981–1985 Planned (original) % | 11th 1981–1985 Achieved (a) % | 12th 1986–1990 Planned (original) % |
|---|---|---|---|---|---|---|
| **Productivity of labour in:** | | | | | | |
| Industry | 132 | 134 | 117 | 123–5 | 115.9 | 123–5 |
| Agriculture | 137 | 122 | 115 | 122–4 | 112.2 | — |
| Building | 122 | 129 | 111 | 115–17 | 113.1 | — |
| **Productivity of labour** | 139 | 125 | 117 | 117–20 | — | 120–3 (b) |

*Sources:* R. Gavrilov, 'Tempy, faktory i novye pokazateli rosta proizvoditel'nosti truda', *Voprosy ekonomiki*, no. 3 (1982), p. 25. Data for 1981–85, N.A. Tikhonov, *Pravda*, 28 February 1981; for 1981–84, *Narkhoz v 1984g* (1985) p. 147. *Sotsialisticheskaya industriya*, 9 November 1985, p. 2.

Notes:   (a)  Calculations based on CIA, *Handbook of Economic Statistics* (1985), Table 1 and *Report of Fulfilment of State Plan of Economic and Social Development 1985(Pravda*,26 January 1986).
   (b)  Subsequently increased to 125 per cent in final draft of plan. *Pravda*, 20 June 1986.

Table 5.2:   Rate of Growth of Labour Productivity by Sector of the Economy, 1960–84 (selected years)*

|  | 1960 | 1970 | 1975 | 1980 | 1983 | 1984 |
|---|---|---|---|---|---|---|
| All industry | 2.96 | 4.92 | 6.57 | 7.69 | 8.35 | 8.66 |
| Food industry§ | 1.9 | 2.81 | 3.53 | 3.68 | 4.07 | 4.21 |
| Machine tools and metal working | 4.7 | 9.38 | 14.19 | 19.17 | 22.00 | 23.34 |
| Light industry | 2.13 | 2.92 | 3.59 | 4.16 | 4.36 | 4.45 |

Source:   Narkhoz v 1984g (1985), p. 145.
Notes:
\*        Base year 1940 = 1.
§        Excluding produce of collective farms.

Table 5.3:   Rate of Growth of Labour Productivity by Sector of the Economy, 1970–84 (selected years)

|  | Base 1970 (= 1) | | | Base 1980 (= 1) | | |
|---|---|---|---|---|---|---|
|  | 1975 | 1982 | 1984 | 1982 | 1983 | 1984 |
| All industry | 1.34 | 1.64 | 1.76 | 1.05 | 1.09 | 1.13 |
| Food industry* | 1.25 | 1.38 | 1.49 | 1.05 | 1.11 | 1.14 |
| Machine tools and metal working | 1.51 | 2.23 | 2.35 | 1.09 | 1.15 | 1.22 |
| Light industry | 1.23 | 1.47 | 1.52 | 1.03 | 1.05 | 1.07 |

Source:   Narkhoz v 1984g (1985), p. 146–7

\*        Excluding produce of collective farms.

measuring the utilization of equipment fell from 1.55 in 1959 to 1.42 in 1972:[18] by 1981 in metal-working it had fallen to 1.35.[19] Caution must be exercised, however, in interpreting such data. As the capital stock grows it becomes increasingly difficult to increase the *rates* of labour productivity and a decline in the rate of growth has occurred in all industrial societies as they have matured.

*Table 5.4: Rate of Growth of Capital (fondovooruzhennosti) of Industrial Personnel, 1970–84*

(Industrial—productive basic capital assets per employee: 1970 = 1)

|  | 1975 | 1982 | 1983 | 1984 |
|---|---|---|---|---|
| All industry | 1.42 | 2.19 | 2.33 | 2.46 |
| Food industry | 1.42 | 2.05 | 2.16 | 2.27 |
| Machine tools and metal working | 1.41 | 2.33 | 2.48 | 2.63 |
| Light industry | 1.44 | 2.21 | 2.36 | 2.53 |

*Source*: *Narkhoz v 1984g* (1985), p. 153

The rate of obsolescence of capital has a direct effect on levels of labour productivity. The introduction of new and better machines raises the productivity of labour through less downtime through fewer workers producing a given output more quickly and with less breakdowns. The use of old and obsolescent machinery is *not* necessarily inefficient. Scrapping of plant is economically desirable when it fails to make a surplus over operating costs. Compared to high labour-cost economies, in low labour-cost ones, it is efficient to use older capital and the capital stock will therefore rationally be composed of much outmoded machinery. When investment is cheap relative to labour cost a high rate of capital retirement takes place. Abandoning 'outmoded methods' is not good management if labour is cheap and capital expensive because new capital may be more expensive to produce a given output, especially if labour is of poor quality and new equipment needs a high level of skill. Studies of British and American industry, for example, have shown that American productivity is higher because the rate of capital retirement is higher. This is not due to 'good management' but is economically justifiable because the USA has a higher level of real wages.[20]

As noted above, in chapter 2, the Soviet Union has had a plentiful supply of labour, and has adopted an extensive rather than an intensive investment policy—i.e. it has added labour to capital rather than substituting labour for capital. However, as the stock of capital increases, the real price of investment relative to labour falls. In a competitive economy, there is a market compulsion to replace obsolete plant because production in old plants is costlier than in more modern ones. In the USSR, however, such market compulsion does not operate. Management has no financial incentive to innovate, to adopt new plant and methods. Management has no material advantage to overcome short-term problems (including labour displacement) and the rising initial costs of introducing new technology. As there is no foreign competition, industrial ministries act as monopolists and retain obsolete plant, this leads to lower output at a higher price than is economically justifiable and technical progress in the economy as a whole is retarded. A further obstacle in the USSR is that capital has no market price and the labour market is imperfect. The price mechanism is not a constraint on firms either to shed labour or to scrap equipment. Rule-of-thumb methods and administrative means are utilized to direct investment. Mistakes at the highest level over the distribution of investment may be a cause of low productivity as well as the economic and political environment in which the economy operates. These underlying factors act as structural limits to possible increases in labour productivity and are the subject of macroeconomic reform. Here we may turn to consider procedures within the given constraints of planning which may influence labour productivity.

While the goal of raising productivity is an agreed objective, the measures to be taken to achieve this goal are matters of controversy. Even in advanced capitalist firms, the quantification of the causes of productivity differentials is at an elemental level.[21] One may distinguish between the underlying factors promoting the 'quality' of labour and the organizational methods intended to translate labour potential into work. Most policy-makers focus on the latter as these are amenable to political decision and should have an immediate positive effect.

## THE QUALITY OF THE LABOUR FORCE

The efficiency of a labour force will vary according to its 'quality' and composition. It is widely accepted that age, industrial experience, sex, skill and education have direct effects on productivity.[22] As Pratten has put it, 'Tradition, custom and education may affect the motivation and performance of managers and workers and so differences in labour productivity can only be fully explained by studying the development of firms and the environment in which firms and their employees have operated over a period of many years.'[23]

In a speech on the intensive development of the economy, Gorbachev pointed out that 'Present-day production, with its complicated and costly equipment, and the nature of labour are making incomparably higher demands on everything that is known as the human factor in the economy: the cultural and technical level, vocational skills, creativity and the discipline of personnel. Without this, neither labour productivity nor output quality may be raised.'[24] In the USSR, interwar industrialization was characterized by a quantitative growth of the urban working class. The peasant stock constituted a poorly educated and inexperienced industrial working class.

The urban immigrants from the countryside possessed a relatively low level of general education, the work skills they acquire usually result from rote learning and experience, not from instruction and knowledge. Among such workers the habit of team work under the conditions of the rhythms enforced by machinery are formed most slowly and consequently they have greater difficulty in mastering the habits of conscious production and labour discipline within the framework of an industrial organisation.[25]

In western societies a universal culture of literacy, numeracy, discipline and punctuality is taken for granted. Learning new skills associated with technical change presents difficulties in western industrial countries but advances are facilitated by a high general level of education and culture. In 1951, for instance, Britain had more than two-thirds of its male labour force with nine or more years of schooling, and in the United States in 1957, 57 per cent of this group had ten or more years of formal education.[26] In the Soviet Union, at the beginning of the 1970s, only half of the workforce had *seven* or more years of schooling and even by the beginning of the 1980s, the figure had only risen to three-quarters. In 1979, as recorded in the census, only 39.2 per cent of manual workers had a full secondary education or more.[27]

While the massive migrations of the early period of industrialization slowed down in the post-Second World War period, even in the 1960s, 60 per cent of the increase in the urban population was made up of rural immigrants, the figure falling only to 55 per cent in the 1970s.[28] This migration was greater in the small towns; in the large ones, especially those with restrictions on residence,[29] the working class was largely self-generating. A common problem in countries experiencing rapid industrialization is the adjustment of peasants to town and factory life. In a study sponsored by the journal *EKO*, a professor of economics from Leningrad is reported as pointing out that enterprises still, despite official restrictions, recruit migrants from agricultural areas who 'bring their unsystematic work habits with them.'[30]

Workers with pre-industrial skills experience frustration in an urban industrial setting. In the Soviet industrial culture, work habits, discipline, punctuality and initiative are not part of the *byt* (way of living) of certain strata of the working class. As Gordon and Nazimova have expressed it: 'Daily experience persuades us that it is precisely this personality element of occupational and production competence that is developing most slowly of all.'[31] The low 'quality' of work habits, noted by Lenin when he pointed out that 'The Russian is a poor worker as compared to the advanced nations',[32] is a legacy inherited by many in the contemporary workforce. Productivity is kept below a level attainable with the equipment available because of the low quality of labour input. As Gorbachev has pointed out, 'Unconscientious work by a person in the sphere of production or services at any workplace . . . hinders not only the interests of society but also the worker's own interests in the form of poor-quality goods and services.'[33]

A survey of 10,150 people aged over 18 years on the Soviet way of life conducted in eight different Union republics in the early 1980s, found that 98 per cent of the respondents considered 'industriousness and a conscientious attitude towards labour to be the most important factors in achieving success and well-being in life.' In practice, however, the researchers found that those with a 'high level of self-discipline' and a 'creative' attitude towards their duties accounted for only 25−35 per cent of the sample who were in employment, while some 20 per cent had a low level, showing 'little initiative, violating labour discipline and frequently failing to meet plan assignments'.[34]

The quality of labour input is lower in the Russian areas of the USSR than in some other republics. Industrial labour productivity is higher in Latvia and Estonia than the USSR average.[35] In these republics, the level of equipment, education and vocational training is similar to the USSR average, yet labour productivity is 10–15 per cent higher.

One may conclude that it is precisely the habituation of personnel of this region, due to actual historical circumstances, to high accuracy and care in their work that is the principal reason for high efficiency of their labour. . . . Shaping of the traits of personality corresponding to the requirements of highly developed industrial production is becoming one of the most important tasks of the social and cultural policy of the Communist Party.[36]

Type and duration of education affect the level of skill, motivation and adaptability of the workforce. As early as 1924, the economic returns to education were noted by Strumilin, who calculated that for every rouble spent on primary and secondary education, the national income would increase sixfold.[37] But educational systems have a tendency to replicate past rather than new knowledge, and in such cases education does not fulfil its potential contribution towards productivity. The length of time in education is generally regarded as being a reliable, though imperfect, index of the capability of the workforce. A better qualified workforce is able to learn about, cope with, and use the most efficient technically-based production practices. Also, in periods of rapid change, the better the educational level of the workforce, the more able it is to respond to innovation and to take up different work. The amount of 'effort' put into work is an obvious determinant of output, but it is notoriously difficult to measure. The pace of work and attention of the employee to detail is influenced by the general level of culture, by the subjective preference given to work as opposed to leisure, by the role of work in bestowing status through earnings, and by the managerial techniques employed to ensure a constant flow of materials and high tempo of operation. Education, experience and cultural background go to make up labour power or the potential of labour; management and work organization turn that potential into actual work.

General educational standards have undoubtedly risen in recent decades in the USSR. The proportion of manual workers having more than primary education rose from 401 per 1000 in 1959, to

760 in 1979 and to 825 in 1984; the comparable figures for non-manual employees are 911, 982 and 987; and for collective farmers 226, 593 and 695.[38] Though I shall mention some reservations below, these advances in educational levels have led to improvements in productivity. Zhamin pointed out in 1969 that workers who have nine or ten years of education master new techniques twice as quickly as those with six or seven years.[39] Other studies have demonstrated that workers with higher grades of general education take less time to master new types of work, and show more initiative; they also work more efficiently, as witnessed by the fact that they make less waste and have fewer breakages.[40]

While the effects on productivity of longer education have been positive, some negative influences may be detected. Workers may underutilize their qualifications by being 'underemployed' on routine work or on jobs which do not require such education.[41] Thus a dissatisfied stratum of workers arises who move from one job to another.[42] The level of general education has risen but the vocational aspects have been neglected. There has been a tendency for students in the general secondary schools to aspire to non-manual work and for skilled manual jobs to be rejected.[43] Up to the mid-1980s, some one third of school-leavers had no vocational training and they lacked knowledge of, and motivation for, the world of work. The educational reforms in the 'Guidelines for the Reform of the General and Vocational School' adopted in April 1984 attempt to improve the quality of schooling and to make it more appropriate to the world of work. In 1984, the numbers of pupils admitted to PTUs[44] for the first time since 1977 exceeded the number of planned places. In that year a quarter of all pupils leaving school after eight years' education started work.[45] The problem with the provision of 'vocational' education is that the skills required in a growing economy often change more quickly than the educational system.

What one may unequivocally conclude is that whatever political regime currently ruled the USSR, the quality of labour is more comparable to Italy or southern Europe countries than to the USA or north-west Europe. For this reason, whatever organization of production is introduced in the USSR, one might confidently expect labour productivity to be lower than in the advanced capitalist countries. Improvements in the educational level, training and experience of the working class should provide the basis for rises in productivity.

## THE TEMPO OF WORK ACTIVITY

In addition to the suitability and type of a worker's education, productivity is determined by the motivation and intensity of activity of the employee. This can be illustrated by considering western economies.

Accepted levels of overmanning to maintain output given irregular material supply, high numbers of 'indirect' employees (canteen staff, welfare workers, office staff), and restrictive practices by unions have been shown to lead to lower productivity in Britain compared to the USA—as have the lower levels of 'control' exercised by management.[46] It is widely recognized that a 'reserve' of labour in the sense of a surplus of people seeking occupations over the supply of jobs available provides a positive spur to labour effort. A conscientious attitude to work is widely believed to be ensured by the fear of dismissal and unemployment. A psychological atmosphere is created which is much wider than the experience of the relatively small number of workers who at any one time are faced with the loss of work and their livelihood. A full employment/labour shortage economy makes labour 'discipline' difficult to enforce. Workers who lack conscientiousness at work are able to procure other work if sacked and management is loath to exert sanctions for fear of losing workers. It is argued by critics that a 'systemic' effect of a labour shortage economy is to create a psychological atmosphere which encourages slackness in general, and a low intensity of work in particular. Kornai points to absolute labour security as promoting irresponsibility at the place of work by anybody susceptible to it— the diligent suffer and the careless and lazy gain.[47]

In the USSR, the extent of production deficits resulting from unproductive working time may be gauged by the fact that the loss of one per cent of worktime in industry can lead to a shortfall of output to the extent of 6.5 milliard roubles.[48] A survey of 10,150 people conducted in the early 1980s found that only 25 per cent of the employees claimed that they were adequately supplied with equipment and the necessary materials, 58.4 per cent regarded supply as 'fair', and one sixth considered supply to be poor.[49] The actual loss of labour time and its economic cost is extremely difficult to estimate. S. D. Reznik, writing in *Ekonomika stroitel'stva*,[50] points that in four building trusts studied the loss of working time due to the 'violation of labour discipline' as a percentage of all time lost was 11.5, 15.9, 17.4 and 31.5 per cent. In house building, another study found that over a four-month period losses of working time came to 1086 days: 48.4 per cent of the lost time was caused by defaulting of subcontractors, 8.2 per cent by delays in deliveries, 6.2 per cent by lack of essential machinery and equipment, 7.2 per cent by the incompetence of foremen and inadequate technical preparation, and only 3.5 per cent by violations of labour discipline.[51] Other authors stress that the magnitude of losses of worktime caused by absenteeism and inner-shift losses is difficult to estimate, since they are often under-reported. Kostin estimates that 'inner-shift' losses amount to 8−12 per cent of worktime, though official figures only register 0.1−0.3 per cent.[52] An editorial in *Izvestiya* in 1985 reported that at numerous enterprises intrashift idle time takes up at least 10 per cent of total time. Reducing it by half would raise labour productivity by 4−5 per cent.[53] Bernd Knabe refers to Soviet estimates that loss of time is equal to 15−20 per cent of total worktime. In addition, on average 15 days a year are lost due to illness, and another five days to administratively sanctioned leave.[54] Absences for shopping and similar activities have been reported to average 1.6 hours per day and to affect 30 per cent of workers.[55]

E.A. Kyuregyan surveyed some 4000 workers at ten representative industrial enterprises in Erevan in 1979−81 on their attitudes to work and level of discipline. He found that 29 per cent of the correspondents had broken labour discipline, 4.6 per cent had not fulfilled the plan, and 44.4 per cent had produced low quality products (presumably products below technical specifications).[56] Such losses of labour time and infringements of discipline are recognized by Soviet economists and sociologists to be associated with inefficiency of the technical organization of the work process (availability of materials; efficiently working machinery) and are defined as the 'objective' conditions. Kyuregyan's research found that the greatest number of breaches of labour discipline had their roots in the breakdown of equipment and insufficient and untimely supply of materials and tools. This was followed by poor organization of labour, and the absence of skilled help, low levels of knowledge and production experience of workers, lack of interest in carrying out the task and the loss of time in changing to other jobs.[57] Kyuregyan points out that the enterprises used out-of-date and worn machinery which was subject to breakdown, and the technical organization of the enterprise (including supply) was responsible for most of the poor work and was an underlying cause of ill-discipline.

Other Soviet statistics are available on idle time in the machine tools industries. Staff shortage was one of the most important causes of time loss, ranging from 16.1 per cent of all time lost in casting equipment to 26.3 per cent in metal-cutting. Planned repair and modernization accounted for 15.1 per cent of lost-time in metal-cutting and 26.5 per cent in casting equipment. Out of order (*neispravnost'* and unplanned repair of equipment ranged from 10.9 to 15.8 per cent.[58] 'Absenteeism' (*proguly*) accounted for a relatively tiny proportion of idleness: 0.1 per cent in the forge and presswork and casting equipment, and 0.2 per cent in metal-cutting and welding machines. Illness, however, is an important cause of absenteeism, accounting for 'the vast majority of working-time losses in many branches'. Conditions of work are often bad, with high levels of dust, gas, noise and poor lighting.[59] Legitimate absence for illness is as much as three times that of absenteeism.[60]

As far as *intrashift* losses are concerned, Soviet studies show that out of order and unplanned repair of machines ranged from 14 per cent to 26.1 per cent of time lost, setting machines from 13.5 to 22.7 per cent, lack of materials, parts, etc. from 17.9 to 22.1 per cent. Delays attributable to workers' ill-discipline was small: 1.1 per cent of time lost in forge and press work, 1.8 per cent in metal-cutting, 1.9 per cent in electronic information machinery, 2.3 per cent in casting equipment. These data may conceal shortfalls caused by indiscipline and absenteeism, as such causes may reflect badly on management[61] and may be under-reported.

## THE CAMPAIGN FOR LABOUR DISCIPLINE

While these quantitative studies suggest that indiscipline is not the most important problem as far as labour productivity is concerned, popular indignation in the Soviet press focuses on such pathologies.[62] Many letters have been published decrying the prevalence and anti-social nature of ill-disciplined workers. 'Violating labour discipline' is a phrase which is applied to almost any activity which may reduce output—particularly individual acts of drunkenness, poor time-keeping and absence, idling on the job, carelessness, and poor performance in general. *Literaturnaya gazeta's* correspondent, G. Popov,[63] writes: 'There can be no doubt that labour discipline and production discipline play an enormous role in everyday life. The economic welfare of the country as a whole and of each of us depends . . . on labour, production, and executive discipline.' The following are typical of letters published:

the struggle against idlers, shirkers, drunkards is our task. Who should punish a violator of discipline? We should. . . . At the factory where I used to work, the practice of 'hidden idling' was common. . . . Do you know of cases when violators of discipline are punished on the request of their comrades at work? They are rare. . . . It is good that [management] considers the labour shortage. But it is not a matter of indifference to us workers whom we work with. Shirkers mean that plans are not fulfilled, that the collective will pay. We should not let individuals speculate on the fact that there are not enough workers. The power of the collective is great. The boss and foreman of a workshop can be told that workers will not put up with a good for nothing. Moral and materials pressure can be used but a conscientious work attitude cannot be cultivated unless the life of an idler or drunkard is made unbearable.[64]

A foreman wrote as follows:

This is what happened a few weeks before New Year at our factory. Seventeen people wrote two identical letters—one to the factory manager and the other to the chairman of the trade union committee. The substance of the letters was:
  'Dismiss Comrade X, he spoils our collective'.
There followed a stormy session of the factory trade union committee. One after another workers and engineers stood up and accused this worker of arriving late at work, taking long lunch breaks, taking no notice of reprimands, constantly doing defective work. . . . In the end the worker was transferred to another section but still remained at the factory. . . . It must be said that our factory [is most efficient]. . . . Why shouldn't we rid ourselves of [a slacker] once and for all? . . . Many laws and regulations today are orientated not so much towards a struggle against violators of discipline as towards their protectors. It seems that the egoistic good-for-nothing is sometimes in a better position than the administration of the factory and the collective. . . .
  Many workers would behave differently, would work as they should, if they did

not know that there was no unemployment in our country. Almost every enterprise needs workers. If a worker leaves one enterprise he will be taken on by the neighbouring factory. He can dictate his own conditions. And the shop foreman has to hold his tongue, be patient . . .[65]

## A lawyer correspondent commented:

I sympathize with the author of the above letter and others who insist on the stepping-up of the campaign against violators of labour discipline. . . . But there is a paradox here. . . . Many leaders who demand new measures in practice do not apply the existing measures . . . We should campaign for better labour discipline strictly within the boundaries of law. Research shows that there is a direct link between the number of cases of indiscipline permitted by the administration and the level of discipline among workers and employees.[66]

Impressionistic study of the Soviet press leads one to believe that labour indiscipline is thought to be rife. This view is substantiated by a survey of 500 readers of the journal *Ekonomika i organizatsiya promyshlennogo proizvodstva* and 300 participants in seminars in the Siberian areas of the USSR.[67] In answer to the question, 'Have any changes occurred—for better or for worse—in the state of labour discipline during your working career?', B.P. Kutyrev, reported: 'Most respondents expressed the view that labour discipline must be steadily improved and that its present level is too low to satisfy the constantly growing demands of production and of society.'[68] A study of the themes on the topic of labour discipline in Leningrad newspapers, analysed between 1982 and 1984, found that 45 per cent of the publications concerned punishments for disciplinary offences and 73 per cent were on education measures to strengthen discipline.[69]

In the late 1970s and particularly in early 1980s with the administration of Yuri Andropov, campaigns were instituted to tighten up and enforce measures against slack labour discipline. These have been carried on by Gorbachev. The Central Committee called for a 'more resolute struggle against all violations of Party, state, and labour discipline', and the Soviet press called for a less lenient attitude towards ill-discipline. 'Labour discipline' refers not just to the observation of the rules of internal work order but also to a 'conscientious, creative attitude to work, high-quality work, and productive use of work time'.[70] Many resolutions were passed and measures were taken to strengthen discipline in the workforce.[71] The main thrust of the drive to improve labour discipline is directed at reducing loss of worktime incurred through absenteeism—i.e. days lost through late arrivals and early departures from work; another target is 'intra-shift' loss of worktime in the form of idling, drinking, playing. But 'discipline' equally applies to the administration which is required to provide the necessary 'organizational and economic conditions for normal highly productive work', the supply of machinery and materials should promote 'rhythmic' (i.e. uninterrupted) work.[72] The administration is not allowed to distract workers from these tasks and to transfer them to carry out 'anything unconnected with production activity'.[73]

The major legal enactments may be adumbrated here. In December 1979, a law[74] was enacted which decreed that workers who leave a job twice in the same year for no good reason lose their continuous labour entitlement (*stazh*). Absentees and those found drunk at work lose their holiday entitlement gained for uninterrupted work. Workers guilty of malicious infractions of labour discipline lose their rights to holidays at enterprise sanatoria and rest homes. They also lose their place in the housing queue.

In January 1983, the Andropov leadership put into effect a campaign to combat absenteeism by administrative means. 'Raids' were carried out in public places and malingerers were flushed out.[75] Such activity performed by the police and volunteers is spasmodic. Typical of such 'raids' is the following, which happened prior to the Andropov campaign in Frunze in January 1982.[76] The 'raiders' were made up of members of the People's Control Committee of the Republican State Committee on Labour, the newspaper *Sovetskaya Kirgiziya* and its local correspondents. In their inquiries they visited 15 enterprises and found that the 'main reason' for poor time-keeping was 'an indulgent, liberal attitude towards violators of labour discipline. As a rule no action at all is taken against them. Some places do not even keep records on them.'[77] At one factory they found that within shift, equipment downtime and breakdowns led to losses of 17 per cent of working time, one-third of which is accounted for by management-authorized absences.

On 7 August 1983 a comprehensive resolution on labour discipline was passed.[78] I shall summarize the 'negative' sanctions, and later I shall turn to the ways that positive administrative encouragement is proposed. For all workers and employees absent without a valid reason, 'their regular vacation time for that year is to be reduced by the number of days they are absent—however, the vacation must not be less than two working weeks'. For those absent

for more than three hours during a weekday without valid reason, the same sanctions are to be applied as those established for absenteeism; workers and employees who commit violations of labour discipline, are absent without a valid reason or who show up for work in a state of intoxication may be transferred to another, lower-paying job for a period of up to three months or moved to another, lower-level position for the same period. A person is not to be released at his own request during this period, and the time spent on jobs to which manual workers or office employees have been transferred for violating labour discipline does not count towards the period of giving notice; workers and office employees who are dismissed for the systematic violation of labour discipline, for absenteeism without a valid reason or for showing up for work in a state of intoxication are to be paid half the regular bonus rate for the first six months at their new places of work. . . . It has been deemed advisable to increase the material liability of workers and office employees for damage they cause to enterprises, organizations or institutions during the performance of their labour obligations, including liability for the production of defective output.

(The worker is required to pay for damage so done, to a maximum of a third of his or her salary). Workers may be sacked on turning up for work drunk.

These are the main lines of legislation and policy which have been continued by Gorbachev. In his election speech, reported on 1 March 1984, he took up many of the points made by Andropov in calling for greater labour discipline, responsibility, exactingness and improvements in 'style and methods of work'.[79] Enhanced standards of socialist legality, and the cessation of embezzlement, parasitism, hooliganism (i.e. general misbehaviour including drunkeness) and various forms of cheating ('padding' of reports) are the thrust of the leadership's thinking in creating the right style of work. Social justice also has a role to play in improving incentive to work; unearned or unjustly earned income militates against the principle of remuneration in accordance with the quality and quantity of work.[80] The attitudes of management also require a significant shift in the direction of greater 'thriftiness', with more emphasis on economizing time and materials; management has to be more 'responsible' and should accept its obligations to combat mismanagement and wastefulness.[81]

Such suppression of *individual* manifestations of ill-discipline (the 'subjective' element) have to be seen in the context of poor conditions at work, of mismanagement and of the insufficient or poor training of workers. While reducing infractions of labour discipline will undoubtedly lead to improvements in morale and increases in labour productivity, indiscipline itself should be analysed as consequences of the operation of the economy (the 'objective' position). Penal sanctions can only have a limited effect.

## MANAGERIAL AND SYSTEMIC CAUSES OF POOR LABOUR DISCIPLINE

L. Kostin, M. Sonin, T.I. Zaslavskaya and many others have emphasized the structural and managerial constraints which predispose workers to bad habits. The full-employment, labour-shortage economy makes it difficult for enterprises to enforce penalties. As Sonin pointed out:

The administration of enterprises and institutions is frequently compelled to hire new personnel and close its eyes to their moral and professional shortcomings. To a certain degree the dismissal of a careless or insufficiently skilled worker may even run counter to the direct interests of the enterprise (better to have a bad worker than no worker at all). Those who violate labour discipline, including chronic absentees, do not fear the gravest consequence—dismissal—since the only threat is transfer to another, frequently better paid job. Any manager will unquestionably think twice before instituting strict discipline for fear that his workers will begin looking for a job where the rules are not as strict. Much loss of worktime is also due to administratively authorised leave.[82]

The survey conducted by Kutyrev[83] gives instances of the strength of the position of workers. The editor of the Metallurgiya publishing house wrote:'It used to be possible to sack or to transfer a person who was working poorly, but now such a decision is costly: you have to find someone new and train him, and your work unit will suffer. Just try to find an excavator operator today! One has to "think three times" before you take such a step. This is where the harmful liberalism one encounters comes from.'

The legal safeguards to workers' employment also hinder management from taking action against mischief-makers. A foreman at the Noril'sk mining and metallurgical combine pointed out that 'complaints about decisions regarding violations of labour discipline are taken seriously [by unconscientious workers]; therefore, even when they are guilty of a violation, they will file complaints with officials at all levels. Repeated efforts to check out such problems may confirm management's view, but at a considerable cost in time and nervous tension.'[84]

Less than a third of the correspondents in the survey conducted by Kutyrev considered weak laws to be a cause of labour discipline. Two-thirds of people polled thought that poor labour discipline was a consequence of the acute labour shortage: 'You can't make proper demands on an employee these days: if you sack him, he'll find another job that's just as good. . . . Employers consider it better to have a poor worker than none at all.'[85]

Managerial and systemic insufficiencies are considered by most Soviet specialists on labour to be much more important determinants of labour ill-discipline than individual behaviour. But Soviet press coverage emphasizes the 'subjective' factor at the cost of objective ones. In Karpov's study of the Leningrad press (1982–84), only 25 per cent of themes on labour discipline were on the improvement of the organization of production, 16 per cent on enhancing the interests of workers and 11 per cent more on widening the participation of workers in administration of production.[86]

The lack of a clear relationship between worker incentive, effort, output and wages is crucial. In the discussion of the survey noted above, A. Ye. Gazaryan of Gomel University pointed out that with the existing ceilings and floors on wages, incentives are not effective. 'A machine-tool operator who is ten times more disciplined and conscientious than a fellow worker with the same job receives only slightly more money and sometimes he even gets the same.' Another contributor argued 'only amateurish efforts have been made to structure the incentive system in such a way as to increase worker motivation, let alone harness it.'[87] Inadequate service arrangements necessitating queuing (waiting for transport, meals, consumer goods etc.) leads to short-time working (leaving early, absenteeism). The major deficiencies mentioned in this survey are: inadequate incentives for conserving labour, underemphasis on final results, the slow pace of equipment renovation, shortcomings in the organization of production, labour and administration, failure to observe the plan and imperfections in the management mechanism. Three-quarters of the correspondents felt that it was outside the power of enterprises to enforce discipline. They lacked control over the shortage of labour, breakdowns in the supply of materials were outside their control, and they had insufficient powers to reward good workers and penalise shirkers.[88] Kutyrev concludes that it is the 'economic mechanism' which is at the root of poor labour discipline.[89] Zaslavskaya cites a sociological study claiming that 90 per cent of executives and 84 per cent of workers believe that under different economic conditions they could work with significantly greater efficiency.[90] These include having greater independence and initiative and making income depend on the quality of work.

Dissatisfaction with work by young workers is another cause of ill-discipline. The main offenders appear to be young (under 30) workers and male. This age group also has the highest turnover rate. It is suggested that violations of discipline committed by them are a reflection of the frustration felt by young workers when their jobs do not live up to the expectations[91] of a better educated and demanding young workforce. 'Dissatisfaction' with existing practice may not be a form of labour 'indiscipline' but an indication of the inadequacy of traditional management. It is also the result of bad planning, since workers are not always given jobs requiring the skills in which they have been trained.

## ORGANIZATIONAL MEASURES TO IMPROVE LABOUR PRODUCTIVITY

Given the constraints discussed above—size and quality of the population stock, and the level of capital investment—planners attempt within the structure of a command economy to devise means to make labour work more efficiently and effectively.

A common assumption underlying Soviet thinking (as indeed managerial thinking everywhere) is that the level of effort of the worker could and should be increased. Measurement of 'effort' and the determinants of effort are notoriously difficult to achieve.

It is generally agreed that individuals have a map of preferences in which work is substituted for leisure. In the Soviet Union, work is regarded as more than an economic necessity. It is part of a good life. Wages in western society are instrumentalities linked to individual striving for status and possessions. It is widely believed that Americans work harder than Europeans because status is seen in terms of individual advancement measured in money.[92] As noted earlier, for the 'incentive' of wages to be effective they must be related to purchasing power as well as the mentality of the worker. Here indeed one may make parallels between Soviet and British industry. Pratten, in his comparative study of labour productivity, found that British workers, unlike Americans, lacked motivation for money income.[93] The provision of many services 'in kind' (or highly subsidized) in the USSR serves at present to diminish remunerative motivation.

Material incentives, in the form of rewarding individual contribution by monetary payments, is one of the guiding principles of the organization of the workforce. This pre-dates the current leadership and goes back to the time of Stalin. Chernenko summed up current policy when he reiterated that

the principle of socialism, which is sacred to us, [entails] from each according to his ability, to each according to his work. This is the foundation of the social justice that our working class and our people, for the first time in history, have converted from dreams to living reality. . . . Those who work at top efficiency should, always and everywhere, be provided with tangible advantages in earnings and in the distribution of housing, vacation accommodation and other social benefits.[94]

Gorbachev has also emphasized the role of Soviet justice in improving the motive to work, he has castigated unearned and unjustly earned income which is contrary to payment according to the quality and quantity of work done.[95]

The objective of wage policy is to use wages as an incentive for greater effort on the part of the employee and to reward the quality as well as the quantity of labour. At the same time, to avoid inflation, planners have to ensure that wages rise less than productivity. Difficulties arise when planners have to reconcile wages paid with the assumptions (a) that higher levels of skill and qualification should be more highly rewarded; (b) that the provision of incentives for motivation has to affect the labour force as a whole; and (c) that an increase in levels of productivity should rise at rates greater than the increase in wage payments.

In market systems, the wage paid may reconcile labour demand with supply, though there are, of course, imperfections caused by wage-fixing, and lags in adjustments of wages. Productivity is ensured by unproductive firms (in the last instance) being bankrupted, and a drive to improve productivity and to minimize wages is derived from the necessity to remain in business at a profit. However much the market is modified in capitalist states— either by government policy or employees' associations—the influence of the market is to pay the minimum acceptable wage to the smallest workforce compatible with maintaining output over a given period. Capitalist firms are not subject to wage and price controls and rises in wages may be passed on to consumers in the form of higher prices. (Wages in the public sector are also indirectly linked to market rates.)

In socialist economic systems, however, wage-scales, the quantity of material inputs and outputs, and their prices are given to enterprises by superior economic organs. The wage fund is one of these inputs. As noted above, socialist enterprises have a propensity to employ as many workers as possible, to spend the wage fund and to make it as large as possible. The wage fund is relatively weakly constrained. In the early 1980s, in order to control wage rises, an attempt was made to gear a one per cent increase in labour productivity to wage increases of 0.35 per cent. This was ineffective and the ratio was raised to 0.4 per cent in 1984.[96] Just as in market societies where there is inflationary drift, in planned ones wage increases are not adequately covered by growth of productivity. In the early 1950s, wages in industry increased by 0.23 per cent for every one per cent increase in labour productivity; five years later, the comparable rise for wages was 0.45 per cent, in 1976 to 1983, it was 0.9 per cent.[97] In the tenth Five Year Plan (1976–1980), the increase in the growth of wages was 0.69 per cent of the planned increase in labour productivity, instead of the planned 0.5 per cent. In some industries (coal, meat and dairy), productivity even fell, while wages rose; in ferrous metallurgy, petroleum, pulp and paper, food and fish, average wages grew faster than productivity; in building the indices were the same; in machine tools, labour productivity overall grew faster than wages.

In the first years of the eleventh Five Year Plan (1981–85), wage drift continued: in 1981 industry recorded an average increase of labour productivity of 2.7 per cent and an increase of average wages of 2.3 per cent—a one per cent increase in labour productivity for every 0.85 per cent increase in wages, as against 0.64 per cent defined by the plan.[98] In 1982 wages rose nearly one third more quickly than labour productivity.[99] This is often caused by adjusting production plans downwards without reducing the wage fund.[100] Ministries and industrial associations redistribute plan assignments, making life easier for those who work poorly and increasing the burden on the more efficient factories.[101] Prices, however, do not respond to shortages and demand cannot be satisfied. The extent of shortages of consumer goods may be gauged by the fact that between 1970 and 1983 the wages fund in the national economy increased by 90 per cent, while trade turnover rose by 81 per cent.[102] In 1984, compared to 1983, the productivity of labour in industry rose 103.8 per cent (in agriculture [*obshchestvennoe proizvodstvo* ],[103] it was 101 per cent, in building 103.1 per cent, in rail transport 102 per cent). The average income of manuals and non-manuals rose by 103 per cent. In 1984, productivity was 0.4 per cent higher than planned.[104]

Systemic labour shortage leads to enterprises bidding up the price of labour. To keep labour in the factory and to prevent the disruptions of labour turnover, wage rates are adjusted and bonuses are paid to bring up wages should there be a shortfall. Hence wage levels became established not by rational norms but by 'unwritten rules' about the standard of living a worker should enjoy.[105] In the electrical equipment industry between 1970 and 1980, the incentive fund rose by 76 per cent while labour productivity rose by 58 per cent. In another enterprise the incentive fund rose by 83 per cent while labour productivity increased by 8 per cent.[106] Wage drift may also be observed with regard to differentials which have narrowed considerably: between 1976 and 1984 the wages of manual workers grew by an average of 40 roubles per month, whereas those of engineers rose by only 20 roubles. The average pay of engineers, according to one writer, is only 10 per cent more than that of workers.[107] This process is said to reduce the material motivation of engineers and to create distortions in the pay scales which no longer in many instances sufficiently reward levels of skill.[108] The lack of consumer goods available at market prices in turn reduces financial motivation—as money is only worth what it can buy.

The essence of current reforms in socialist societies is to stimulate the labour force to work harder and to encourage the enterprise to increase productivity without significantly weakening the planning constraints on the enterprise noted above. One important means to combat the tendency of wage 'drift' and the lack of correlation between wages and effort is the improvement of norms in deciding wage rates.

## NORMS

'Norming' or 'norms' (*norma*) refers to the amount of time necessary for the fulfilment of a particular work activity, given the qualifications of a worker and the level of technology. Wages are paid on the basis of such norms. The value of output is then fixed in relation to the norm, and wages are directly linked to the normative net output of labour. Determining norms is similar to time and motion studies in the West. In socialist states, the notion of the 'socially necessary' labour time embodied in a product, derived from the Marxist labour theory of value, legitimates this process. It is assumed that there should be a technologically-determined 'norm' for each work process. Such norms determine what workers should receive as a fair reward for their effort, they shape relativities between workers as well as being a measure for the improvement of productivity. (Norms are separate from bonuses which are paid out of profits.)[109] Once norms have been worked out, the size of the wage fund for an enterprise may be determined by the volume of net output. The wage fund should only rise in proportion to achieved production and labour productivity growth.

Economists and planners regularly call for the re-examination and setting of norms on 'technically-based' criteria on a branch and inter-branch scale. The objective here is for a given job to be paid identically wherever it is located (subject, of course, to planned regional supplements) rather than being determined by individual factory management decision. In the ninth Five Year Plan (1971–1975) it is claimed that 1.706 million piece-workers were made redundant as a result of revision of norms.[110] Norms are often set too low and are regularly overfulfilled from 150 to 200 per cent;[111] in 1981, more than one third of all piece-rate workers in industry fulfilled their output norms by 110–130 per cent and another third by more than 130 per cent. Norms which are fulfilled qualify for a bonus of 20 per cent of the basic wage rate even though the norms may be fixed too low.[112] Norms also 'nearly always fail to take into account the equipping of production with new machinery and . . . the improvement in workers skills'.[113] To stop this practice many writers call for a limit to the overfulfilment of norms. A correspondent writing to the newspaper *Literaturnaya gazeta*, summed up the situation as follows:

The loss of work time in industry is great. But on the other hand is it normal that at some enterprises output norms are constantly being overfulfilled by 20–40 per cent without any great strain, and with considerable inner-shift loss of work time? Use of these reserves alone would give us a huge number of additional work hands. At present, enterprises have to have hidden reserves to compensate for inadequacies in planning material—technical supply, use of workers and employees for agricultural work, construction etc. However, freeing [i.e. making redundancies]and realising manpower reserves does not improve the financial-economic position of an enterprise, on the contrary, it usually worsens considerably. We must find a way out of this vicious circle. It can be said without doubt that without making enterprises interested economically in saving labour, all other measures will not provide a solution to the problem.[114]

Clearly, workers often attempt to negotiate the lowest norms to secure the highest pay for the minimum amount of work. To counter this tendency, the *Aksay* method was introduced in 1968 in a plastics factory in the Rostov province. The object of the scheme was to encourage workers to revise labour norms on their own initiative. It is claimed that at the plastics plant out put rose by 14 per cent per annum between 1972 and 1982,[115] which is three times the average in this branch of industry. The director saw 'norming' as the crucial variable to increase productivity. He points out that norms reconcile the interests of the individual, the factory collective and society: 'if norms are set low, the individual worker may be at an advantage—but not society and the collective . . . if the norm is high, the material and moral interest of the individual is reduced.'[116] When norms are always overfilled by 130 to 140 per cent, the usual procedure is for a norm-setter (*normirovshchik*) to advise the director to increase the norm. If he does so, workers become dissatisfied and wages fall, though later they normally rise. There is a constant process of norm-fixing and revisions. The *Aksay* director, N. Nagibin, points out that this creates a bad psychological atmosphere. While norms are revised 'from above' when new technology or machinery is introduced, at other times workers initiate increases. The immediate incentive is that the worker is paid on the introduction of the new norms a bonus equal to half of the anticipated saving for a six-month period. When accepted, such increases in productivity lead to a continuous rise in wages. Since 1978, piece-workers have had a threefold increase in wages and productivity has grown six times. Discipline in the factory has improved and labour turnover has declined from 30 per cent to 6 per cent.[117]

It is recognized, however, that the method has not been widely adopted. Factory director Nagibin concedes that disruption of supplies may lead to norms (and output) not being fulfilled and thus managers and workers have a common interest in maintaining hidden reserves of labour which can be called on to maintain sudden bursts of production (storming) and low norms can be grossly exceeded thereby compensating for idle time. In some cases, when the scheme was introduced bonuses have been lowered to exact even greater savings for the factory: this goes against the spirit of the scheme and leads to resentment. But workers become wary of initiating and accepting the revision of norms, despite initial material incentives of 50 per cent of the value of resources saved. As a weaver put it in a letter to *Literaturnaya gazeta*:

I am weaver . . . and on average a weaver today may manage 26 to 28 looms. It would be possible to do more, but people don't want to. Why? Because it's not worth it. . . . Let us assume that workers agree to supervise an extra 4 machines. Their pay increases . . . and does so for 8 to 10 months. Then output norms are increased. Wages stay the same as they were before the extra machines were taken on, but the work is more difficult. As a result many people refuse to man more machines.[118]

The system of individually-based norms has some intrinsic difficulties. Workers concentrate on their individual tasks to the detriment of the collective interest. They may show less care for equipment. Defining the correct norms, moreover, is a highly complicated process. The materials and machinery used by workers vary greatly, making it difficult to fix equitable rates.

Even when it is possible to ascertain what a worker could reasonably be expected to do, the organization of production often means that norms are not enforced. Lack of supplies, holdups and breakdown of machinery restrict output and, if norms were strictly applied, wages would fall. Hence management often resorts to paying bonuses to workers, not as a reward for extra effort but in order to make up the wage to the average level of pay.[119] In the early 1980s, in many industries, bonuses came to the maximum limits of 40–60 per cent of pay; in industry more than 90 per cent of all workers (on piece-rate and time-rate) receive bonus payments.[120] Fixing the wage fund on the basis of 'norms' would also make life more difficult for management whose wages fund would be determined by an 'objective' criterion. Hence there is resistance to their introduction and adoption. The brigade system, described below, is one way around these problems.

## CONCLUSIONS: PRODUCTIVITY IN A LOW PAY/FULL-EMPLOYMENT ECONOMY

The maturation of the Soviet economy in the 1980s has brought in its train not only new economic problems but also a different pattern of needs on the part of the population. It is impossible to increase growth extensively by adding to the labour force because the supply of labour cannot be significantly increased. The economy now requires intensive growth entailing an increase in labour productivity. Labour productivity and motivation to work are systemic properties of a social system which limit the opportunities of the political leadership to raise productivity through its own actions. The Gorbachev administration, however, has inherited an economic system which provides opportunities for labour productivity to rise. From a social point of view, it will benefit from a population which is much better educated and able to adjust to changes in technology. One current cause of low labour productivity is overmanning and there is currently a surplus of employed labour to meet administrative inefficiencies. In the short run, labour productivity can be improved by reducing the age of retirement of capital. This will lead to shorter periods of machinery downtime and to a reduction in the number of auxiliary workers. Relatively small improvements in administration also can lead to rises in productivity: these are to do with delivery of materials and using the workforce more effectively. Such changes can be achieved without any significant reform of the existing 'economic mechanism'. The impact of the campaign to increase 'labour discipline' is limited to short-term improvements in labour productivity. Increased motivation to work in the long run is largely conceived of in material terms—of more appropriate payment 'according to one's work'.

Material 'stimulation' of labour to achieve greater efficiency has many implications for social policy. First, wage payments linked to 'material incentives' may give rise to socially and politically unacceptable differentials between groups of workers, thereby undermining the principles of distribution thought appropriate for the development of 'mature socialism'. While reward according to the principle of desert has been a component of policy since the time of Stalin, those of need and equality of consideration are also motivating principles of socialism. Secondly, the utilization of wages as a stimulus will only be effective if payment can be realized through consumption. This is not just a problem of adjusting the economic mechanism but involves the development of new and different products with an appeal to the higher income groups. A consumer society fulfils a particular pattern of needs: it encourages production to respond to the pattern of demand given by the distribution of income. The consumption needs of the richer groups might be met at the cost of those of the poorer ones. Such a policy is at variance with the political goals and ideological outlook of the Soviet political leadership (or at least with elements of it). A consumer society also entails the reconciliation of demand and supply through the use of money, rather than administrative allocation. Thirdly, improving material incentives involves not only rewarding those who work efficiently, but penalizing workers who default. The organization of work on the basis of efficiency, where for the enterprise marginal cost equals marginal revenue, is likely to involve a reduction in the workforce. Unemployment may follow in the train of a move to an economy based on maximizing the efficiency of production units and giving priority to consumption needs. Unemployment is not only a consequence of substituting capital for labour but it also acts to discipline the labour force and as a reservoir to meet changing industrial requirements for labour (by sector and geographical location). For reasons to be discussed below, it seems unlikely that a western-type labour market will evolve. More likely will be an increase in the number of redundancies which will be handled through labour exchanges with enhanced powers. Individual security of employment will be weakened in the context of economic planners maintaining full employment at the macro-level.

## REFERENCES

1. W.E.G. Salter, *Productivity and Technical Change* (Cambridge: Cambridge University Press, 1960), p. 1.
2. A. Bergson, *Productivity and the Social System—the USSR and the West* (Cambridge and London: Harvard University Press, 1978), p. 93.
3. N.A. Tikhonov (Chairman of the Council of Ministers), 'Osnovnye napravleniya ekonomicheskogo i sotsial'nogo razvitiya SSSR na 1981-1985g. i na period do 1990 g', *Pravda*, 28 February 1981.
4. M.S. Gorbachev (Speech to Stakhanovites), *Pravda*, 21 September 1985.
5. Ibid.
6. M.S. Gorbachev (Speech to Plenum of Central Committee), *Pravda*, 16 October 1985.
7. *Draft Basic Guidelines, Pravda* 9 November 1985 (*CDSP*, vol. 37, no. 45, pp. 10-11).
8. Gorbachev's speech to Plenum of Central Committee, *Pravda*, 16 October 1985.
9. *Pravda*, 23 April 1985.
10. *Pravda*, 15 October 1985.
11. *Pravda*, 12 June 1985.
12. Ibid.
13. Speech on fundamental problems of the Party's economic policy, reported in *Pravda*, 12 June, pp. 1-2.
14. L. A. Kostin is the First Vice-Chairman of the USSR State Committee on Labour and Social Questions. The following is drawn from *Trudovye resursy v odinnadtsatoy pyatiletke* (Moscow: 1981), Chapter 3; *Planovoe khozyaystvo*, no. 12 (1978), pp. 16-27; 'Reservy ispol'zovaniya trudovykh resursov', *EKO*, no. 1 (1984), pp. 22-38.
15. See, for example, A. Aganbegyan (then Director of The Institute of the Economics and Organization of Industrial Production), *Trud*, 12 December 1982.
16. *Narkhoz v 1983g* (1984), p. 135.
17. *Narkhoz v 1984g* (1985), p. 417. Calculated on figures for income in cash and in kind, excluding collective farmers.

18.  I.S. Maslova, 'Effecktivnost' ispol'zovaniya trudovykh resursov', *Voprosy ekonomiki*, no. 8 (August 1978), p. 54.
19.  Tikhonov (1981).
20.  W.E.G. Salter, *Productivity and Technical Change* (Cambridge: Cambridge University Press, 1960), pp. 70-3.
21.  C.F. Pratten, *Labour Productivity Differentials within International Companies* (Cambridge: Cambridge University Press, 1976), p. 24. Managers, however, do have 'clear views' on the causes of low productivity.
22.  Ibid., p. 1.
23.  Ibid., p. 22.
24.  *Pravda* 23 April 1983 (Speech commemorating Lenin's birthday).
25.  L.A. Gordon and A.K. Nazimova, 'The Productive Potential of the Soviet Working Class: Tendencies and Problems of Development', *Soviet Sociology*, vol. 19, no. 4 (1981), p. 33. (Translation of article appearing in *Voposy filosofii* (1980 no. 11, pp. 26-40.)
26.  E.F. Denison, *Why Growth Rates Differ* (Washington, D.C.: Brookings Institution, 1967), p. 80.
27.  See D. Lane and F. O'Dell, *The Soviet Industrial Worker* (1978), pp. 9-10; Gordon and Nazimova, p. 42; *Vestnik sttistiki*, no. 5 (1981), p. 64.
28.  Data cited by Gordon and Nazimova, p. 35.
29.  A permit is necessary to move to, and settle in, large towns.
30.  Participant in seminar on labour in discipline, cited in B.P. Kutyrev, 'Ditsiplina truda v dinamike', *EKO*, no. 9 (September 1981), p. 45.
31.  *Op.cit.*, p. 48.
32.  *P.S.S.*, vol. 11, p. 108. Cited by Gordon and Naximova, pp. 51-2. For Lenin on the work ethic, see also D. Lane, *Leninism: A Sociological Interpretation* (1981), pp. 72-4.
33.  M.S. Gorbachev, *Pravda*, 23 April 1983.
34.  No further definitions of activeness are given here. Interview between V. Ivanov (researcher) and A. Lepikhov, in *Izvestiya*, 3 May 1985.
35.  Growth in industrial labour productivity in the USSR averaged 8.35 in 1983 taking 1940 as base 1. The corresponding figure for Latvia was 13.37 and Estonia 15.75. *Narkhoz v 1983g* (1984), p. 136. However, growth of labour productivity using a 1980 base (1) was not much different in 1984 from the USSR average: USSR 1.09, Latvia 1.09, Estonia 1.08. *Narkhoz v 1984g* (1985), p. 149.
36.  Gordon and Nazimova, pp. 50-1.
37.  S.G. Strumilin, *Problemy ekonomiki truda* (Moscow: 1957), p. 598.
38.  Date given in the annual statistical handbook combine into one figure, higher and secondary education, including 'incomplete secondary'. *Narkhoz v 1983g* (1984), p. 30.
39.  V.A. Zhamin, 'Contemporary Problems of the Economics of Education', in D. Noah, *The Economics of Education in the USSR* (New York: Praeger, 1969), p. 9.
40.  P. Kaydalov and E.I. Suymenko, *Aktual'nye problemy sotsiologii truda* (Moscow: 1974), p. 91.
41.  See E. Gloeckner, 'Underemployment and Potential Unemployment of the

Technical Intelligentsia: Distortions between Education and Occupation', in D. Lane (ed.), *Labour and Unemployment in the USSR* (Brighton: Wheatsheaf Books, 1986), Chapter 13.

42. Kaydalov and Suymenko, p. 91.
43. For a discussion of incompatibilities between school-leavers' aspirations and work opportunities, see S. Marnie 'Transition from School to Work: Satisfying Pupils' Aspirations and the Needs of the Economy', in Lane (ed.) *Labour and Employment in the USSR*, Chapter 12.
44. *Prof-tekh uchilishche*, vocational-technical schools.
45. *Uchitel'skaya gazeta*, 23 March 1985; *CDSP*, vol. 37, no. 12, p. 23.
46. See Pratten, pp. 51-4. See also the comparative study of German and British industry by I. Maitland, *The Causes of Industrial Disorder* (London: Routledge, 1983).
47. J. Kornai, *The Economics of Shortage*, vol. A (1980), pp. 255-6.
48. Kostin, 'Tsena rabochey minuty', *Khozyaystvo i pravo*, no. 11 (1982), pp. 35-6.
49. Lepikhov and Ivanov (interview), *Izvestiya*, 3 May 1985.
50. No. 3 (1980), p. 51.
51. *Stroitel'naya gazeta*, 10 June 1983. Cited by E. Teague, *Labour Discipline and Legislation in the USSR: 1979-85* (Munich: RL Supplement 2/85), p. 39.
52. *Loc.cit.*, p. 36.
53. *Izvestiya*, 19 March 1985. English translation in *CDSP*, vol. 37, no. 11 (1985), p. 5.
54. B. Knabe, 'Arbeitstatigkeiten und Arbeitskraftepolitik in der UdSSR zu Beginn der 80 er Jahre', *Verichte des Bundesinsituts fur ostwissenshaftliche und internationale Studien* (Koln: no. 35, 1981), p. 13.
55. *Trud*, 29 December 1982. Cited by E. Teague, 'Labor Discipline and Legislation in the USSR: 1979–85' (Munich: RL Supplement 2/85), p. 4.
56. E.A. Kyuregyan, 'Otnoshenie k trudu i distsiplina promyshlennykh rabochikh', *Sots. issled*, no. 2 (1983), pp. 129-30.
57. Kyuregyan gives the ranking of deficiencies. Technical inadequacies, poor repair of machines had a scale of 3.42 on a five-point scale; insufficiencies in supply 3.21, poor labour organization 3.09, low levels of knowledge 2.98, lack of interest in the task 2.97 and time lost changing jobs 2.69; *loc.cit.*, p. 130.
58. These data relate to a 24-hour period: *Vestnik statistiki*, no. 4 (1983), p. 69.
59. Editorial, *Izvestiya*, 19 March 1985.
60. i.e. 7 per cent of the workforce was absent sick compared to 2 per cent. Data cited by Teague, *loc.cit.*, p. 18.
61. M. Ya. Sonin has estimated that downtime during shifts attributable to violations of discipline (including absenteeism) amounts to 30 per cent of losses, while shortcomings of organization account for 70 per cent. 'Zametki o trudovoy distsipline', *EKO*, no. 5 (1981). English translation in M. Ya. Sonin, 'Notes Regarding Discipline', *Problems of Economics*, (April 1982), vol. 24, no. 12, p. 12.
62. For a review of labour discipline and legislation on it between 1979 and 1985,

see Teague, *op.cit.*

63. G. Popov, '. . .Ne tol'ko prikhodit' vo vremya na rabotu', *Literaturnaya gazeta*, April 1983, p. 13. Popov contrasts this with other letters stressing the role of management.
64. D. Moiseev (a Moscow electrician), 'Otvetstvennost' rabochego', *Literaturnaya gazeta*, no. 29, 20 July 1983.
65. 'Kak spravit'sya s lodyrem?', *Literaturnaya gazeta*, 12 January 1983.
66. V. Nikitinski, ibid.
67. B.P. Kutyrev, 'Distsiplina truda v dinamike', *EKO*, no. 9 (September 1981), pp. 17-45. The press varies in its coverage, Slider's study of six national newspapers' coverage of the labour law found that 30 per cent of letters to *Izvestiya* (the government paper) referred to discipline proposals, in *Trud* (the trade union paper) the share fell to 12 per cent and in *Literaturnaya gazeta* (the organ of the Writers' Union) much favoured by intellectuals, it dropped to 8 per cent. On the 'participation' proposals, the proportion of letters for the three newspapers was 18 per cent, 20 per cent and 85 per cent respectively. D. Slider, 'Reforming the Work Place: The 1983 Soviet Law on Labour Collectives', *Soviet Studies*, vol. 37, no. 2 (April 1985).
68. No quantitative results were reported, though many responses were cited (ibid., p. 24).
69. V.G. Karpov, 'Distsiplina truda kak tema gazetnykh publikatsiy,' *Sots, issled*, no. 2 (1986), p. 125.
70. 'Tipovye pravila vnutrennego rasporyadka dlya rabochikh i sluzhashchikh predpriyatii, uchrezhdenii, organizatsii', *Byulleten' Goskomtruda*, no. 11 (1984), item 1.
71. A review of changes may be studied in S. Karinski, 'Razvitie trudovogo zakonodatel'stava v usloviyakh zrelogo sotsialisticheskogo obshchestva', *Sots. trud*, no. 9 (1981), pp. 3-10.
72. 'Tipovye . . .', items 1 and 2.
73. Ibid., item 19.
74. 'O dal'neyshem ukreplenii trudovy distsipliny i sokrashchenii tekuchesti kadrov v narodnom khozyaystve', *Sobranie postanovlenii pravitel'stva SSSR* (1980), no. 3, p. 17. See also the comprehensive regulations on work order, in *Tipovye pravila vnutrennego rasporyadka dlya rabochikh i sluzhashchikh predpriyatii, uchrezhdenii, organizatsii* Byulleten' Goskomtruda, no. 11 (1984).
75. For a description see E. Teague, 'Crackdown on Labor Discipline Proposal', RFE/RL 302/83, 10 August 1983.
76. Reported in *Izvestiya*, 14 January 1982; excerpts in *CDSP*, vol. 34, no. 2 (1982), p. 9.
77. Ibid.
78. *Pravda*, 7 August 1983. A full translation of the text (cited here), 'On Stepping up work to Strengthen Socialist Labor Discipline' is to be found in *CDSP*, vol. 35 (1983), no.32, pp. 4-7.
79. *Pravda*, 1 March 1984, p. 2.
80. Ibid.
81. These points were emphasized in Gorbachev's discussions with workers in

Leningrad, reported in *Pravda* on 16 may 1985, p. 1.

82. 'Zametki o trudovoy distsipline', *EKO*, no. 5 (1981). English version (cited here), 'Notes Regarding Labor Discipline', *Problems of Economics* (April 1982), vol. 24, no. 12, pp. 6-7.
83. *EKO*, no. 9 (September 1981), p. 25.
84. Ibid.
85. Ibid., p. 32.
86. Karpov, p. 125.
87. *EKO*, no. 9 (1981).
88. Ibid., p. 45.
89. Ibid.
90. T. Zaslavskaya, *Sovetskaya Rossiya* (7 January 1986). English summary in *CDSP*, vol. 38, no. 2 (1986), pp. 1-3.
91. M. Ya Sonin, 'Notes Regarding Labor Discipline', p. 10.
92. E.F. Denison, *Why Growth Rates Differ* (Washington, D.C.: 1967), p.112; Pratten, p. 53.
93. Partly because (like Soviet workers) they had low-rent council houses, free health and education: Pratten, p. 3.
94. K.U. Chernenko (speech), *Pravda* and *Izvestiya*, 6 October 1984; *CDSP*, vol. 36, no. 40 (1984), p. 5.
95. *Pravda*, 1 March 1984, p. 2.
96. E. Rusanov, 'Proizvoditel'nost' truda i zarplata', *Sotsialisticheskaya industriya*, 24 January 1985.
97. Ibid.
98. D. Karpukhin, *Planovoe khozyaystvo*, no. 10 (October 1983), pp. 87-92. Abstract in *CDSP*, vol. 36, no. 10 (1984), p. 5.
99. Rusanov, *loc. cit.*
100. K. Volkov, *Ekonomicheskaya gazeta* (31 July 1983); *CDSP*, vol. 35, p. 10.
101. Karpukhin, p. 5.
102. Rusanov, *loc.cit.*
103. i.e. excluding production of private plots.
104. *Voprosy statistiki*, no. 4 (1985), pp. 67-8.
105. L.S. Byakhman and T.S. Zlotnitskaya, 'Differentsiatsiya zarabotnoy platy kak faktor stimulirovaniya truda', *Sots. issled*, no. 1 (1984), p. 40.
106. V. Parfenov, *Pravda*, 29 August 1983, p. 2; *CDSP*, vol. 35, no. 35, (1983), p. 19.
107. Rusanov, *loc.cit.*
108. Blyakhman and Zlotnitskaya, *op.cit.*
109. K. Volkov, *Ekonomicheskaya gazeta* (31 July 1983), p. 10; *CDSP*, vol. 35, no. 31, (1983), p. 10.
110. A. Kotlyar, 'Polnaya zanyatost' i sbalansirovannost' faktorov sotsialisticheskogo proizvodstva, *Vop. ekon*, no. 7 (1983), p. 110.
111. Rogovski, *loc. cit.*: *Vop. ekon.*, no. 1 (1982), p. 9.
112. Karpukhin, p. 6.
113. E. Rusanov, *Sotsialisticheskaya industriya* (24 January 1985).
114. V. Savich, 'Mneniya', *Literaturnaya gazeta*, 26 November 1980, p. 11.
115. See full account of interview with director of the enterprises in 'Na odnikh

vesakh', *Literaturnaya gazeta*, 3 August 1983, p. 13.
116. Ibid.
117. Ibid.
118. Lida Malikhova, 'Defitsit kadrov', *Literaturnaya gazeta*, 24 December 1980, p. 11.
119. See, for example, V. Parfenov, *Pravda*, 29 August 1983, p. 2.; *CDSP*, vol. 35, (1983), no. 35, p. 19.
120. Karpukhin, p. 10.

# 6 The Process of Redundancy, Displacement or 'Freeing' of the Workforce in Conditions of Labour Shortage

## OCCUPATIONAL AND SECTORAL LABOUR MOBILITY

Western commentators justify levels of unemployment on the grounds that industrial change and economic efficiency require a responsive labour force. The market, it is held, is a regulator. Declining industries shed labour which is absorbed by growing ones. The supply of labour has to respond to demand through retraining and changing jobs. Both Soviet and western writers have said that the Soviet labour market lacks flexibility and that labour mobility is sluggish. Garnsey[1] points out that employment in manufacturing has been greater, and in the service sector lower, than in the West. A similar conclusion has been reached by E. Manevich, who unfavourably contrasts shifts between sectors of the Soviet economy with those in capitalist countries.[2] The immobility of a large number of unskilled manual workers in many areas of production acts as a brake on the rise of labour productivity. At the level of the enterprise when mechanization has occurred, the numbers of workers have only decreased marginally.[3] Study of the occupational structure of the labour force, however, shows that considerable changes in the structure of employment have taken place in recent years.

Table 6.1 shows the number of workers in different industries in the USSR for certain years between 1940 and 1982. The table shows first, a reduction of 5.3 million in the agricultural workforce between 1940 and 1982 and a concomitant rise in industry, building and transport; second, it shows the slow increase in the service sector between 1965 and 1982. Unlike in western capitalist countries, however, the proportion of employees in industry,

131

*Table 6.1: Distribution of Employment by Branch of Economy 1940–82 (000s)*

|  | 1940 | 1965 | 1975 | 1980 | 1982 |
|---|---|---|---|---|---|
| Total | 62.926 | 95.815 | 117.560 | 125.998 | 128.263 |
| Manual and non-manual | | | | | |
| workers | 33.926 | 76.915 | 102.160 | 112.498 | 115.163 |
| Manual workers | 23.860 | 56.389 | 72.281 | 78.830 | 80.353 |
| Collective farmers | 29.000 | 18.900 | 15.400 | 13.500 | 13.100 |
| Industry (industrial | | | | | |
| production personnel) | 13.079 | 27.447 | 34.054 | 36.891 | 37.610 |
| Manuals | 11.113 | 23.495 | 28.487 | 30.479 | 30.950 |
| Agriculture (state farms) and | | | | | |
| Forestry | 2.983 | 9.330 | 10.974 | 12.108 | 12.478 |
| Manuals | 2.491 | 8.567 | 9.807 | 10.713 | 10.988 |
| Transport and | | | | | |
| communications | 4.009 | 8.259 | 10.743 | 11.958 | 12.337 |
| Manuals | 2.997 | 6.644 | 8.450 | 9.466 | 9.732 |
| Building | 1.993 | 7.301 | 10.574 | 11.240 | 11.299 |
| Manuals | 1.704 | 6.012 | 8.143 | 8.460 | 8.533 |
| Trade, public catering, supply | 3.351 | 6.009 | 8.857 | 9.694 | 9.863 |
| Manuals | 2.322 | 4.555 | 6.921 | 7.681 | 7.816 |
| Other aspects of activity in the | | | | | |
| sphere of material production | 166 | 775 | 1.250 | 1.436 | 1.495 |
| Housing and utilities, | | | | | |
| 'unproductive' services | 1.516 | 2.386 | 3.805 | 4.512 | 4.612 |
| Manuals | 1.095 | 1.857 | 3.142 | 3.696 | 3.751 |
| Health, physical education | | | | | |
| and social insurance | 1.512 | 4.277 | 5.769 | 6.223 | 6.448 |
| Education | 2.482 | 6.044 | 8.135 | 9.166 | 9.454 |
| Culture (*kul'tura*) | 196 | 556 | 1.056 | 1.290 | 1.362 |
| Art (*iskusstvo*) | 173 | 370 | 446 | 457 | 463 |
| Science (*nauka*) | 362 | 2.401 | 3.790 | 4.379 | 4.475 |
| Banking, insurance | 267 | 300 | 519 | 649 | 676 |
| Administrative (government | | | | | |
| and voluntary bodies) | 1.837 | 1.460 | 2.188 | 2.495 | 2.591 |
| Manuals in above | 2.138 | 5.259 | 7.331 | 8.335 | 8.583 |
| Agriculture* Total personnel | 31.300 | 28.300 | 26.600 | 26.000 | 26.000 |
| of which: Collective farms | 29.000 | 18.900 | 15.400 | 13.500 | 13.100 |
| State farms | 1.800 | 9.400 | 11.000 | 12.000 | 12.300 |
| *Percentage of workforce (including collective farmers) engaged in:* | | | | | |
| Agriculture | 49.7 | 29.5 | 22.6 | 20.6 | 20.2 |
| Industry, building, transport | 30.3 | 44.8 | 47.1 | 47.6 | 47.7 |
| Services | 20.000 | 25.700 | 30.300 | 31.800 | 32.100 |
|  | 100.000 | 100.000 | 100.000 | 100.000 | 100.000 |

* This figure excludes persons solely engaged in private agricultural production and includes personnel on farms engaged in repairs, building and services.

*Source: Narodnoe khozyaystvo SSSR v 1982g* (1983), pp. 287, 364-5, 367.

building and transport has risen, albeit very modestly between 1975 and 1982. Agricultural employment has only fallen slightly between 1975 and 1982 (from 22.6 per cent to 20.2 per cent). By contrast, in 1975, the USA agricultural labour force was only 3.8 per cent, the British 2.7 per cent, and Japan, which started its industrialization from a similar base to that of the USSR, reduced its agricultural labour force from 50.1 per cent in 1950 to 12.5 in 1975. These changes refer to annual average levels of employment. *Prima facie*, and bearing changes in western societies in mind, the general distribution of the Soviet workforce would appear to be changing less rapidly in the past twenty years: the total workforce in industry, building and transport increased from 43 millions to 61.2 millions between 1965 and 1982.

It would appear that workers are retained in positions, even after capital investment takes place. Study of the data in Table 6.1 shows that the ratio of manual workers to the total number of non-manual has remained constant, or has even increased between 1940 and 1982. Taking the total number of manuals to the total number of workers the ratio was 1.4:1 in 1940 and 1.4:1 in 1982; in industry the ratios were 1.1:1 and 1.2:1 on the two dates respectively.[4] In industry in the RSFSR the number of manual workers was planned to be reduced from 53.6 per cent in 1981 to 49.7 per cent in 1985—a reduction of 0.7 per cent annum, and even in factories which will come on-stream in 1981—90, one third of the labour force will be manual workers.[5] Economic plans usually define the level of labour displacement (or 'freeing'[6]) at some one per cent of the workforce a year, whereas many specialists argue that it should be more like three per cent.[7] Possibly there are too many jobs in the USSR. Are more jobs created than are necessary and are jobs maintained that should be eliminated?

## AN OVERSUPPLY OF JOBS?

Levels of employment are directly related to the supply of jobs. Western and Soviet economists agree that the Soviet economy, in a macro sense, is a labour shortage one. A labour shortage may be said to exist when the number of vacancies is greater than the number of workers presenting themselves for employment; i.e. the effective demand for labour outstrips its supply. This is illustrated by Figure 6.1. At wage W, $N_2$ is demanded and O $N_1$ is notionally supplied. $N_1 - N_2$ is the labour shortage. $N - N_1$ represents the level of frictional unemployment, as described above (see Chapter 4).

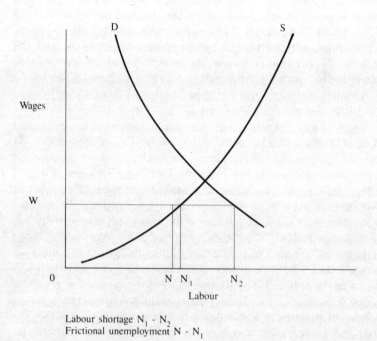

Labour shortage $N_1 - N_2$
Frictional unemployment $N - N_1$

*Figure 6.1  Demand and Supply of Labour*

A labour shortage can be characterized at different levels: (a) in the economy, (b) in industrial sectors and regions, (c) in particular trades or jobs, and (d) in certain enterprises. Due to imperfections in the labour market, shortages at one level may not affect other levels. Conceptualizing 'shortage' is complicated by considerations of the efficient use of labour, by whether the supply of jobs is artificial and by whether requirements of production can be met by fewer workers. The latter considerations are not only technical and managerial ones but are also linked to the training, ability, motivation and culture of the worker or employee.

Estimates of 'overmanning' and 'underemployment' are fraught with methodological problems. Notions of what is a 'reasonable' or 'efficient' work rate are not simply technological measures of work output, but also involve socially construed beliefs about work norms. Even under capitalism, work rates vary greatly between societies, though management is impelled to increase work effort. How then do Soviet economists justify their assertion that the workforce is 'underemployed'? There is, first, direct evidence of the inefficient use of labour time, and secondly, economic analysis pointing to the inefficient combinations of factors of production and the low productivity of labour.

There is a paucity of detailed statistics showing the extent and nature of the supposed shortages: no comprehensive and regular surveys of job vacancies are published. In total the number of vacancies is approximately two per cent.[8] This is not a particularly high figure as one would expect, with normal turnover and the creation of new jobs, vacancies to be about this proportion. At the macro-level we know that labour demanded by enterprises continually exceeds Gosplan's calculations. In 1971, the planned number of workers was 92.7 million. In practice, employment totalled 94.1 million; in 1975, 101.4 million places were planned and 104.1 million were employed; i.e. plans were exceeded by 1.4 and 2.7 million in the two years respectively.[9] In 1981, Manevich reiterated the fact that the 'inflation' of the workforce regularly exceeds the plan by 2−2.5 million.[10]

Estimates made by central planners at the macro-level of the numbers of jobs in the economy are not coordinated with the number of jobs created by enterprises. Numbers of jobs are not calculated centrally for enterprises which are able to employ the numbers of workers they require, subject to not exceeding the wage fund (i.e. the total planned expenditure on wages).[11] However, the size of the wage fund indirectly regulates the size of the workforce and, since 1980, ceilings have been set for the total numbers employed. Such limits are enforced by the local councils' executive committees (*ispolkoms*) but their monitoring and enforcement are ineffective. In 1983, it 'frequently happened that union-republic ministries ratified manpower increases without consulting local organs'.[12] In 1982, one-third of enterprises in four production ministries of the Russian Republic (RSFSR) exceeded the labour targets; and one fifth of all industrial enterprises in that republic employed more workers than authorized in the plan.[13] Local agencies of control have no effective power over ministries and can only petition them and the organs of people's control. Reducing bonuses of management (as a penalty) is counter-productive—it weakens morale and lowers output. I. Malmygin, in the Soviet planning journal *Planovoe khozyaystvo*,[14] points out that in industry the number of jobs regularly increases in the USSR, much more than the number of workers available for employment. From this viewpoint, the demand for labour—the creation of jobs—is the crucial factor. The Soviet economic mechanism operates to increase the supply of jobs. Enterprises have no interest to adopt manpower ceilings. Widespread shortages of labour are reported. In 1979, 197 industrial enterprises were surveyed: at 179 there was a shortage of workers.

Agriculture is short of skilled and semi-skilled labour. An article by V. Golubev and L. Tyangov pointed out that in the Non-Black-Earth zone in 1973 there were 116 farm machinery operatives per 100 machines, by 1980 this ratio had fallen to 104:100. In 1980, 72-3 per cent of farms in Novgorod and Pskov provinces had less than one machine operator per piece of equipment.[15] The exodus from rural areas leads to labour shortage and this in turn requires the towns to send workers to the countryside to help with the harvest and other urgent jobs. The training of more skilled workers (*mekhanizatory*) in rural areas does not solve the problem. In the Amur region, for example, 7000 people are trained yearly, but most leave agriculture.[16] The building industry is also short of skilled workers, particularly bricklayers, carpenters, erectors (*montazhniki*) and concrete layers.[17] Such building workers have a high turnover as conditions of work and pay are poor. While posts appear to be vacant throughout the USSR, regional imbalances exacerbate the problem.

## THE UNDERUTILIZATION OF LABOUR

The present high levels of labour utilization and the apparent shortage of labour have been interpreted by many commentators, especially but not exclusively in the West, as being indicative of the inefficent use of labour, of underutilization and overmanning and of being a hidden form of unemployment or underemployment. Western writers conceive of such employment to be deleterious to production and public welfare: 'It contributes to slow and undemanding work rhythms, slack work discipline, low productivity, low average wages, high production costs etc. . . . It is one of the factors that enables workers to husband their energies for private ventures. It has a adverse impact on work habits and attitudes toward work. And it results in wages being insufficiently linked to performance.'[18] It is not only western critics of socialist societies, however, who point to the widespread 'overmanning'. Economists in the USSR and other socialist countries point to the paradox of 'labour deficits' coupled with the abundance of reserves. Such writers would deny that the demographic tendencies noted above (see Chapter 4) are the chief cause of labour shortages, but point to chronic overmanning and uneconomic deployment.

Comparative studies with western countries suggest that for similar types of production Soviet enterprises are 'overstaffed'. Myasnikov and Anan'ev point out that in the Soviet small tools industry there are 30−50 per cent more workers than in comparable enterprises abroad.[19] G. Kulagin has remarked that in chemical plants bought from abroad more than 1.5 times as many operatives are employed, 3.5 times as many engineering, technical and administrative staff and eight times as many auxiliaries.[20] Manevich has said that Soviet machinery plants employ 30−50 per cent more personnel than similar factories in the major capitalist countries: Japan and the Federal Republic of Germany require only a quarter to a third as many designers and researchers to develop comparable new machinery. Soviet factories, too, have many more 'auxiliary' workers (repairmen, toolmakers, materials handling workers). Manevich argues that they account for 38 per cent of the total number of workers in Soviet machinery plants, but only 11 per cent in American factories.[21] He concludes that the causes of inadequate labour resources are the low levels of mechanization and automation. In 1974, 45 million people were engaged in unskilled manual labour; this represented about 44 per cent of employees in industry, 66 per cent in building and 75 per cent in agriculture. Furthermore, he points out, even when labour-saving machinery is introduced, 'excess employees' are maintained on the payroll.[22] (This may be somewhat misleading, as western factories are able to scrap and replace parts rather than repair them. American plants also have more machinery for lifting and transfer, whereas in the USSR this has to be done manually.) Much of the mechanization of production is haphazard. In one automatic production facility, it took 120 workers to operate the machinery and 1500 to do the despatch, packaging, stores and repair work.[23] In total, about half of all manual labour in the Soviet Union is engaged in auxiliary production.[24] The economic effectiveness of investment is 2.8−3.5 times greater in auxiliary than in basic production.[25] Numbers in auxiliary work, however, grow because of the need to repair and service machinery. (Spare parts have to be made in the users' workshops.) In 1979, there were 35 million people in repair work and 14 million workers employed in loading and unloading (i.e. 22−33 per cent of workers employed in the various industrial branches).

Seasonal shortages in agriculture have 'knock on' effects in industry. The system of *shefstvo* or *shefskaya pomoshch'* involves enterprises helping out with agricultural labour bottlenecks. Kostakov has estimated that some two per cent of all industrial personnel are maintained at enterprises so that sponsorship work may be carried out.[26] This leads to inefficiency in industry. A writer to *Pravda* expressed his frustration as follows:

Everyday many tens of thousands of people leave their places of work to do jobs that are inappropriate for them. . . . For the third week now . . . our enterprise's employees have been going out into the radish fields, where the radishes are not even ripe. But no matter what work there is to be done or what we have accomplished, they don't release us earlier than the set time. Isn't this absurd? Who is supposed to design new equipment? Who is supposed to put it into production? How much is a bunch of radishes costing the state?[27]

A director of a plastic and polymer factory reported that the enterprise had to send 400 people to harvest tomatoes, 120 people per day from November to May to agriculture depots, and 50 workers were engaged on building houses and silos. In eleven months in 1982, it was estimated that in this enterprise alone 90,000 working-days (7 per cent of total labour time) were lost by such activities. A contributor to *Literaturnaya gazeta* estimates that about 1.5 million people per month may be absent from their main tasks in order to perform *shefstvo* activity. This form of activity makes for poor discipline—workers do not work properly at their place of *shefstvo* and often request time off from their home enterprise in lieu of work performed at weekends.[28]

To meet this kind of labour demand, enterprises hold on to reserves of manpower to send quotas for agricultural and construction work. This partly explains the large numbers of manual workers retained in industry, described above. Economists such as Manevich and Kostin call for such practices to be dropped, or at least curtailed, since it is uneconomic in the long term. They point out that if agricultural labour were better organized, and such work more mechanized, there would be no need to import such large numbers of helpers from industry. Agro-industrial complexes or associations, it is suggested, should be created to reduce the seasonal fluctuations in the employment levels for agriculture.[29] Manevich points to the instrumental rationality of this process for the factory manager: 'enterprises keep certain reserves of workers to enable them to send workers for agricultural work without placing the fulfilment of their own production plan in jeopardy. . . . The recruitment of workers and white-collar workers for agricultural work is not economically viable. As a rule, the agricultural output attributable to these workers is two times more expensive than that produced by agricultural workers, and their labour efficiency is four times less than at their normal workplace.'[30]

Overmanning is widespread in the USSR and, moreover, is recognized to be so. Over 1000 people participated in a forum on labour organized by the weekly *Literaturnaya gazeta*, of whom 80 per cent said that there was no 'real' labour shortage.[31] In the discussion of labour utilization, an economist wrote from Alma Ata that the 'planned' workforce could be reduced by 6.4 per cent and he alleged that generally work for a planned workforce of 100 could be done by 60.[32] A western study conducted in 1983/84 of 2900 former Soviet citizens found that 75 per cent believed that productivity in the USSR was declining and 49 per cent felt that the plan could have been fulfilled with 5 per cent fewer workers. (Eleven per cent felt that it could have been completed with 50 per cent fewer employees.) A contributor to the *Literaturnaya gazeta* debate emphasized that inefficiency was due to lack of financial incentives. It was pointed out that many enterprises exceed plans by 30−40 per cent without any strain on the workforce.[33]

Production is not carried out evenly throughout the month; rather, it is clustered in the last few days. As V. Parfenov has put it: 'if a plant fulfills 60–70 per cent of its monthly plan in the last 10 days of the month that means that the enterprise has a considerably greater number of people than it needs if work were to be organized at a regular pace . . .'[34] Labour reserves are also necessary to help cope with changes in plan assignments and to be 'in reserve' to help overcome bottlenecks caused by irregular supplies and breakdowns.

## THE PROCESS OF JOB CREATION

There are two main reasons for the excessive number of jobs created. First, the level of new investment is high and creates its own demand for labour. New capital investment is sanctioned by Gosplan and is administered through the control of local agencies of USSR Capital Investments Bank. They are supposed to 'establish clear-cut criteria for the economic effectiveness of new construction and of expansion, reconstruction and re-equipment'. The USSR State Construction Committee and its local agencies have oversight over new construction projects. Though the total amount of investment is controlled by Gosplan, investment and construction organs ignore the labour implications of new investment. The Ukrainian Minister of Industrial Construction has pointed out that new construction is required by 'powerful organizations at all levels . . .. Reconstruction is unprofitable for builders . . .. We build mainly new plants.'[35] Second, production enterprises have little incentive to economize on labour. The wage fund is given by higher authority, and the larger this is, the easier it becomes for the enterprise to meet its production targets. The essence of Soviet planning is the fulfilment of production targets in quantitative terms. Enterprises are not rewarded if their wage fund is not used up. Enterprises (with the exception of some 'experiments' described below) have no financial incentives to 'shed labour'. Sonin has pointed out that authorities at all levels in the enterprise (foremen, shop superintendents and enterprise directors) have a stake in not reducing manpower reserves, but in 'retaining extra workers, saving them for peak periods and for periodic assignments to agricultural work'.[36] In planning negotiations, therefore, the need for workers by enterprises is inflated.

The existing shortages of labour have a ratchet effect: shortage creates further shortage. New enterprises tempt labour by offering higher wages. Managers in practice have some leeway in fixing wages. A writer to *EKO* describes the process whereby new enterprises inflate their wage funds. Such factories make claims to their administrative superiors for labour-intensive processes. These they use for non-labour-intensive ones and thus are able to pay wages which are 40–50 roubles greater than other factories.[37]

The numbers in the workforce are an important determinant of the resources made available to the enterprise in the economic plan: they determine the size of the wage fund, the material incentives fund, the socio-cultural and housing construction fund, the bonuses for introduction of new technology, the bonuses for socialist competition, and (in the machine tools and metal-working industries) the salaries of managerial and engineering-technical personnel.[38] The 'brigade' and Shchekino methods studied below are advocated to overcome these problems.

Administrative controls are ineffective in reducing manning levels. In 1982 the planned growth of labour resources was reduced by the planners by a third in the RSFSR and by a quarter in Lithuania. However, it was found that about a fifth of industrial enterprises in that year had exceeded their labour quotas, yet the same proportion of enterprises had a shortage of trained workers.[39] Labour organs of Goskomtrud and Gosbank USSR have the right to exert economic sanctions against enterprises which exceed the limit of workers' places. They may reduce the wage fund by up to 50 per cent and by up to 50 per cent of the bonus fund for management. In practice, however, such sanctions are only applied when enterprises do not fulfil their plan for the increase of labour productivity. In 1981, it was reported that 2000 cases of exceeding labour employment limits were known to the labour authorities of the RSFSR but only in 564 cases were material sanctions applied.[40]

Attempts by enterprise managers to plan the number of workplaces through a process of 'certification' have been made. This process tries to relate manpower available in a given area to the needs of the individual enterprises. The local authority's planning commission takes over responsibility for checking the manning levels in factories. For instance, in the Voroshilov factory in Dnepropetrovsk, a 'certification' of the number of workplaces was reported in March 1984: it found that of 2789 jobs, 528 were only partially necessary and 92 were unnecessary and were eliminated.[41] Such 'experiments', however, have not yet been adopted on a wide-scale level and have met with resistance by managers.[42]

The availability of 'surplus' labour at enterprises concurrent with an insatiable demand for labour by the enterprise poses the problem of whether the Soviet authorities may improve productivity of labour through redundancy while avoiding mass unemployment. Answers to this question may be sought at the macro-level with changes in the 'economic mechanism' and the planning process, and at the micro-level in the enterprise and work unit. We shall take up the macro-analysis in the final chapter and outline in this and the next two methods that have been introduced at the workplace: the 'Shchekino experiment' and the work brigade.

## THE 'SHCHEKINO EXPERIMENT'

Localized 'experiments' may be introduced in the Soviet Union without seriously disturbing the institutionalized patterns of control and traditional planning procedures. They can be used as instances of what might be called 'good practice' in British government—a model to be emulated by others and on which existing activity may be evaluated. They may be initiated by local political interests (the local party apparatus) or by management. The Shchekino experiment takes its name from the *Shchekino khimkombinat imeni 50—letiya obrazovaniya SSSR*[43] in Tula which in 1967 introduced a number of local reforms aimed at improving labour productivity.

Tula is an urbanized and industrialized province in central Russia. It has a very high labour participation rate—97.4 per cent of the economically active population[44] is either at work or study. The size of the population of the area is declining. Extensive forms of economic development (adding more labour to capital) had to be replaced by intensive ones. From 1966 to 1968–70, the rate of growth of labour productivity fell from 8.8 per cent to 7.2 per cent a year and wage rises were greater than productivity increases.[45] The chemical industry in Tula was an expanding one as mineral fertilizers were in great demand for agriculture. Expansion of production, then, was limited by labour shortages both within existing enterprises and for meeting the needs of newly constructed ones. In April 1967, representatives of the USSR State Committee on Labour and Wages and the Ministry of the Chemical Industry visited the Shchekino chemical factory.[46]

Following their visit the Shchekino experiment[47] was instituted. It sought (a) to increase output of an enterprise with a given number of employees, and (b) to increase output and simultaneously reduce the number of staff.[48] As P. Sharov, the manager of the enterprise pointed out, the established planning procedures entailed that the larger number of workers employed, the greater the material incentives fund. The crux of the experiment was to maintain the size of the wage fund while decreasing the number of workers employed; under the routine form of planning, of course, the number of workers would entail a fall in the wage fund. The scheme envisaged that (a) the Shchekino wage fund was to remain unchanged for three years (1968–70), (b) the production plan was to be stable during this period, and (c) the enterprise had to increase labour productivity. The fixing of levels of production targets together with a constant wage fund meant that improvements in labour efficiency through labour losses would not lead to hikes in targets with a lower wage fund.

The incentive for (c) was that all savings on labour would accrue to the enterprise's funds. Fifty per cent of savings would be the responsibility of the workshop head who could give bonuses to workers for combining jobs or increasing output. Wages could rise by up to 30 per cent of basic pay. The other half of savings made would be controlled by the factory director and could be used as financial incentives for punctuality, to enhance the quality and quantity of production, and to improve amenities—factory housing, holiday facilities and so on.[49]

A number of suggestions were made as to how productivity should be increased. The most important ways to reduce staff were to combine jobs (*sovmeshchenie professii*), to mechanize labour-intensive work, and to 'expand zones of service' (*rasshirenie zon obsluzhivanie*), i.e. to supervise or operate more working units. In addition, other procedures of a technical and administrative kind were advocated: (i) the 'scientific organization of labour' (NOT), (ii) introduction of normatives for labour, (iii) automation of production processes, (iv) simplification and improvement of the administration structure, (v) centralization of auxiliary services, and (vi) provision of training for all categories of workers to enable them to have knowledge of technological processes involved in production, and to keep up with technical innovations.[50]

The immediate results of the experiment were hailed as impressive. The enterprise manager reported that, in the first two years, more than 1000 workers took on a second or 'mixed' job, more than 4000 workers improved their qualifications, the number of workers was reduced by 870, in two years productivity increased by 87 per cent and the volume of output by 80 per cent.[51] Between 1967 and 1974, the volume of production increased 2.5 times and labour productivity by 3.1 times; total personnel employed fell by 1324 and expenditure on wages per rouble of goods produced fell from 13.9 copecks to 5.3 copecks; the average wage increased by 43.1 per cent. Labour discipline also improved, turnover was reduced and fringe benefits were also better.[52] The destination of labour that was shed will be discussed below; here we may note that the demand for similar types of labour continued in an adjacent newly constructed plant.

The first period of the Shchekino experiment lasted from 1968 to 1972, during this time the method was adopted by 22 enterprises responsible for about a third of industrial output in the province.[53] This period saw productivity rising mainly through combining jobs and the expansion of 'zones of service'. By 1974 in the 22 factories adopting the methods, 7421 employees were laid off: 5991 manual workers, 1127 engineering technical workers and 160 office (*sluzhashchie*) personnel. This represented about 8 per cent of the total number employed in industrial production, 19.4 per cent were laid off at the Shchekino plant, 19.7 per cent at Novomoskovski and 11 per cent at Tulasantekhnika.[54]

The second stage of the Shchekino experiment occurred between 1972 and 1976. This coincided with the spread of the movement to other industries and to further developments in the modernization of production, improvements in the management structure, updating technology and better training for the work force. By the end of the ninth Five Year Plan (1975), Parfenov and Shvetsov report that some 1000 enterprises had adopted the method of which only 150 were in the chemical industry; 45,500 manual workers and 10,600 technical and office workers had been made redundant.[55] During this stage the introduction of new methods and the 'freeing' of workers was accompanied by the construction of new combines which were staffed by workers from the old plants.[56] In the machine tool industry, personnel cuts occurred among auxiliary workers, whereas at Shchekino production workers were affected.[57]

The adoption of the Shchekino method appeared to make a difference to the efficiency and productivity of labour. A study of 326 enterprises between January and October 1975 found that 91.7 per cent of the increase in production was derived from an increase in labour productivity compared to 80.5 per cent in industry as a whole.[58] The tempo of work and discipline improved with the introduction of the Shchekino method. In the Artemov GRES, turnover fell from 17 per cent in 1973 to 8.7 in 1975. In the Angarsk petrochemical plant absenteeism fell by 40 per cent between 1970 and 1975.[59] At enterprises studied which had adopted the method, wages on average had a 7.8 rouble additional payment and the average bonus for workers was 8 per cent.[60]

In the second phase of the experiment, low-powered and antiquated equipment was 'reconstructed'; technology and the introduction of labour-saving machines became of prime importance. A study of the Shchekino method adopted at the Perm Mashinostroenie factories found that at one factory between 1969 and 1972 increases in labour productivity were derived from the following: mechanization and automation of production (29 per cent), perfecting organization, adjusting norms and pay (22 per cent), introduction of new technology (20 per cent), improvements in product design (18 per cent), perfecting administration, combining jobs and widening job content (11 per cent).[61]

Taking the period 1967−80, under the chemical and mineral fertilizer industries, 83,000 people were displaced: 19 per cent through combining jobs, 23 per cent as a result of expanding 'zones of service', 17 per cent through improving the form of administration, 8 per cent from progressive labour norms, 15 per cent were due to transfer to the brigade form of organization, 5 per cent resulted from the centralization and specialization of auxiliary services, 12 per cent through the mechanization of labour-intensive work; in all, 30 per cent were 'freed' as a result of technical factors and the remainder from organizational-economic measures.[62]

The method was adopted in Ministries concerned with motor car production (23 enterprises), chemical and oil industry machine tools (46), chemicals (150), tractors and agricultural implements (1).[63] Others ignored the scheme. Data given in an overview article in *Sotsialisticheski trud* showed that the method had been adopted in the paper-making industry (54.3 per cent of the enterprises), chemical production (46 per cent), microbiological industry (*glavmikro-bioprom*) (41.7 per cent), oil refining and petrochemicals (30.1 per cent). These industries were ones where regulated technological processes occurred and were paid on day rates; here 'technical-organizational measures' are utilized to combine tasks and reduce the number of jobs. In machine tool, coal and light industry workers use one machine and are paid piecework and output is increased by the intensity of machine working and hence the Shchekino method is less useful.[64] In 1981, ministries not adopting the method included: the Ministry of Energy Machinery, Ministry of Oil Production, Ministry of Gas Production, Ministry of Heavy Machinery Production, and the Mining Industry.[65] Different forms of labour-saving are appropriate for different industries. A survey of eighteen Leningrad factories in different branches of production found that displacement of workers could be analysed into three groups. First, in machine tools, 30 per cent of the 'freed' workers were as a result of mechanization and automation of production and only 9.9 per cent from combining jobs and widening the sphere of activity. Secondly, in the chemical industry, combining jobs and widening the 'zone of service' accounted for 41.9 per cent of those displaced, and only 10.1 per cent of displacements were due to mechanization and automation (for the third group, metallurgy, no data are given).[66]

By 1980, however, the full scheme had been adopted in 2003 production enterprises, and 7251 enterprises had adopted elements of the method, particularly combining jobs and extending the sphere of operations.[67] It was claimed that such devices in the period of the tenth Five Year Plan had freed 968,000 workers—

6 per cent of the industrial production personnel and 433,000 had been transferred to new workshops to take up vacant posts.[68] In 1980, the freeing of workers led to savings in the wages fund of 287 million roubles.[69]

As to redundancies, though no comprehensive statistics are available, the Central Statistical Agency, surveyed a sample of factories using the Shchekino method. The results were as follows: in the Ministry of Light Metallurgy 15.3 per cent of the total employed, Ministry of Chemical Production 10.3 per cent, Ministry of Energy 10.4 per cent, Ministry of Oil Extraction 6.4 per cent and the Ministry of Heavy Metallurgy 6 per cent.[70] In auxiliary work (repair, transport, packeting, control) combining jobs and extending job content, reductions in personnel were much lower: Ministry of Oil Extraction 1.8 per cent, Ministry of Energy of USSR 1.1 per cent, Ministry of Paper Production 0.8 per cent, Ministry of Chemical Production 0.7 percent, at the Ministries of Heavy Machinery, Electrical-Technical Industry, Leather and Footwear and Fur industries 0.4 per cent, Automobile Production 0.3 per cent and Sewn Goods Industry 0.2 per cent.[71]

The scale of laying off may be gauged by a survey of 326 industrial enterprises studied on 1 November 1975, which since introducing the experiment had 'freed' 4.5 per cent of their workforce—47,400 personnel.[72] The destinations of the workers so made redundant by changes in the 326 enterprises studied were as follows: 22.4 per cent took up jobs in new workshops (presumably within the same enterprise) and 52.4 per cent were assigned to vacant positions in existing workshops, 25.2 per cent went to other enterprises and organizations with vacancies.[73] At Shchekino, V.M. Suslyak, the Secretary of the Tula obkom, points out that the local party organization and the trade union branches 'were obliged to help the leadership of the combine to find work for displaced manual and non-manual workers'.[74] In an overview article, V. Fil'ev points out that when redundancies are properly planned workers can have a choice of two to three jobs.[75]

## LIMITATIONS ON THE SPREAD OF THE METHOD

The experiment was unevenly adopted. By the end of the 1970s, the method was used in full at 1500 enterprises in the USSR and only in part at another 8000.[76] During the whole period of the tenth (1976–80) Five Year Plan, R. Batkaev and S. Semin, estimate that 968,000 people were 'freed' in 11,710 enterprises using the Shchekino method. The growth in productivity at such enterprises averaged 3.4 per cent compared with 1.5 per cent not on the system. This was widely regarded in the Soviet press as disappointing. In the second phase of the scheme, some of the initial conditions were either changed by the higher authority, or enterprises were unable to implement the method because of regulations imposed by their ministries. The USSR Committee on Labour and Wages in 1973 changed the rules. They forbade the transfer of wage savings to the material incentive fund; profits from savings were taken by the central authorities (from Shchekino itself, 4 million roubles). The promised stable five-year wage fund and production targets were not maintained.[77] The authorities found it necessary to change supply targets. A. Radov, the *Pravda* correspondent who investigated the fate of the experiment in 1981, reported that if a head of a *glavk* (administration) had non-fulfilment of the plan by one enterprise, the targets would have to be 'redistributed'[78] to other enterprises, including those on Shchekino. Ministries which started new units in enterprises did not provide them with additional wage funds and thus savings from productivity had to be used to finance the wage outlays for the new units.[79]

In the Cherkass chemical plant 'Azot', for instance, the wage fund was set for the period 1971–75, but adjusted 17 times during the period of the experiment.[80] At the Shchekino plant, after economizing on labour and saving on the wage fund, the enterprise found that the wage fund for subsequent years was cut. During the ninth Five Year Plan (1971–75), the fund lost 3 million roubles: 'This led to a situation in which, with the introduction in 1975 of new base wage and salary rates, the combine was forced by a lack of money to cancel the intended pay increments and rates for 1700 employees. During the past five-year plan, the Shchekino workers' planned wage fund decreased by 1.3 million roubles.'[81] Ministries also required enterprises to reduce engineering, technical and office staff, quite independently of reductions made internally as a result of the introduction of the new methods.[82] These procedures, of course, severely discouraged their introduction. In other enterprises, even when considerable rises in productivity had been achieved, the Ministry discontinued the scheme and in some cases refused the adoption of the method.[83]

The introduction of general regulations allowing enterprises to give extra material incentives for work with fewer staff led to enterprises ignoring the need to introduce the Shchekino principle.[84] Ministries and Departments did not press the method, presumably because production would be fixed for five years and therefore supply would be inflexible. As Academician A. Aganbegyan put it, when an enterprise has a stable plan for a number of years, the Ministry loses room for manoeuvre, complicating its own life. When one enterprise does not fulfil its plan, another one is given an additional assignment and its plan revised upwards. This completely undermines the Shchekino experiment. The Deputy Minister of the chemical Industry, K. Cherednichenko, asserted in March 1977 that the instructions sent to enterprises by the central authorities 'gradually reduced the interest of enterprise collectives in introducing the Shchekino method'.[85] Enterprises, for instance, were required to set labour norms on a branch and inter-branch basis as a condition for introducing the method; yet even in the Shchekino combine itself by 1977 only 30 per cent of personnel were working on confirmed norms. Thus, this regulation 'will prevent most enterprises from introducing the Shchekino workers' experiment during the tenth Five-Year Plan'.[86] While the regulations formally said that enterprises could independently decide to adopt the experiment, 'other paragraphs indicate that no step can be taken without a higher department's approval'.[87]

In 1978, Goskomtrud, Gosplan, the Ministry of Finance and the trade unions' organization approved new regulations on the application of Shchekino. Such methods would be introduced by management with the agreement of the trade union committee.[88] While the methods were not universally put into effect, this decree marks the acceptance of the Shchekino experiment as part of the system of economic administration. In December 1981, a resolution of the Council of Ministers gave managers the right to give supplementary payments for combining jobs and for expanding zones of service as well as for increases in the volume of work done.[89] This resolution provides the basis for increasing effectiveness and efficiency of labour under the brigade system. The resolution gave management greater powers over the distribution of material benefits and the displacement of workers. By the mid-1980s, the following elements derived from the Shchekino method had been incorporated in the practice of many enterprises: the setting of stable wage normatives, the transfer of unused savings from the wage fund to the fund for material incentives, the setting of supplementary payments for combining skills, the simultaneous payment of rewards for measures undertaken to guarantee reductions in staff, the planning of basic indicators for the Five Year Plan with divisions for each year. Until 1981, these rights had been given only to enterprises officially designated as working '*po-shchekinski*'.[90] By the early 1980s the scheme had been revitalized and in 1984, practically all enterprises in the chemical industry had adopted the method.[91]

## RESISTANCE TO CHANGE

The reluctance on the part of the Ministries to implement Shchekino may also be seen to have a political significance: the greater the independence of enterprises, the lesser the need for ministerial tutelage and direction. Ministries probably regarded an extension of the method as an infringement of their own rights. Some indication of this view is the statement by S.Z. Kossoi, the deputy director of the Ryabikov machinery factory in Tula, when he said, 'the clear, well-defined nature of the rights won by the Shchekino method is apparently not to the liking of certain planning and economic agencies . . .'.[92] When the scheme went through difficult periods, the Party again seems to have been the major force in Shchekino for keeping it going. Under the town Party Committee was formed a council composed of Party, Soviet, Komsomol workers and other specialists. J. Grotseskul, the First Secretary of the Shchekino town Party Committee points out that 'due to lack of support from the Ministry [the method] began to crumble. It was clear that without Party action, the innovation would go no further . . .'.[93] The Party was responsible for reviving the scheme in the late 1970s.

The implications of the Shchekino method become clearer when we consider its further developments. V.V. Semenov, the head of the Tula Province Party Committee advocated that the method be spread 'horizontally' to other enterprises in the city. From a labour utilization point of view, he argued that it was hardly an economy of labour if, after being displaced from Shchekino, the workers were used inefficiently in other city enterprises. By 1982, 90 per cent of the city's industrial output was on the Shchekino method and this equilibriated labour supply and demand. The First Secretary of the Shchekino City Party Committee advocated that the system be extended to a regional basis and he further advocated it be introduced in the Tula province as a whole.[94] If such proposals were to be adopted, adjustments between enterprises and labour supply problems would be determined locally and the supervisory powers of the centre would be reduced. By the mid-1980s, the Shchekino 'experiment' was sufficiently adopted for it to be considered no longer at the experimental stage and, as noted above, many of its conditions have been generally adopted.[95] The brigade system (see Chapter 8) in which workers are paid for 'end results' to some extent supersedes the 'Shchekino' method.[96]

Opposition also came initially from the workers at the Shchekino plant and presumably was also a factor when introduced elsewhere. But 'displacement' involved by the method does not have the connotation of 'redundancy' as in the West. It means for an employee his or her departure from a given production collective and/or his or her movement to a different type of work.[97] Such labour movement has to be seen in the context of enterprises having an obligation to give work to those displaced through the introduction of new technology.[98] It is recognized, moreover, that there are conflicts of interest between the individual and society: 'freeing of workers may correspond to the interests of society and to the labour collective but not to the interests of those who have to transfer to a different section, or to a different enterprise.'[99] On the positive side, the benefits of a rise in labour productivity accrue to the economy and to society as a whole. The individual worker who remains in employment has a rise in wages, his qualifications may be improved and it is possible that the 'content of labour' will also be more acceptable.[100] For workers 'displaced' from their enterprise, however, the benefits may not be direct and—should they be unable to find satisfactory work—they may even become worse off. The introduction of the method 'directly impinged on every employee's personal interests. Some had to be persuaded to transfer to a neighbouring plant'.[101] Parfenov and Shvetsov refer to the resistance as follows:

In accordance with dialectical laws, every innovation encounters psychological barriers of negation, doubt and attachment to the old ways. The Shchekino innovation was also complicated by the fact that it directly impinged on every employee's personal interests. Some had to be inspired voluntarily to assume additional workloads, others had to be persuaded to transfer to a neighbouring plant. For a full six months prior to the first release of production workers, hundreds of communists conducted exploratory work in the collective. Twelve combine committees and dozens of shop committees searched for optimal variants of organising labour at each work-place and endeavoured to solve complex and subtle social problems . . . .[102]

Overcoming such problems, the prevarication of the higher administrative personnel, and inertia probably account for the inability and unwillingness on the part of some managers to adopt the Shchekino method.[103] A spokesman of USSR Goskomtrud has pointed out that many enterprises initially refused to try the experiment. The personal influence of the Deputy Minister, K. Cherednichenko, and the active support of the Party organizations in Tula provided the energy for the introduction of the scheme.[104] The Party Second Secretary of Tula *obkom* (province) is reported as saying that the Party had to persuade people in the factory that the practice of planning from the achieved level would cease. After convincing them, the practice recommenced and at many of the province's enterprises, plans were revised upwards six to seven times per annum.[105] A spokesman of Gosplan pointed out that such changes are caused by unforeseen changes in the economy:[106] from the planners' point of view having 'slack' at enterprises helps them to reschedule supply.

A report by *Sovetskaya Rossiya's* correspondent from Tula recorded that supervisory staff were afraid to try new methods as long as the old ones worked. As one collective put it: 'They're somewhat fearful . . . when there is a surplus of employees, it's more peaceful to work . . . '.[107] Labour reserves are used to prevent interruptions of work when workers are on leave or absent. The Second Party Secretary in Tula reported that local managers preferred the old system which they found easier.[108] Radov recalls that when he was at the enterprise, 'the chairman of the *kolkhoz* under the factory's patronage came there. . . . He reminded them that he was expecting 100 workers daily and that a hostel had to be built for them. The factory management was not against this . . . . But the trouble was to procure the helpers. For the *kolkhoz* was not the only enterprise under its patronage. It had to send people to the brick works, to construct roads and to pick vegetables.'[109] Hence the rationale of the local management and its opposition to 'freeing labour' is clear.

Another important reason for the reluctance of enterprises to adopt the method is that 'it is more advantageous even in economic terms for an enterprise to have a surplus than a shortage of manpower. The enterprise's status is determined according to numbers. The more people there are, the bigger the wage fund and likewise also of the bonus resources.'[110] Radov points out that the managers' salaries depend on the size of the workforce, not on how effectively it is used. As the factory administration and the Ministry officials had some fear of change, it is understandable that the Party organization played an important part in pushing such reforms. Radov points out that economic organs (economists and managers of enterprises) had almost to be forced into applying the method by the local Party organs.[111]

## DISPLACEMENT OF LABOUR AT THE ENTERPRISE

Comprehensive statistics have not been collected on the numbers of workers 'displaced' 'redistributed', 'freed', 'transferred' or plainly made redundant as a result of economic change, particularly following the introduction of labour-saving machinery or improved work organization. In the period 1971–75 enterprises under the USSR Ministry of Ferrous Metallurgy shed 350,000 jobs as a result of increased labour productivity. Of these, 270,000 workers were 'transferred to other sectors of production'.[112] The guidelines for the formulation of the Five-Year Plan (1976-80) for the Production Association recommended that a plan be drawn up for an absolute and relative reduction of the manual labour force for each year of the Five Year Plan. But in practice, reductions in the numbers of manual workers have been unevenly distributed over the USSR. In Latvia, a 'complex' programme for the contraction of physical labour was drawn up in 1976 by Gosplan, Goskomtrud and the Central Statistical Agency. It covered 14 republican ministries and departments and 65 enterprises under All-Union jurisdiction. Between 1976 and 1978, 12,900 workers doing physical labour were made redundant, the work of 14,300 was mechanized and 19,400 were redeployed to other jobs.[113] By 1980, however, it was reported that 'the majority of enterprises have not developed such plans'.[114] For the period 1981–85 many regional schemes were being put into effect which aimed to maintain planned growth with the same or a smaller labour force.[115] In this plan period ministries, association and enterprise have been required to cut their manual labour force.[116] Some positive results have been reported. In the Ukraine between 1980 and 1983, 2.4 million full-time workers' positions were eliminated (*n*) against 1.9 million planned.[117] Subjecting production to 'the scientific organization of labour' (time and motion studies) led to the elimination of 4600 jobs in the Ukraine (1983) and more than 8000 more were expected to be lost in 1984.[118]It is confidently stated that one fifth of required labour productivity may be achieved by means of the 'scientific organization of work'.[119] But L.A. Kostin reports that the experience of 35 industrial ministries in the eleventh Five-Year Plan showed that in the first two years of the Plan they were unsuccessful in reducing the labour force by the planned number of 1.2 million manual workers.[120]

The data and opinions cited above would indicate that the 'freeing' and redeployment of labour in the Soviet Union is occurring, though at too slow a rate to meet adequately the advances in technology which are taking place.

## HOW DISPLACEMENT AFFECTS THE WORKER

We have noted that 'displacement' in the USSR does not result in an unemployed status, as in capitalist societies. A study of the effects on the worker of 'freeing' through the Shchekino method has been reported by L. Gol'din in the journal *Sotsialisticheski trud* (no.3, 1980). A questionnaire was completed anonymously by 'several thousand' respondents at enterprises adopting the Shchekino method. Though this is by no means comprehensive it gives many insights into how the Soviet authorities went about reducing and redirecting the labour force.

Study of the workers' responses, according to Gol'din, showed that none had any fear of being unemployed.[121] Prior to the introduction of the method, Party and other groups spent a considerable time explaining to the workforce the advantages of the system. Six months prior to the first release of production workers, 'hundreds of communists' conducted exploratory work in the factory. Twelve factory committees were formed in addition to many workshop committees. These groups solved 'subtle social problems' including presumably decisions about who should be made redundant.[122] Before the method was introduced it was agreed by the members of the whole collective and not just introduced by the management.[123] Considerable on-the-job training in other skills was given at the various enterprises: at the *Azot* combine, every machine operator had to learn another job over a two to three-year period and at the *Polimir* factory, most of the workforce had retraining before and during the introduction of the method.[124]

As noted above, the problem of unemployment did not arise because an enterprise producing synthetic fibre was being built in the vicinity of the combine. Many workers, however, did not want to leave as they were uncertain of whether they would have similar jobs and the same rates of pay.[125]

Women and older workers were not interested in changing their place of work. It was the younger workers who left. At the beginning of the experiment, the average age of the factory personnel was 27, in 1981 it was 41. This was due to the ageing of the staff and the lack of new young recruits to the enterprise.[126] Gol'din points out that, on the whole, workers 'approve of the introduction of the Shchekino method'. They are interested in the material rewards and later improvements in the work process are of most concern.[127] In all, in the period 1971–75, 3313 workers at the Shchekino enterprise were displaced (*vysvobozhdenny*), of whom only 554 left the enterprise.

A survey of nine enterprises on the Shchekino method delineated the form taken by the 'displacement' of workers. Table 6.2 shows that most of the displacement occurred through the redefinition of the jobs of workers (combining activities and overseeing more units) rather than through the introduction of new technology and new processes. The total of 873 workers displaced through mechanization and automation was made up of a single, large contingent of 454 workers at the Furmana textile mill. In a study of 25 oil-extraction and refining enterprises it was found that combining jobs accounted for 11 per cent of the displacements (760 people), widening the sphere of operations 46.2 per cent

*Table 6.2:* Forms of Displacement of Labour in Nine Enterprises, (1969–71)

| | Total displaced | Widening sphere of operations | Combining jobs | Introduction of new technology | Automation of production | Raising of technical norms | Improvement in administrative apparatus |
|---|---|---|---|---|---|---|---|
| Omsk oil refinery | 1469 | 733 | 84 | 125 | 88 | 258 | 181 |
| Angarsk petrochemicals | 1078 | 168 | 170 | — | 103 | 74 | 245 |
| Mogilev synthetic fibre plant | 800 | 311 | 131 | 13 | 20 | 50 | 79 |
| Gusev glassworks | 222 | 60 | 60 | 39 | 18 | 18 | 27 |
| Saratov industrial glassworks | 348 | 100 | 84 | 37 | 100 | 27 | 6 |
| Gomel glassworks | 152 | 30 | 44 | — | 72 | 2 | 6 |
| Furmana spinning and weaving factory | 1027 | 175 | 191 | 59 | 454 | — | 78 |
| Darinski silk factory | 624 | 345 | 76 | — | 9 | 28 | 81 |
| 'Marat' Manufacturing | 218 | 68 | 2 | 19 | 9 | — | 42 |
| | 5938* | 1990 | 842 | 292 | 873 | 457 | 745 |

* Totals of columns do not sum to 5938.

*Source:* Material of NII cited in E.I. Ruzavina, *Zanyatost' v usloviyakh intensifikatsii proizvodstva,* (1975), p. 69.

(3200) improving the organization of the engineering and the structure of the administration of labour 20.8 per cent (1400), improving the structure of laboratory control and transport 10.8 per cent (738) (the figure of 4.2 per cent was wrongly calculated in the original), other activities 7.7 per cent (487).[128] Ruzavina, taking into account other studies, concludes that for the period up to 1972, displacement on account of 'technical progress was insignificant' and she gives examples of factories where the plan for technical advancement was not fulfilled.[129]

A study by Dolishni of the introduction of new technology in the Ukraine, though not indicating the total number of workers displaced, shows the relativities betweeen different types of technology and the attributed increases in labour displacement.[130] These are shown in Table 6.3. Dolishni notes that in the industry of the Ukraine, more than 8 per cent of the average number of workers were displaced during the period of the ninth Five Year Plan; as a result of the introduction of new technology, the numbers of displaced workers increased 39 per cent between 1971 and 1975.[131] Table 6.3, however, shows that displacement originating from the introduction of automated systems and computers between 1971 and 1975 was insignificant, accounting for only 1.3 per cent of labour displaced. Dolishni points out that their introduction even leads sometimes to an increase of personnel to service them.[132]

The industry in which labour displacement was greatest was coalmining, and light industry machine-tools and metal-working also lost relatively much labour.[133] Table 6.4 shows the numbers of workers displaced at various factories in 1975. Automation and computer systems played very little role: they accounted for 50 per cent of displaced labour at the instrument factory, at the Mikronpribor plant 10 per cent, at the carriage works 15 per cent, at Lvovpribor 13 per cent, at the bio-physical instruments factory 10 per cent. Automated systems of management were introduced at only 3 out of the 17 factories quoted in the table.[134]

The vast majority of workers displaced by the Shchekino method were absorbed on other work within their own enterprises. In the Shchekino enterprise itself during the period 1971–75, 3313 workers were displaced, of whom only 554 (16.7 per cent) left the enterprise.[135] A study of 14 enterprises reported by Ruzavina showed that the Shchekino enterprise was exceptional, with a

Table 6.3: Shedding of Workers in Industry in the Ukraine 1972–1975 (in percentages compared to 1971)

| Measure | 1972 | 1973 | 1974 | 1975 | Relative no. of workers 'freed' in 1971–75 as a % of total |
|---|---|---|---|---|---|
| Introduction of advanced technology | 106.5 | 136.5 | 154.7 | 136.8 | 37.6 |
| Mechanization of production | 111.0 | 110.6 | 133.6 | 137.6 | 35.7 |
| Automization of production | 103.4 | 123.6 | 119.1 | 110.0 | 7.1 |
| Introduction of automated systems of management and computer technology | 96.7 | 153.9 | 189.4 | ×2.3 | 1.3 |
| Assimilation of new industrial production | — | — | ×25 | ×31 | 0.4 |
| Modernization of existing equipment | 114.5 | 126.5 | 159.5 | 129.9 | 1.9 |
| Other | 136.8 | 143.9 | 145.1 | 148.9 | 16.0 |
| Total | 112.4 | 126.8 | 144.1 | 139.0 | 100.0 |

Source: M.I. Dolishni, *Formirovanie i ispol'zovanie trudovykh resursov* (1978), p. 74.

much higher than average dispersal of workers to other enterprises: out of a total of 1052, 24.3 per cent went to other plants, most of the enterprises, however, shed less than 5 per cent in this fashion, as is illustrated in Table 6.5. The difficulty of mobility, notes Ruzavina, is that it involves the mobility of other members of the worker's family. The high labour participation rate, therefore, makes movement from the existing place of work more difficult than in capitalist countries where fewer wives work in paid employment as a main occupation.

The destinations of the displaced workers are shown on Table 6.6. Remarkable again is the very small number who took up work in other factories. The table also shows that many workers left voluntarily, some presumably retired and others found jobs. However, most workers were absorbed by their own enterprise, either on newly created positions or on vacant ones. Ruzavina

Table 6.4: *Reductions in the workforce in enterprises of L'vov oblast' in 1975 (people\*)*

| Enterprise | Total | As a result of: | | | | | |
|---|---|---|---|---|---|---|---|
| | | Application of new technology | Mechanization of production | Automation of production | Application of automated systems of management | Modernization of equipment | Other measures |
| Conveyor-building factory | 53.0 | 28.0 | 21.0 | — | — | — | 4.0 |
| Production association 'Iskra' | 24.6 | 6.3 | 17.3 | — | — | — | 1.0 |
| Fittings factory | 22.8 | 6.0 | 16.8 | — | — | — | — |
| Stryy Kirov factory for forge-press equipment | 51.4 | 30.2 | 21.2 | — | — | — | — |
| Artificial diamond and diamond instrument factory | 35.0 | 21.9 | 9.5 | 3.6 | — | — | — |
| Instruments factory | 32.2 | 6.7 | 9.5 | 16.0 | — | — | — |
| Milling machine factory | 60.0 | 54.8 | 3.2 | 2.0 | — | — | — |
| Science production | 15.8 | 1.6 | 4.2 | — | 2.5 | — | 7.5 |
| Production Association 'Mikropribor' | 432.0 | 306.0 | 73.0 | 42.0 | 4.0 | — | 7.0 |
| Biophysics instruments factory | 224.4 | 99.4 | 53.0 | 24.0 | — | — | 48.0 |
| 'L'vovpribor' | 410.0 | 194.3 | 159.4 | 54.3 | — | — | 2.0 |
| L'vov car factory | 107.0 | 36.0 | 47.0 | 4.0 | 7.0 | — | 13.0 |
| Carriage factory | 272.0 | 45.0 | 153.0 | 41.0 | — | 9.0 | 24.0 |
| Tractor spare parts factory | 4.0 | 1.0 | 2.0 | 1.0 | — | — | — |
| Fork-lift truck factory | 56.5 | 50.5 | 2.0 | 4.0 | — | — | — |
| Production Association 'L'vovkhimsel'khozmash' | 148.9 | 88.1 | 46.1 | 1 | — | 0.7 | 13.0 |
| Drogobych chisel factory | 81.0 | 81.0 | — | — | — | — | — |

*Source:* Dolishni, *Formirovanie i ispol'zovanie trudovykh resursov* (1978), p. 77.
\* Fractions in the table probably refer to positions manned for part of a person's working time.

points out that where displacement occurs due to 'intensive' growth (i.e. introduction of new technology), workers may need to be geographically mobile. (As noted in chapter 3, the present Soviet system has no institutions to cope with such movement and no plans for such geographical mobility.) She calls for a special office to be concerned with labour mobility and movement between enterprises.[136]

*Table 6.5: Occupational destinations of displaced workers, engineering and technical workers and white collar workers at enterprises working on the model of the Shchekino combine (as at 1 January 1972)\**

| | | Found work | | | |
|---|---|---|---|---|---|
| Enterprise | Total no. of displaced workers | At the same enterprise absolute no. | % | In other organisations absolute no. | % |
| Shchekino chemical combine | 1052 | 533 | 50.7 | 256 | 24.3 |
| Gorlovka chemical combine | 511 | 413 | 76.4 | 1 | 0.18 |
| Mogilev factory for man-made fibres | 800 | 358 | 44.8 | 64 | 8.0 |
| Omsk oil-refining combine | 1469 | 702 | 47.8 | 49 | 3.3 |
| Angarsk petrochemical combine | 1078 | 607 | 56.3 | — | — |
| Kotlass cellulose and paper combine | 673 | 323 | 48.0 | 22 | 3.3 |
| Kudinovski factory of ceramic blocks | 94 | 70 | 74.5 | 3 | 3.2 |
| Kremenchug car factory | 354 | 214 | 60.5 | 18 | 5.1 |
| Minsk refrigerator factory | 101 | 59 | 58.4 | 3 | 3.0 |
| Sverdlovsk factory of medical preparations | 94 | 28 | 29.8 | 29 | 30.9 |
| Spinning factory 'Krasnaya Vetka' | 206 | 202 | 91.8 | 2 | 1.0 |
| Darnitski silk combine | 905 | 285 | 31.5 | 35 | 3.9 |
| Dedovsk spinning textile factory | 296 | 257 | 86.8 | 32 | 10.8 |
| Minsk meat combine | 65 | 64 | 98.5 | 1 | 1.5 |

\*  Information from NII of Labour.
*Source*:  E.I. Ruzavina (1975), p. 72.

*Table 6.6: The transfer of 'freed' workers in a group of enterprises (as at 1 January 1972)*

| Enterprise | Transferred to work in production newly introduced within the enterprise | Transferred to vacant positions in production | Left work voluntarily | Found work at another enterprise | Left the enterprise for other reasons |
|---|---|---|---|---|---|
| Mogilev man-made fibre factory | 66 | 292 | 61 | 64 | 168 |
| Omsk oil-refining combine | 245 | 457 | 293 | 49 | 165 |
| Angarsk petro-chemical combine | 134 | 452 | — | 3 | 26 |
| Minsk refrigerator factory | — | 59 | — | 3 | 26 |
| Gusev glassworks | 38 | 130 | 52 | 2 | — |
| Saratov glassworks | 44 | 250 | 60 | — | 29 |
| Gomel' glassworks | 5 | 25 | 88 | — | 34 |

From NII of Labour.
*Source:* Ruzavina (1975), p.73.

## RETRAINING

Retraining of workers is an important way to increase productivity. The objective of the Shchekino and other schemes is to train workers with a second or third trade. At the Angarsk petrochemical combine from 1971 to 1975, some 10,000 workers attended courses on which 1300 learned a second or third trade. This factory also shed 3400 workers between 1971 and 1975. At the Alma-Ata plant *Kzyl-Tu* during the ninth Five Year Plan, 20 per cent of the workers upgraded their qualifications.[137] A report on Radio Moscow[138] described the introduction of robots in a heavy-engineering plant in the Ukraine, in which forty press workers were displaced. All were retrained within the enterprise for other trades and during the retraining they received their previous wages. Over a five-year period 500 workers were displaced, retrained and employed within the enterprise.

In the ferrous metallurgy industry in the period 1971–75 over 350,000 workers were 'freed' as labour productivity grew. These were primarily auxiliary and administrative personnel. The process of redirection, however, does not channel workers to places where they are needed. Retraining is done within enterprises. Movement between enterprises is 'insignificant' and there are no effective economic and organizational-legal prerequisites for interplant redistribution.[139]

In the early 1980s, research was carried out in 13 enterprises in various industries. It was found that of those who had transferred from manual to mechanized work, 38.7 per cent had completed a training course, 52.3 per cent had 'individual' or 'group' training lasting two to three weeks, and 8.9 per cent had no training at all.[140]

A study of jobs that were eliminated completely (*absolyutnoe vysvobozhdenie*) in a Leningrad area factory in the 1980s shows that most workers are retrained and absorbed in their own factory, very few were transferred to others—of a total of 98 redundancies only 16 moved to another enterprise. The type of retraining for such workers is shown on Table 6.7.

Each year, new factories coming on stream, require 500–600,000 workers in the USSR. The absence of channels of redistribution, however, means that these factories with new and complicated technology are short of workers. Also when

*Table 6.7: Retraining and Relocation of Redundant Workers in the Volkhov Factory (Leningrad)*

| Job | Total made redundant | Retrained in the factory | | | | Transferred to other factories by the planning commission of the town council |
| | | Total | Flux operators | Rolling-mill operators | Others | |
| --- | --- | --- | --- | --- | --- | --- |
| Pickling and acid storage operators | 22 | 20 | 8 | 9 | 3 | 2 |
| Laboratory assistants | 19 | 13 | 5 | — | 8 | 6 |
| Duty electricians | 29 | 24 | 7 | 12 | 5 | 5 |
| Duty fitters | 28 | 25 | 3 | 19 | 3 | 3 |
| | 98 | 82 | 23 | 40 | 19 | 16 |

*Source*:  G. Gendler, 'Rabota s men'shey chislennost'yu personala', *Planovoe khozyaystvo* no. 11, (1984), p. 101.

workers leave enterprises because of the introduction of new technology, the most efficient workers are kept and the less effective freed.[141] As early as 1965, E. Manevich advocated that unemployment benefit should be paid to those made redundant due to 'technological progress', but this suggestion has not been taken up.[142] In 1978, he called again for forms of material support to be given to workers who move to new jobs, for training to be given and help also for their move.[143] Displaced workers do not have the right to the same conditions or income as before, though it seems likely that the administration will attempt to find suitable work. The regulations for the further introduction of the Shchekino method introduced in January 1977 stipulated that enterprises freeing labour in order to reduce the number of personnel should retrain them and find them alternative jobs.[144] Other commentators have advocated the introduction of unemployment benefit. G. Popov (a professor at Moscow University and a key figure in present discussions) arguing for a significant reduction in the surplus workforce and the payment to redundant workers of a minimum wage of 80 roubles, points out that 'a clear distinction must be made between the right to work and the right to a certain wage level. A worker who leaves a plant retains his right to work, but no one is obliged to guarantee him anything above the minimum that the country is able to afford today.'[145]

Such views undermine the present security and conditions of employment in the USSR. A lawyer, V. Malakhin, replying to Popov's article, argued in *Pravda* that paying 80 roubles (half the average wage) 'would be a flagrant violation of labour legislation and Article 40 of the USSR Constitution, which guarantees not only the right to work, but the right to choose one's occupation'.[146] Soviet officials have made it clear that unemployment benefit will not be introduced in the USSR.[147] The evidence points to a great reluctance to shed labour in those enterprises which might cause difficulties for the further absorption of displaced workers. Most of the 'shedding' has taken place in expanding industries and the bulk of the workforce, as noted above, has been transferred to work on new units in the same or nearby enterprises. Under the Gorbachev leadership one might expect greater flexibility in the movement of labour. In 1985, in the resolution 'On the Further Improvement of the Management of the Agro-Industrial Complex', people displaced through reorganization are to retain their pay for no longer than three months.[148]

## RAISING PRODUCTIVITY THROUGH DISPLACEMENT WHILE MAINTAINING FULL EMPLOYMENT

The significance of the Shchekino methods lies in the management of labour and the attempt to reduce labour costs in the production process. The displacement of labour has had positive though limited effects in improving labour productivity. The greatest saving in labour has been in the area of workers' combining jobs and taking on more jobs. But this is not the limit of the method. It is clearly not the case that the system is limited by 'the level of underutilized capacity within the plant'.[149] Technical advance entails that the introduction of new technology will always enable savings in labour to be made.

As a managerial device to reduce the cost of labour, however, the initiative to reward labour for greater intensity of effort comes into conflict with the principle derived from NOT (the Scientific

Organization of Work) that norms should be 'technically validated', i.e. that there should be one technically validated rate for a job wherever it is. While it is true that the extra pay given for increased productivity is limited, it does to some degree undermine the universality of labour norms and increases the differentials between enterprises.

'Displacement' has not led to unemployment as understood in the West. Unlike under capitalism where profit is dependent in part on lowering labour costs because price is determined by demand, in the Soviet Union there is no market compulsion for managers to minimize total labour costs. In an administrative system, labour costs are given, and supply determines the price of commodities. Producers seek to maximize the inputs, not the surplus between costs of production and the selling price. 'Scientifically determined norms' for work should provide a common basis for the level of wages for all kinds of labour. In practice, however, this is difficult, if not impossible, to achieve. The resort to allow enterprises greater initiative is a short-term solution to the problem of reducing labour levels, but is at the cost of violating the principle of the consistent application of labour norms.

The absence of a labour market enables the planners to provide occupations for all who seek work—something which evades governments in advanced capitalist states. It does this, however, at an economic cost of underemployment and the inefficient use of labour. The use of a labour market in the western sense would destroy the planning system. Administrative measures are the only feasible way in which greater efficiency can be achieved.

The rises in productivity planned in the current (twelfth) Five Year Plan will lead to a reduction estimated at between 13 million and 19 million people at present employed in the primary and secondary sectors, with the number of manual labourers falling between 15 and 20 per cent.[150] This will involve a major shift of manpower between sectors. The service sector will grow considerably and greater mobility between occupations will be necessary.

One may optimistically forecast that such labour shifts will occur without the development of mass unemployment. Kostakov, in an interview with Tass (subsequent to the article cited above) has argued that displaced workers should be retrained on full pay.[151] The Soviet economy will continue to pay a social cost for the employment of people at a full wage for less than a full workload. Further reductions could be made in the length of the working week, in the provision of part-time employment, and in increasing the length of full-time education. The systemic character of underemployment is an advantage in maintaining high levels of labour utilization if a high level of formal employment is considered to be morally desirable and politically feasible.

However, the increasing pace of technological change and the requirement to displace labour to ensure increases in productivity will undermine job security. It seems likely that jobs will be lost and that workers will be required to find new ones through the labour exchange and to move, if necessary, to places where jobs are available. Extended severance pay and retraining allowances will probably be introduced as substitutes for unemployment benefit, which for ideological and political reasons will be impossible to introduce.

## REFERENCES

1. E. Garnsey, 'Occupational Structure in Industrialised Societies', *Sociology*, vol. 9, no. 3 (1977).
2. E. Manevich, 'Ratsional'noe ispol'zovanie rabochey sily', *Voprosy ekonomiki*, no. 9 (1981), p. 56.
3. L.A. Kostin, 'Rezervy ispol'zovaniya trudovykh resursov', *EKO*, no. 1 (1984), pp. 24-6.
4. Manevich, p. 57.
5. P. Shumenkov, 'Ratsional'no i ekonomno ispol'zovat' trudovye resursy', *Sots. trud*, no. 4 (1981), p. 111.
6. Displacement (*vysvobozhdenie*) refers to movements *within* enterprises as well as between them.
7. E.R. Sarukhanov, *Sotsial'no-ekonomicheskie problemy upravleniya rabochey siloy pri sotsializme* (Leningrad: 1981), p. 137.
8. Data based on bureau of labour supply: *Trud*, 17 July 1979. L. Kostin reported the number at about 2 million, with a yearly demand by new enterprises or extensions coming on stream of 750–800,000 hands. *Tass*, Russian service, 29 June 1980, cited in R/L 308/80, p. 1. This is just under two per cent of the employed workforce of 112 million in 1980. We have no data on the duration of unfilled vacancies.
9. A. Myasnikov and A. Anan'ev, *Trud*, 17 July 1979.
10. Manevich, p. 55.
11. A. Bachurin, 'Problemy uluchsheniya ispol'zovaniya trudovykh resursov', *Planovoe khozyaystvo*, no. 1 (1982) p. 29.

12. A. Tkachenko, B. Veretennikov and L. Belkina, 'Voprosy opredeleniya i vnedreniya pokazatelya limita chislennosti rabochikh i sluzhashchikh', in *Planovoe khozyaystvo*, no. 11 (November 1983).
13. Ibid.
14. I. Malmygin, 'Sbalansirovannost' rabochikh mest i trudovykh resursov', *Planovoe khozyaystvo*, no. 8 (1982) p. 55.
15. How many and for how long is not defined. V. Golubev and L. Tyanov, 'Nechernozem'e: pochemu ne izzhit defitsit kadrov?', *Molodoy kommunist*, no. 8 (August 1981), pp. 41, 42.
16. M. Lavrinenko, 'Trudovye resursy priamurskogo sela', *Trud*, no. 9 (1984), p. 88.
17. V. Yaborov, 'Kto poydet na stroyku?' *Sots. trud*, no. 9 (1974), p. 76.
18. J. L. Porket, 'The Shortage, Use and Reserves of Labour in the Soviet Union', *Osteuropa Wirtschaft*, vol. 29, no. 1 (1984), p. 17.
19. *Trud*, 17 July 1979.
20. *Sotsialisticheski trud*, no. 7 (1980), p. 105. A comparison of the staffing of Moscow's *Rossiya* hotel has illustrated the high staff complement compared to comparable western hotels. The *Rossiya* has an establishment of 2137 for 5354 beds—a ratio of 1 to 1.7. In 1980, it was 700 short of staff giving a ratio of 1 to 2.1 guests (assuming 100 per cent occupancy). The Munich Hilton has 350 staff for 1000 residents, a ratio of 1 to 2.8. Soviet data from *Literaturnaya gazeta*, no. 2 (1980), p. 13. Cited by A. Tenson, (Munich, RL 60/80). Calculations added.
21. E.L. Manevich is a Professor of Economics. In addition to the article cited above, see also 'Vosproizvodstvo naseleniya i ispol'zovovanie trudovykh resursov', *Voprosy ekonomiki*, no. 8 (1978), pp. 38-48, and 'Ratsional'noe ispol'zovanie rabochey sily', pp. 55-66.
22. Manevich (1978), p. 42.
23. E.R. Sarukhanov, *Sotsial'no ekonomicheskie problemy upravleniya rabochey siloy pri sotsializme* (Leningrad: 1981), p. 123.
24. L.S. Sbytova, *Struktura zanyatosti i effektivnost' proizvodstva* (1982), p. 105. Similar data are given in I. Tratsevski and A. Zhuk, 'Opyt mekhanizatisii ruchnogo truda v promyshlennosti Gomel'skoy oblasti', *Sots. trud*, no. 1 (1983), esp. p. 27.
25. Data based on 1979 census of jobs, cited in L.S. Sbytova, *Struktura zanyatosti i effektivnost' proizvodstva* (1982), p. 105.
26. *Sovetskaya kultura*, 1 February 1986; *CDSP*, vol. 38, no. 3, p .23.
27. V. Egorov, *Pravda*, 7 July 1985; *CDSP*, vol. 37, no. 27, p. 16.
28. Taken from readers' letters: A. Shokhin, 'Privlekat' ne otvlekaya', *Literaturnaya gazeta*, 31 August 1983, p. 13.
29. Manevich (1981), p. 61; and L.A. Kostin, 'Upravlenie trudovymi resursami strany', *Planovoe khozyaystvo*, no. 12 (1978), p. 25.
30. Manevich (1981), p. 60.
31. N. Alekseev, 'Defitsit kadrov', *Literaturnaya gazeta*, 24 December 1980, p. 10.
32. V. Volodarski, 'Defitsit zdravogo smysla', *Literaturnaya gazeta*, 24 September 1980, p. 10.

33. Paul R. Gregory, 'Productivity, Slack and Time Theft in the Soviet Economy: Evidence from the Soviet Interview Project', Working Paper no. 15 (University of Illinois at Urbana-Champaign, 1986), pp. 9-10.'Mneniya', *Literaturnaya gazeta*, 26 November 1980, p. 11.
34. V. Parfenov, 'Chelovek krasit mesto', *Pravda*, 5 April 1982, p. 2.
35. 'Rekonstruktsiya: opyt i problemy: *Pravda*, 30 July 1984.
36. M. Ya. Sonin, 'Effecktivno ispol'zovat' trudovye resursy', *EKO*, no. 4 (1977) pp. 9-10. English translation in *CDSP*, vol. 29, no. 38, p. 10.
37. V.V. Ustimenko, 'Kadry primamim!', *EKO*, no. 9 (1983), p. 155.
38. T. Baranenkova, 'Reserves for Economizing the Workforce', *Voprosy ekonomiki*, no. 5 (1980), English Translation, *Problems of Economics*, February 1981, p. 12.
39. L.A. Kostin, 'Rezervy ispolzovaniya trudovykh resursov', *EKO*, no. 1 (1984), p. 35.
40. A. Kotlyar, 'Polnaya zanyatost' i sbalansirovannost' faktorov sotsialisticheskogo proizvodstva'; *Vop. ekon.*, (1983), p. 155.
41. V. Parfenov and V. Cherkasov, *Pravda*, 9 March 1984; *CDSP*, vol. 36, no. 10.
42. On Leningrad, where only 20,000 jobs during the twelfth Five Year Plan are being lost, see V. Volostnykh, 'Skol'ko nuzhno rabochikh mest', *Pravda*, 4 May 1985. for an overview, see P. Hanson, 'Work Place Attestation: Attempts at Labor-Saving in a Labor-Hoarding Economy' (Munich: RL 316/85), September 1985.
43. Now called *Shchekinskoe obedinenie Azot*. For an excellent account in English, see Peter Rutland, 'The Shchekino Method and the Struggle to Raise Labour Productivity', *Soviet Studies*, vol. 36, no. 3, (July 1984), pp. 345-65.
44. *Eksperiment-opyt-resul'tat* (Tula 1975), p. 8.
45. *Eksperiment...*, p. 9.
46. V. Parfenov and V. Shvetsov, *Pravda*, 28 March 1977. Translation in *CDSP*, vol. 29, no. 13 (1977), p. 14.
47. The Shchekino method's full title is *Kompleksnaya sistema organizatsii truda material'nogo stimulirovaniya i planirovaniya*.
48. P. Sharov (Manager of the Shchekino chemical factory), 'Put' k visokoy effektivnosti', *Pravda*, 12 October 1969, p. 2.
49. These details are given in Sharov, *loc.cit*. Parvenov and Shvertsov (*Pravda*, 28 March 1977) claim that the 1966 wage fund was stable as was the production plan for a five-year period.
50. *Eksperiment...*, p. 11.
51. Sharov, *Pravda*, 12 October 1969.
52. *Eksperiment...*, p. 12.
53. Ibid., p. 13.
54. Ibid., p. 19.
55. *Pravda*, 28 March 1977.
56. *Eksperiment...*, p. 16.
57. Ibid., p. 17.
58. 'Ekonomika proizvodstva i organizatsiya zarabotnoy platy', *Sotsialisticheski*

trud, no. 4 (1977), p. 13.
59. Ibid., p. 14.
60. Ibid.
61. *Shchekinski metod na Permskikh predpriyatiyakh* (1974), p. 19.
62. V. Fil'ev, 'O dal'neyshem vnedrenii shchekinskogo metoda', *Voprosy ekonomiki*, no. 2 (1983), p.67.
63. *Eksperiment* . . ., p. 16.
64. 'Shchekinski method v desyatoy pyatiletke', *Sotsialisticheski trud*, no. 4 (1977), pp. 10-11.
65. R. Batkaev and S. Semin, 'Shchekinski metod v usloviyakh sovershenstvovaniya khozyaystvennogo mekhanizma', *Sots.trud* (1983), no. 1. p. 46.
66. V. Fil've 'O dal'neyshem vnedrenii shchekinskogo metoda', *Voprosy ekonomiki*, no. 2 (1983), p. 61.
67. V. Fil'ev, 'O dal'neyshem vnedrenii shchekinskogo metoda', *Voprosy ekonomiki*, no. 2 (1983), p. 59.
68. Ibid.
69. Ibid. The chief form of saving came from combining jobs and widening the sphere of activity.
70. *Sots. trud* (1977), no. 4, p. 11.
71. Ibid., p. 12.
72. 'Ekonomika . . .', p. 13.
73. Ibid., p. 14.
74. 'Eksperiment-opyt-resul'tat' (Tula), (1975), pp. 11-12.
75. V. Fil'ev, 'O dal'neyshem vnedrenii shchekinskogo metoda', *Voprosy ekonomiki*, no. 2 (1983), p. 60.
76. A. Radov, 'paradoksy eksperimenta', *Sovetskaya Rossiya*, 19 July 1981. R. Batkaev and S. Semin, 'Shchekinski metod v usloviyakh sovershenstvovaniya khozyaystvennogo mekhanizma', *Sots. trud*, (1983), no. 1, p. 44.
77. V. Parfenov and V. Shvetsov, *Pravda*, 29 March 1977, p. 2; *CDSP*, vol. 29, no. 13, p. 15.
78. Radov, *loc. cit.*
79. Mirgaleev says this happened at 18 enterprises in Sverdlovsk and used up to 40.5 per cent of the savings from the wage funds: 'Shchekinski . . .', p. 109.
80. 'Shchekinski metod v desyatoy pyatiletke', *Sots. trud*, no. 4 (1977), p. 17.
81. A. Nikitin and V. Shevtsov, *Pravda*, 14 June 1982; *CDSP*, vol. 34, no. 24 (1982).
82. Ibid.
83. Radov, *loc. cit.*
84. 'Shchekinski method. . .', p. 14.
85. A. Aganbegyan, *Trud*, 12 December 1982. K. Cherednichenko, cited by V. Parfenov and V. Shvetsov, *Pravda*, 29 March 1977, p. 2; *CDSP*, vol. 29, no. 13, p. 15.
86. Parfenov and Shvetsov, p. 15.
87. S. Kossoi, cited by Parfenov and Shvetsov, ibid. The regulations are conveniently translated in *Soviet Statutes and Decisions* (Summer 1979), pp.

363-73.
88. R. Batkaev and S. Semin, 'Shchekinski metod v usloviyakh sovershenstvovaniya khozyaystvennogo mekhanizma', *Sots. trud*, no. 1 (1983), p. 43.
89. 'O poryadke i usloviyakh sovmeshcheniya professiy (*dolzhnostey*)'; Batkaev and Semin, p. 48.
90. Ibid., p. 50.
91. V. Listov, 'Planirovanie razvitiya otrasli na sovremennom etape', *Planovoe khozyaystvo*, no. 9 (1984), p. 20.
92. Reported in A. Nikitin and V. Shevtsov, *Pravda*, 14 June 1982; *CDSP*, vol 34, no. 24, p. 11.
93. 'Ostaetsya v deystvii', *Pravda*, 18 October 1983, p. 2.
94. Speeches reported in Nikitin and Shevtsov, *Pravda*, 14 June 1982, *CDSP*, vol. 34, no. 24, p. 11.
95. Fil'ev, pp. 64-5.
96. Ibid., p. 168.
97. Either within an enterprise, or to another one. Sarukhanov, p. 130.
98. Ibid., p. 71. One experiment, instituted in five engineering factories in Leningrad in July 1983, relieved the enterprises of responsibility for finding new work for redundant workers; presumably this was taken over by the labour exchanges. Example cited in E. Teague, *Labour Discipline and Legislation in the USSR 1979-85* (Munich: RL Supplement 2/85), p. 28.
99. Sarukhanov, p. 71.
100. L. Gol'din, 'Sotsial'nye posledstviya primenenya Shchekinskogo methoda', *Sots. Trud*, no. 3 (1980), p. 97.
101. V. Parfenov and V. Shvetsov, *Pravda*, 28 March 1977; *CDSP*, vol. 29, no. 13 (1977), p. 14.
102. Ibid.
103. I.Gol'din,'Sotsial'nye posledstviya primeneniya Shchekinskogo metoda', *Sots.trud*, no. 3 (1980),p. 103.
104. Radov, *loc. cit.*
105. A. Radov, *Sovetskaya Rossiya*, 24 July 1981.
106. Ibid.
107. A. Radov, *Sovetskaya Rossiya*, 22 July 1981.
108. A. Radov, *Sovetskaya Rossiya*, 24 July 1981.
109. A. Radov, *Sovetskaya Rossiya*, 22 July 1981.
110. Radov, *Sovetskaya Rossiya*, 22 July 1981, p.2.
111. Ibid.
112. T. Baranenko, 'Reserves for Economizing the Work Force', *Voprosy ekonomiki*, no. 5 (1980). English translation in *Problems of Economics*, February 1981, p. 4.
113. *Sots. trud*, no. 1 (1980), pp. 70-1.
114. Baranenkova, p. 7.
115. On Latvia see M. Dzliev, 'Programma sokrashcheniya ruchnogo truda: kakoy ey byt', *Sots. trud*, no. 1 (1983), p. 22. Programmes for reductions are mentioned in E. Sarukhanov, *Sotsial'no-ekonomicheskie problemy*

*upravleniya rabochey siloy pri sotsializme* (Leningrad: 1981).
116. See *Sovershenstvovanie khozyaystvennogo mekhanizma* (Sbornik dokumentov), 1982.
117. V. Folkin (Vice-Chairman of the Ukraine Republic State Planning Committee), *Pravda*, 30 July 1984; *CDSP*, vol. 36. no. 30, p. 14.
118. N. Panteleev (Chairman of the Ukraine Republic State Committee on Labour), *Pravda*, 30 July 1984), p. 14. (At the same time, however, 300,000 jobs remained unfilled in the Ukraine.)
119. Sbytova, p. 12.
120. L.A. Kostin, 'Rezervy ispol'zovaniya trudovykh resursov', *EKO*, no. 1 (1984), p. 25.
121. p. 99. No actual questions and specific details of responses are recorded here by Gol'din.
122. Parfenov and Shvetsov, p. 14.
123. Radov, 19 July 1981.
124. Gol'din, p. 100.
125. L.S. Kheifets, *Uvelichenie vypuska produktsii s men'shey chislennost'yu rabotnikov* (1974), p. 17. Other factory workers did not want to transfer because of the receiving plant's location on the outskirts of the town.
126. Radov, 19 July 1981; Gol'din, p. 99.
127. Gol'din, p. 102.
128. E.I. Ruzavina, *Zanyatost' v usloviyakh intensifikatsii proizvodstva* (1975), pp. 69-70.
129. Ibid., p. 70. Similar data, showing the small proportion of displaced labour through technical advances and the large share through economic organization factors, are cited in M.I. Dolishni, *Formirovanie i ispol'zovanie trudovykh resursov* (1978), p. 84.
130. He later estimates that the number of displaced workers was 68,000 to 76,000 people per annum in the years of the ninth Five Year Plan: Dolishni, p. 83.
131. Dolishni, p. 74.
132. Ibid., p. 75.
133. Ibid., p. 76.
134. Ibid., p. 77.
135. A.Z. Dadoishev, *Problemy ispol'zovaniya trudovykh resursov v SSSR* (1975), p. 60.
136. Ruzavina, pp. 75-6.
137. 'Ekonomika . . .', pp. 12-13.
138. 'Technical Progress in the Interests of Workers', 28 August 1981. Reported in *FBIS: USSR National Affairs, Economic Developments* (1981).
139. M. Ya. Sonin, 'Effektivno ispol'zovat' trudovye resursy', *EKO*, vol. 40, no. 4, (July–August 1977), p. 11.
140. L. Danilov and V. Karev, 'Tekhnicheski progress i vysvobozhdenie kadrov', *Sots. trud*, no. 5 (1983), pp. 102-3.
141. Sonin, pp. 11, 9.
142. E. Manevich, *Voprosy ekonomiki*, no. 6 (1965).
143. E.L. Manevich, 'Defitsit i reservy rabochey sily', *EKO*, no. 2

(March–April 1078), p. 83.

144. English version printed in *Soviet Statutes and Decisions* (Summer 1979), p. 365 (Article 4).

145. G. Popov, *Pravda*, 27 December 1980. English translation in *CDSP*, vol. 32, no. 52 (1980), p. 11.

146. *Pravda*, 31 December 1980; *CDSP*, vol. 32, no. 52 (1980), p. 23.

147. Head of Social Security Directorate for USSR. K.V. Protsenko, 'Social Security in the USSR', Moscow Radio, 31 October 1983. Reported in BBC *Summary of World Broadcasts*, SU/7479/B/2, 1 November, 1983.

148. *Pravda*, 23 November 1985; Translation in *CDSP*, vol 37 (1985), no. 48, p. 4.

149. Bob Arnot, 'Soviet Labour Productivity and the Failure of the Shchekino Experiment', *Critique*, no. 15 (1981), p. 50.

150. V. Kostakov, *Sovetskaya Kultura*, 4 January 1986; *CDSP*, 38, no. 3, p. 1. In his report to the 27th Party Congress, Gorbachev also mentioned that 'around 12 million' existing jobs will be saved through investment in new machinery: *Pravda*, 26 February 1986.

151. Reported in Radio Liberty (Munich) 35/86, p. 11.

# 7  Distinguishing Features of the Soviet Labour Market

## EMPLOYMENT AND THE DUAL LABOUR MARKET

The main thrust of recent scholarly western writing on labour has been in terms of dual and segmented markets.[1] Such paradigms cannot be applied to Soviet-type societies without considerable modification—if they can be said to be relevant at all. Western writers who point to similarities between the capitalist and the Soviet labour market ignore the context in which labour is employed.[2] While we may not dwell here on the economic and political system in which labour is engaged under capitalism and state socialism, some of the major contrasts may be summarized before we consider problems of productivity and work organization.

A 'market' in its most general sense is a mechanism which reconciles supply and demand. It is assumed that there are specific and opposed interests which constitute the forces of demand and supply. The market as an arena of exchange reconciles the interests of the bargaining parties. Many theorists interpret such market exchanges as being to the mutual advantage of both parties: when equilibrium is reached each side has a satisfactory outcome. The effects of market activities, it is asserted, are to coordinate and distribute resources in an optimum way; efficiency and effectiveness are achieved. As a result of market exchange, the worker receives his just desert.

Other writers on the labour process, however, deny both the reciprocity of exchange and the justice of market outcomes (see below pp. 218–19). From such viewpoints markets are regarded as mechanisms which lead to the domination of one group over the

other and it is concluded that the exchange relations are unequal
and outcomes are to the advantage of the powerful (capital). The
labour market is constituted of mechanisms through which the
hiring of labour is arranged; wages or salaries reconcile the
interests of employer and employee. Many theorists of labour
markets conclude that the employer is dominant. Under capitalism
surplus has to be extracted from the employee. The reserve army
of unemployed severely weakens the bargaining power of labour.
Labour markets, however, are more complex than a mere
confrontation of worker and employer. To ensure a stable and loyal
work force some firms under capitalism replace personal forms of
control (hiring 'at the factory gate'; firing on the factory floor)
with bureaucratic control.

Two types of labour market are thus established. The
'secondary' market in which personal control continues: workers
are hired with no security or provision for a career or
advancement; the level of skill typically is low, turnover is high
and wages are poor; workers in such jobs usually have little
education and are often recruited from certain social groups—
ethnic minorities, school-leavers, women. In the 'primary'
market, however, security of tenure for the employee is achieved
and promotion within the firm is possible; turnover is low, wages
are high, employees are usually recruited from established social
groups with good levels of education.

The primary labour market reduces levels of uncertainty for
employer and employee. It does not, however, entail an equality of
exchange. Labour market theorists would interpret the primary
market as a sophisticated device to ensure the control of the
employee by the management of the firm. As Edwards has put it:
'The new system of control, devised both as part of the
corporation's response to the general worker threat to capitalist
hegemony and as a specific strategy to ameliorate the crisis of
control in the firm, was bureaucratic control'.[3] In essence, in
return for relative security of employment, good working
conditions and career prospects, the firm is ensured a stable, loyal
and hardworking labour force. Wages and conditions of work are
not determined 'on the market' (i.e. external to the firm) but are
regulated internally. The firm, being in control of the labour
process, is able to exert sanctions (rewards, responsibility, wages)
over the 'captive' labour force.

In a command or planned economy of the Soviet type the labour market is not characterized by secondary or primary markets analogous to those under capitalism as described by Edwards, Reich and Gordon. The data we have considered lead me to conclude that labour markets are of a differentiated form, similar in limited respects to dual markets under capitalism. The most important differences affecting the labour market are threefold: first, production does not take place for profit realizable through commodity markets: second, the labour force is fully employed; and third, there is an absence of a national labour market.

Management has no incentive to minimize labour costs. The absence of production for profit and of the need for accumulation to take place at the level of the enterprise significantly changes the pattern of management motivation. For reasons adumbrated above, management seeks to enlarge and spend its wages fund. It acts like a public sector institution in a western economy. Also, management is severely circumscribed in its power over the labour force. Edwards points out that under capitalism *the firm* is a 'system of control'.[4] Under state socialism, it is the Ministry which has analogous power; and Ministries work in conformity with the economic plan, which defines inputs, outputs, the wages fund and prices. To overcome the 'distortions' caused by market forces in determining the 'true' deserts of employees (e.g. monopoly tendencies by certain groups of workers) wage *rates* for various skills are given to the enterprise. They are based on 'norms' which are part of national job evaluation intended to secure equality of desert.

It is not market uncertainty that threatens Soviet management but administrative uncertainty. Soviet enterprises are motivated to expand their workforce. To maintain a stable labour force they undermine the regulations (stipulated by the state committee on prices and wages) applicable to wages to reward workers with scarce skills. Hence in a limited respect some Soviet enterprises operate like primary labour markets as in the West. They provide out of their surpluses welfare services, and through their administrative control they seek to distribute rewards of a material and welfare kind. This process applies, though in different degrees, to all enterprises, not just to big monopolies which characterize the primary labour market in the West. (Small enterprises, as noted earlier cannot compete with large ones on the scale of provision.) Moreover, as there is no ultimate threat of unemployment and as the enterprise is not evaluated by market performance, management does not regulate the workforce with Taylorist rigour. At the point of production, on the shopfloor, the 'brigade' method, to be discussed below, seeks to reward workers on the basis of their individual skill and collective performance. Hence administrative control is replaced by social control based on self-interest. This in turn, however, creates a contradiction in the administration of the enterprise: the notion of universal norms for a given job is undermined by the ability of production teams to 'overfulfil' their plans and by the interest of management (for the sake of stability) to pay over the planned rates. Also, Soviet-type management does not have the authority of their counterparts in western firms and workers effectively have greater control over the process of production.

Soviet employees, unlike their counterparts in the West, have less effective choice of occupational mobility. There is no national labour market and recruitment of labour takes place through local informal networks and to a lesser extent by administrative placement. Mobility is restricted in three ways: recruitment of many entrants to the labour market is controlled administratively, geographical mobility is subject to administrative ratification (and some cities and areas are effectively restricted to their existing population), the high full-time employment levels make husband and wife the unit of employment.

The secondary labour market, as described above, does not exist in any significant way in the Soviet Union. The major reason for this is that uncertainty of employment does not occur for the employee. Management cannot reduce labour costs by the recruitment of cheaper labour at the factory gates. On the contrary: the unemployed are likely to be 'undisciplined' and minimum wages are laid down by the state committee. Even managements employing unskilled workers in low-paid sectors of the economy will attempt to provide conditions which will keep a stable labour force. From the supply side of labour, administrative controls prevent the immigration of a 'reserve army' of people seeking work. Whilst we have noted that there is a pool of underutilized rural labour in some areas of the USSR, procurement prices of agricultural products are such that underemployment is sustained in such areas. The inability of enterprises to 'push up' wages to act as a carrot and the absence of the sticks of unemployment and rural poverty, deter labour mobility, the growth of a secondary market and its associated ethnic underclasses as found in the West.


## A DIFFERENTIATED LABOUR MARKET

Labour in the Soviet Union is not a homogeneous product. Even workers with identical skills have different conditions, prospects and wages. The labour market is differentiated. On the side of production, certain sectors enjoy higher wages and better conditions irrespective of the skill levels of employees. One may observe social statuses grouped in occupational clusters. Women, for instance, are less skilled than men and are concentrated in low-paying industries (textiles, catering, teaching, administration); Central Asian ethnic groups remain in traditional agriculture. The differentiation of the labour market is the consequence of complex interchanges between administrative decision, traditional values and market shortage.

Wage *rates* are determined by state committees for wages and prices in collaboration with the state planning committee (Gosplan). Such rates are not fixed in a vacuum. They reflect social and political priorities. Marxism as economic theory posits the source of wealth to be productive labour in the sense of the creation of commodities that can be exchanged for a price. Politically, men in 'productive' industries have been regarded as the core of the working class which ideologically is regarded as the dominant class. The promotion of political stability and social solidarity underlies the financial rewards of this group. 'Direct' producers of wealth, therefore, receive higher rewards than providers of services. Hence manual workers in general and in extractive industries (for example, mining) in particular have higher wage rates than non-manual professionals (physicians, teachers). Men traditionally work in such industries and this gives rise to differentiation by sex. Wage differentials have progressively moved away from non-manual workers to manuals as shown by Table 7.1.

Marxism as an ideology, however, does not legitimate differential rewards on the basis of sex. Traditional views about the

*Table 7.1:   Wage Ratios of Managerial/Technical, Manual and Office Workers in Soviet Industry, 1932—84*

| Managerial/Technical | 1932 | 1940 | 1950 | 1960 | 1970 | 1975 | 1981 | 1984 |
| --- | --- | --- | --- | --- | --- | --- | --- | --- |
| Workers | 100 | 100 | 100 | 100 | 100 | 100 | 100 | 100 |
| Managerial/Technical | 263 | 210 | 175 | 148 | 136 | 124 | 112.7 | 111.1 |
| Office workers | 150 | 109 | 93 | 82 | 85 | 82 | 77.9 | 77.3 |

*Sources*:   Calculated from *Narkhoz 1922—82* (1982) p. 405; and *Narodnoe Khozyaystvo SSSR* for relevant years. See also D. Lane, *Soviet Economy and Society* (Oxford: Blackwell, 1985), pp. 177-82.

position of women in society have influenced their work role. The feminist argument has some force here. The economic and political apparatus which regulates wages and job recruitment is dominated at the higher levels by men and they, subconsciously perhaps, take it for granted that women are rightly engaged in more menial jobs and in less well paid industries and services.

The operation of the laws of a 'shortage' economy favours the production sector. In the negotiation of a wages fund with higher administrative bodies, the managements of industrial distribution enterprises are able to bargain for a large fund. The uneven distribution of administrative power between industrial ministries (with heavy industry, machine tools and defence having priority), gives rise to distortions in the distribution of the wages funds. Hence, though notionally wages should reflect general principles concerning skill, experience and work effort, in practice wage rates provide only 'floors' below which wages do not fall. Groups of workers in well-endowed enterprises are able to negotiate higher income. This bargaining position is furthered by the labour shortage which induces management to hike wage payments to maintain a stable and financially motivated labour force. In this way, however, distortions in wages occur—workers with given skills find that wages vary between different enterprises. The absence of trade unions as effective levers of wage payments (within and across industries) helps maintain such distortions and anomalies.

In the services sector, the strength of employing units is weaker. These ministries have lower prestige and political muscle and this is compounded by the feminization of the workforce.

Consumers are treated with indifference and bear the social cost of inadequate provision. Wages rise more slowly. The workforce is highly feminized, and politically women are unable to bring sufficient administrative and political pressure to raise the standing of their services. A vicious circle occurs with low-paid workers and underfinanced enterprises unable to provide comparable welfare and social facilities (housing, holidays, childcare, clinics) to the well-endowed factories.

The poor servicing of consumers in many sectors (car, house-building and repair) leads to suppressed demand and creates a market for certain skills (mechanics, plasterers, plumbers, painters). The market asserts its own priorities on the price of labour: individuals and groups of *shabashniki* (self-employed) mop up excess spending power. The market effectively fixes a wage rate. Ironically, this reverses the planners' priorities, for it creates an aristocracy of labour not in the industrial sector but amongst workers, including the unskilled, such as building labourers and taxi-drivers who can serve the retail consumer. In doing such part-time jobs they move out of the public sector creating further labour shortage and distortions in the administered ordering of the labour market. Tradesmen capable of finding work in the 'private' sector are able to bargain for higher wages in the public sector—or in those parts of it with the ability to pay. Skilled workers who lack negotiable skills (e.g. librarians, laboratory technicians, engineers, teachers, clerks) and the semi-skilled (machine operators, assemblers, fitters, panel operators, computer technicians) become captives of the public sector. Divergences between their income levels and those exercising 'private initiative' lead to charges of 'injustice' in the distribution of rewards.

The planners are thus faced with trying to resolve many contradictions. To further social justice they advocate the strengthening of scientifically worked out norms. But to meet production workers' demands for realistic wages and to improve labour productivity they concurrently advocate the *khozraschetny* brigade (see below, Chapter 7). Efficient workers with negotiable skills are able to maximize their personal advantage akin to similar workers exercising private initiative. In doing so, however, the socialist goal of equality of distribution is undermined by the excessive fulfilment of the principle of payment by results. The system punishes employees who do not produce an 'object' but who provide services—social workers, librarians, teachers, clerks, technicians, scientists.

To conclude, the labour market under Soviet socialism is differentiated. Some industrial sectors are well-endowed and workers in them are relatively privileged. They operate in a similar way to primary labour markets under capitalism: workers in them have a real income above the average for a given level of skill, conditions are superior and a job for life may be pursued. This is not only for foremen and supervisory staff, but also for manual workers; indeed, Soviet enterprises cultivate 'workers' dynasties' across generations. The absence of competitive recruitment and a national (All-Union) labour market promotes internal promotion, as does the chronic labour shortage in general. Secondary labour markets, however, do not have the same character as in the West. There is an absence of migratory labour: immigration is strictly controlled and has an insignificant impact on the labour market. Internal migration is limited: pockets of underemployment in the countryside are perpetuated but are not characterized by rural poverty. Full employment at a macro-level makes the labour market a sellers' market. The labour shortage concurrent with administrative formation of wages obviates the development of a qualitatively separate secondary labour market. Nevertheless, poorly endowed industries and services have below-average levels of pay and poorer conditions. We may call this sector a quasi-secondary labour market. From the labour supply side, it is distinguished by feminization of the labour force. Administrative regulation of the services and retail sectors involving lower average wages and poorer conditions has led to the growth of 'individual initiative' in some trades and services. This has created a market in which labour is able to bid up its price. This in turn undermines the bureaucratic system of wage and price formation. Its logic, in a context of full employment and in the form of *khozraschetny* brigades, will be to undermine seriously the administrative determination of wages.

# REFERENCES

1. R. C. Edwards, M. Reich, D. M. Gordon, *Labor Market Segmentation* (Lexington, Mass.: D. C. Heath, 1975). R. C. Edwards, *Contested Terrain* (London: Heinemann, 1979). D. M. Gordon, R. C. Edwards, M. Reich, *Segmented Work, Divided Workers* (Cambridge: Cambridge University Press, 1982). David Stark 'Re-thinking Internal Labor Markets: New Insights from a Comparative Perspective', *American Sociological Review*, vol. 51 no. 4 (August 1986).
2. See for example, Paul Gregory, 'The Earnings of Soviet Workers: Human Capital, Loyalty and Privilege', Soviet Interview Project, Working Paper No. 13 (University of Illinois at Urbana-Champaign, 1986), pp. 7-9. Gregory notes institutional differences, but these do not appear to have much effect on the market (e.g. p. 9).
3. R. C. Edwards, 'The Social Relations of Production in the Firm and Labor Market Structure', in Edwards, Reich and Gordon (1975), p. 9.
4. Loc.cit., p. 4.

# 8 The Brigade System and the Work Process

## TAYLORISM AND THE LABOUR PROCESS

The brigade system, as currently advocated, is a form of work organization which modifies in many significant respects the dominant paradigm of Taylorism[1] which has had an enormous impact in the USSR. Taylorism is not just a theory of work organization and control but is a perspective on work and production which has been adopted in one form or another by both western advanced capitalism and by socialist countries. Taylorism is open to many interpretations: it is often viewed as an 'ideas system', as a form of work organization or job design, as a form of structure of control to extract surplus[2] (through pay, time and motion study, fragmentation of work) and as an organizational theory to enhance productivity and economic efficiency.[3] Such approaches are not mutually exclusive.

Kendall E. Bailes has shown that in the early days of Soviet power, Alexei Gastev, a self-styled disciple of Taylor, emphasized the fragmentation of work turning the workers, even under socialism, 'into mechanized and standardized cogs in a vast machine'.[4] Capitalism and socialism share in common Taylor's goal of achieving prosperity through the increases of productivity. This is the objective which has commended itself not only to western capitalists but also to Lenin and his followers. The controversy over Taylorism turns on the duality between its function of improving productivity through the scientific study of the work process and its effects of making employees work harder and thus extracting more profit under capitalism.[5]

Henri Savall[6] itemizes four propositions derived from Taylor which, I believe, inform western and Soviet practice. First, scientific management implies a reciprocity of relationships between workers, foremen, technicians, engineers and employers. Second, efficiency in work may only be achieved through the application of 'scientific principles' to analyse methods of work. Taylor believed that there was only one way to achieve efficiency with a given process. Third, Taylor believed that the management had the responsibility to give workers technical assistance. The hierarchy was important in the transmission of knowledge and organization of training essential to optimize efficiency. Fourth, work has to be a cooperative venture undertaken in the spirit of collaboration. Specialization of work has to take place within the context of the development of a cooperative spirit.

This summary of Taylor's principles brings out four affinities with Soviet Marxism—Leninism. First, it is compatible with the Leninist organizational precepts of democratic centralism and central planning. Authority is hierarchical and centralized. Second, like Soviet Marxism, Taylorism is steeped in notions of scientism, i.e. the application of scientific principles to human behaviour. Third, both Taylorism and Marxism-Leninism have materialist philosophies. Finally, as noted above, both socialism and capitalism are predicated on the belief that material abundance may be achieved through increased productivity which in turn can only be achieved through collaboration between management and labour. As a writer in *Pravda* has put it:

The objective conditions for the moulding of voluntary, conscious discipline are inherent in the very nature of socialism, above all in public property, production relations and the objectives of production, and in the unity of the fundamental interests of the individual and society. By increasing public wealth, the worker, to an ever greater degree, satisfies his own requirements as well. . .[7]

There is a duality in Taylorism between, on the one hand, its concern for efficiency, with the reduction of costs and the rationalization of movement and, on the other, the control of the workforce to secure greater exchange value or, in the Soviet context, value for investment and the control of the workforce by management.

The brigade system in the USSR attempts to use the positive elements of Taylorism which have been absorbed into the movement called 'the scientific organization of work' (NOT— *nauchnaya organizatsiya truda*). NOT is concerned with 'the process of organizing labour in a precise and calculated way', its objective is to save on 'time, effort and materials'.[8] However, the brigade system takes into account many of the criticisms which have been made of the negative and unsatisfactory elements of Taylorism. Alexei Gastev himself was subjected to the criticism that his concept of labour involved its 'militarization' and denied it any creativity.[9] Bogdanov argued on the contrary that industrialism created workers who could share in 'the planning, regulating and fulfilling functions of industry'.[10] Bogdanov conceded that fragmented work and detailed control might be necessary in an undeveloped economy with an abundant supply of unskilled labour but with the development of the Soviet economy a form of 'comradely cooperation' would arise with organizing and executive tasks becoming combined.[11] Gastev was also criticized on the grounds that he neglected the psychological and physiological aspects of labour.[12] His opponents argued that workers under socialism should develop initiative and participation in production.[13]

In analysing Soviet work methods and job design one should not identify aspects of the Taylor system with their American counterparts as the context of production in the USSR is quite different. In the USSR a major role of NOT has been to create an ethic of labour in place of the laggardly, slapdash attitudes of the newly-mobilized Soviet peasantry.[14] Gastev made it explicit that NOT was 'a means for raising culture in general and a method of struggle against remnants and survivals of the peasant, Asiatic culture of old Russia'.[15] Education, training and induction into a work culture have played a more important role (though often overlooked in the West) in NOT than they have in Taylorism in the West. NOT has always encouraged participation by the worker in the organization of things. This has been a goal, even if it has not been fulfilled, which is not the case for the American version of Taylorism.

Taylorism is widely criticized in the West for taking too instrumental a view of people at work. As Savall[16] has pointed out, people expect a great deal from work and have had a long period of preparation for it. People have high expectations: the work should develop their intelligence and imagination; the development of technology leads to greater cooperation in work. Taylor has been found to be wrong in assuming that there is only *one* 'scientifically determined' way to do a job. Mass-production processes have only a limited application and 'small-batch' production is less amenable to the high degree of specialization assumed by Taylor. The need for quality requires workers who are conscientious and have a commitment to, and sense of pride in, their work. The brigade system in the USSR has affinities with Taylorism, and in its contemporary form seeks to avoid some of its drawbacks.

## THE SYSTEM OF BRIGADES

The brigade system is intended not only to improve labour productivity (its main aim) but also to motivate workers, to constrain the labour policy of managers, and to reconcile the interests of individual workers with those of the industrial enterprise and society as a whole.[17]

Work methods based on the self-interest of workers which had been developed in the 1930s with the introduction of Taylorism had often led to a conflict between individual and collective interest. As a writer in *EKO* described it:

Social ownership of the means of production under socialism created the necessary basis for the fusion of social and personal interests. However, the interests of society, the collective, and the individual do not always coincide. Specialization of production and further deepening of the division of labour means that the interests of society, the collective, the shop, the section, and the individual are not always in agreement. For example, to assemble a machine it is necessary to have all the component parts. For individual shops it is not equally economically advantageous [*vygodno*] to produce all the parts to make up a set [*komplekt*], therefore there is a surplus of some parts ['paying well'] and a deficit of ['poorly paying'] others. A worker doing individual work is interested in overfulfilling the plan not for the parts necessary for assembly, and thus for the end product of the enterprise, but in the most 'advantageous' [*vygodnye*] ones, the ones which pay best. In such cases material interest is at odds with the organizational ones of the administration. A mechanism is necessary which can unite the interests of every participant in the production process with the interests of the enterprise. One such mechanism . . . is, the brigade subcontract [*podryad*].[18]

Changes in the organization of production requiring workers to have not one skill but many and to exercise a wider responsibility over production tasks make *individual* job assignments less appropriate and collective (or brigade) methods more appropriate.[19]

Since the Second World War, collective forms of labour have had ups and downs in the USSR. In 1951, in the Kharkov turbine factory, multi-shift brigades similar to the present ones were formed.[20] Brigades of the contemporary type began to be introduced in industry in the early 1970s, but it was not until later that decade that they were widely advocated and adopted as the principal form of work collective in the USSR.[21] Factories introducing this system in the late 1970s include VAZ (Volga automobile plant), the Kaluga turbine factory, the Perm' engine building factory, Uralmash, the Gomel electrical equipment factory, Yuzhuralmash and the Konakovo mechanical instruments factory.[22]

The objectives of the brigade system are (a) to encourage maximum effort by individual members, (b) to provide an incentive to economize on labour employed, (c) to stabilize labour mobility and enhance labour discipline, (d) to involve workers in management, to increase their personal responsibility for state affairs in the collective, and (e) to make the labour collective not only a unit of production but also a social unit.[23] As a brigade leader put it in an article in *Kommunist*: 'Contemporary production demands that every worker be able to picture his place in the work process, to know on what and for what he is working, what depends on him, and to feel that his labour is a necessary part of the overall work. There is a need to organize labour and pay so that a worker is interested not only in fulfilling his own assignment, but also in achieving optimum end-results.'[24] While brigades have existed in the USSR since the 1930s, the contemporary form of brigade labour is wider in scope and significance.[25]

The 1979 resolution on the economic mechanism decreed that the brigade form of labour organization would become the 'basic' type of labour unit in the eleventh Five Year Plan.[26] The earlier brigade methods were a collection of individual job specifications with workers having individually targeted assignments and being paid according to their personal output. The contemporary system, however, seeks to specify inputs, output and wages for a group of workers (the brigade) as a whole. They work on a given contract (*ediny naryad*), rather than on individually priced tasks. Such brigades may be organized by a given shift[27] or 'vertically',[28] the latter being appropriate when the process of production transcends more than one shift. Such brigades have the advantage of being able to include not only line workers, but technicians and auxiliary workers—loaders, controllers, crane operators, machinery maintenance and repair personnel.[29] Specialized and complex brigades may be organized on a shift basis or across several shifts. They have been found to operate successfully in both mass and small-batch production.[30]

By 1984, 18.4 million industrial production workers out of a total of 37.9 million were organized into 1.519 million brigades. While the desired size of brigade should be about 25, in 1983, it averaged eleven and a third of all brigades had less than five members.[31] There were 732,000 'complex' brigades with 10.6 million workers, and 787,000 'specialized' brigades with 7.7 million participants. In 1984, 15 million brigade members (1.21 million brigades) were on 'single contract' (i.e. they were given a total sum for completion of the output target).[32] By 1984, it was reported that 65.6 per cent of workers in brigades were on job assignments linked to final pay.[33] While these data show a considerable rise in the number of brigades,[34] even in 1984 half of the total number of production workers were not organized in them.

A distinguishing feature of the contemporary brigade method is that management gives the brigade a volume production target and goals for numbers of workers employed, and quality.[35] It takes responsibility for arranging the organization of inputs—use of materials, deployment of labour and the distribution of wages. The brigade has a yearly subcontract on the basis of which a monthly assignment for output is given; it also has a wage fund, an average wage, a given workforce, a labour productivity growth quota, and expenditure for tools and supplies.[36] This is known as a full accounting (*khozraschetny*) system which is often regarded as the essence of the new type brigade system.[37] In cases where time is essential to the contract (e.g. completing buildings), bonuses may be given for early finishing; this is called *akkordnaya oplata*. An assumption of the system is that the factory management does not interfere with the organization and work process of the brigade. Intermediate calculation by the management of payments for fulfilling operations is superseded by the brigade which distributes pay among its members. Hence the brigade, rather than the individual, becomes an accounting and work unit. However, Yu. Balatin (Chairman of the USSR Committee on Labour and Wages) pointed out that in 1983 only 15 per cent of brigades were working to *khozraschet*.[38] By 1985 this figure had reached only 20 per cent, to the concern of Gorbachev.[39]

It is well known in all industrial societies that when workers are priced on individual piecework rates, they maximize wages by working slowly when tested. Thus a rate for the job is secured by a minimum of effort at the cost of low productivity. A brigade contract, it is believed, will overcome this underworking. In order to maximize income, fellow workers will 'pressurize' each other to work harder and to increase productivity. As Gorbachev has put it:

In a brigade every person is on view, and the members of the collective themselves evaluate the extent of everyone's participation in joint work. Here the principles of social justice are more fully realised, both in earnings and in other material and moral forms of incentives. Here it is difficult to frinagle and hide behind the backs of others; the link between pledges and the final results of production is more clearly evident.[40]

Incentives should be determined collectively by the brigade council (*sovet*). Such payments should reflect effort and skill on the part of individual workers. If wages accurately reflect effort and work, it is believed that workers will be more satisfied and the psychological well-being resulting from membership of a brigade will lead to reduced labour turnover.

There are many forms that brigades may take.[41] Specialized (*spetsializirovannye*) brigades are formed of workers with the same trade (e.g. lathe operators). These are not the most appropriate for the goals of contemporary brigades as they tend to be based on individual job assignments—disaggregated by the brigade—rather than on combined work contributing to a whole product. Complex (*kompleksnye*) brigades are made up of a group of workers having many skills covering the production of a given product or of one component part of a product. In these brigades, workers combine many tasks and skills.

## CALCULATION OF WAGES

There is no standardized formula for the distribution of pay within the brigade. The brigade soviet, or council, is responsible for distributing if not the overall wage, then at least the bonus part. In practice, there are three ways in which workers are remunerated. First, equally to all members—this method is often adopted in small brigades with undifferentiated levels of skills and experience.[42] Second, and most generally, workers are paid the basic rate for their skill category (*razryad*), but their bonuses are calculated according to their contribution to the brigade's work. Third, a system of coefficients has been introduced at some enterprises to determine each individual's contribution to the collective's work. This is called the KTU (*koeffitsient trudovogo uchastiya*, or coefficient of labour participation): by this method, workers are evaluated on the basis of their work effort by the brigade council. This involves estimating initiative used, capacity for work in other jobs, intensity of work and conscientiousness; and the KTU may be reduced for poor discipline or poor work.[43] The value of defective work may be calculated and not only will an individual's KTU be reduced but also the whole brigade may suffer a loss. This encourages workers in brigades to reduce defective products and to pass on skills to inexperienced workers.[44] But in 1983, such coefficients were used only by 30.6 per cent of all brigades.[45] Coefficients are set monthly for members by the brigade council. This not only attempts to distribute wages more equitably to the workforce but also attempts to eliminate the practice of the 'levelling' of wages:

Unfortunately at many enterprises it is normal to 'pull up' [*vyvesti*] wages, using every possible supplementary payment, bonus etc. . . . so that a worker does not get less than a certain level. This means that payment is not made for 'concrete' work, but on the basis of an 'average', so that a worker is not offended, and does not go off to another factory - this leads to 'levelling', the 'stimulating' role of the rouble is reduced and labour is less efficient. . . . A worker knows that if he works badly, his wage will nevertheless be raised. One way of solving the problem is to have brigades with 'economic accounting' [*khozraschet*]* which ensures that one receives according to one's labour, providing that brigades are guaranteed normal work. The brigade system of payment is also designed to eliminate 'peak' wages, earned by favoured workers doing well paid [*vygodnye*] operations.[46]

---

* 'Economic accounting' (*khozraschet*) means that the cost of all production inputs (materials, energy, labour) are considered in the calculation of the brigade's earnings.

Brigades receive bonuses for the overfulfilment of targets and for savings in materials and, by the same token, deductions in remuneration are made for non-fulfilment of targets and for excessive expenditure on materials.

## PARTICIPATION IN ADMINISTRATION

The brigade method should not be conceived of as solely an instrumentality to get workers to work harder. It is also thought that it may overcome the 'dissatisfaction' with work experienced in the advanced division of labour and the 'fractioning' of the process. Western firms in the 1970s and 1980s have attempted to improve productivity, reduce turnover and motivate the workforce by various forms of job design and work organization. Job enlargement schemes involving workers combining similar types of jobs (horizontal job rotation) and job-enrichment (combining different jobs such as maintenance, service and repair— vertical regrouping) have been successfully practised.[47] The introduction of 'semi-autonomous groups' or 'group technology' has been advocated and tried. Briefly, such schemes in the West give the responsibility to a group of workers to rotate jobs (they have been trained to do all the jobs required) and work as they wish to meet their production targets.[48] These experiments are similar to those tried in the USSR. The foreman is made redundant and workers are given greater responsibility for their work. Such schemes in the West, however, have had only limited success. Trade unions particularly have been opposed to their introduction as they are believed to infringe union power. Management has also had reservations: the schemes destroy the traditional forms of control both by the foreman and by management's control of job design. Western firms are also subject to intense competition and the short-term costs of such initiatives cannot be passed on to consumers, however desirable the forms of work reorganization from a social point of view.

In the USSR, O.F. Balatski, writing in *EKO* points out:

The fractioning of the work process leads on the one hand to an increase in efficiency but, on the other hand, work becomes more and more monotonous— research shows that after a certain stage has been reached in the division of labour, productivity stops growing or even drops . . . . In order to make labour more attractive, to give it more content, it is necessary to look for new forms of labour organization such as the 'complex' brigade, based on an end product . . . . The growth in the volume of production, the more complicated links between enterprises and sub-divisions, narrow specialization and differentiation of operations, all complicate the management process . . . . The active participation of all workers in management increases their creative interest in the results of labour and forces them to make more effective use of the reserves of productivity growth.[49]

Balatski points to the example of American and Japanese motor companies creating work teams for assembly and the consequent rise in work satisfaction.

The importance of the system of production relations is emphasized by Pavlov and Gavrilenko. Writing in *Literaturnaya Gazeta*,[50] they point out that unless workers participate in administration, they may 'feel like hired [*naemny*] workers'. Having drawn attention to the fact that wage rates have risen faster than productivity, they point out that a real *khozyain* (boss, or owner) would not pay himself more than he produced. They point out that the link between collective ownership and management of production is weak. Hence workers consider not the end-product and the interest of the production unit as a whole (*obshchego dela*) but their own individual interest. Participation in the management of production is advocated to heal this rupture. The objective of reform on the shopfloor should be to create a subjective feeling on the part of the worker of being an owner (*khozyain*) of the enterprises. The brigade system is advocated as a means to this end. It may overcome the disjunction between management and workers to some extent by devolving many of the decisions of the management to the work unit. At the Kaluga turbine works, which is often cited as an example of good practice,[51] brigades not only linked wages to production tasks but improved the participation of management in production at all levels.

In many cases, as at Kaluga, members of the brigade councils are elected by open ballot at general meetings of the brigades. Each council must include a production foreman, a trade union organizer, and a *brigadir* as chairperson.[52] The brigade councils have to be distinguished from the council of brigade leaders (*brigadirs*).

Brigade leaders are a crucial link in the chain. Ideally, conscientious and efficient workers are selected and some have been assistant foremen; full-time training of two to three months is sometimes carried out by the Ministry.[53] The *brigadirs* also have their own factory council to which they are elected (presumably by all the *brigadirs*) for a two-year period; the council operates under the leadership of the factory trade union committee and the section of the administration concerned with labour and wages.[54] The yearly plan is confirmed by a general meeting of all *brigadirs* and quarterly ones by the council of *brigadirs*.[55] *Brigadirs* and budding *brigadirs* attend courses, organized by the appropriate Ministry, where they learn good practice. Some schools for *brigadirs* have been founded under the auspices of various Ministries.[56] The brigade leaders report directly to the factory director with whom they should have a good rapport.

At some enterprises, the functions of foreman and *brigadir* are combined. Obviously, the rise of the *brigadir* seriously affects the position of foreman and Yu. Batalin has noted the need for a new definition of the latter's role.[57] B. Molodtsov, writing in *Pravda*, suggests that the role of the *brigadir* will be to take over the personnel and disciplinary functions, leaving the foreman to deal with the engineering aspects of production.[58] In many cases the brigade council has taken upon itself as much as 70 per cent of the decisions previously made by the foreman.

A more collective attitude towards work may be engendered by the brigade system and workers may begin to feel more like 'masters' of their enterprise, reflecting collective ownership of the means of production. The effects then should be to increase labour productivity. A workers' assembly (*sobranie*) is held monthly, allowing discussions by the rank and file of production assignments, quality of product, productivity, waste, discipline and the distribution of wages.[59] Mutual help becomes more of a feature of the brigade method. After studying brigade and individual work at 21 factories in Irkutsk, Bronshtein points out that it is normal with piece-work organization for members of the collective to go home and leave one comrade and the foreman to complete unfinished work. In brigades, the *brigadir* and all members have the responsibility to complete the work and consequently all are prepared to 'muck in'.[60]

The brigade system should bring together leading personnel

within the enterprise to help liaise with the management. The factory director should participate in the deliberations of the council of *brigadirs* and the chairperson of the council of *brigadirs* should be in 'constant contact with the factory chief'.[61] Brigade councils (*sovets*) composed of the *brigadir*, the representatives of the Party, trade union and Komsomol and leading (*peredovye*) workers are formed which help integrate the workers into the factory administration.[62] The participation of Party and trade union representatives ensures consistent administrative and political control and prevents the brigades from becoming competing political units to Party and union.[63] The presence of such influential people helps to make the brigade councils authoritative.[64]

The initiative for the formation of a brigade soviet is often taken by the factory Party group.[65] The *brigadir* is appointed by the management of the enterprise, after consultation with the foreman and members of the brigade,[66] and this procedure is in keeping with the principle of 'one man management'. The brigade system is introduced by a decision (*prikaz*) of the management and not at the initiative of the workforce;[67] however, the trade union committee should be consulted.[68] When the brigade system was introduced at the *Krasny Ekskavator* factory, for example, it was planned by the factory's general director, the Party Secretary and the chairman of the factory trade union committee.[69] The *prikaz* defines the composition of the organizational committee responsible for the planned changes.[70] At this preparatory stage intense campaigns (*agitkampaniya*) take place to break down psychological opposition to change.[71] Once brigades are formed the administration still retains authority over signing on new workers, though the views of the brigade may be taken into account.[72] At the Frunze bicycle factory former employees are only taken on if a particular brigade will accept them.[73] The management thus remains in control of personnel and planning of the enterprise targets. The brigade possesses devolved authority over the work activity of its members and over levels of pay of individuals. At Kaluga, meetings took place twice a month between the heads of brigades and the factory director. Decisions made by the brigade leaders' council, after confirmation by the director, have the force of orders of the combine.[74]

A form of social control is established by members of the brigades. As researchers writing in *Sotsiologicheskie issledovaniya* put it: 'no one is interested in having a poor worker in the brigade, as this affects the "end results" and overall brigade pay'.[75] The brigade heightens the effectiveness of the teaching of new workers for 'practically the entire brigade acts as a collective mentor to new brigade members'.[76] For the same reason, job demarcation disputes are avoided and members have an interest in developing multiple skills in order to substitute for each other. Sociological research conducted in machine tool factories in the Ukraine found that 84 per cent of workers in brigades working on a single contract thought it normal to help their fellow workers, compared to 42 per cent working on individually priced jobs. It was also found that workers in brigades began on their own initiative to learn other jobs, so that they could stand in for each other.[77] On the basis of a survey of workers in 21 factories in Irkutsk, it was found that many more workers in brigades intended to learn another trade. The reasons differed considerably: for 'individual' piece workers (i.e. not in brigades) the main motivation (41 per cent of respondents) was at the request of the foreman (master) and next (29 per cent) was to fulfil the plan; for brigade workers, 62 per cent said it was the fulfilment of the plan for the collective, the second most frequently cited reason (17 per cent) was to make work more interesting.[78] This in turn may increase job satisfaction and reduce turnover.[79]

## LABOUR PRODUCTIVITY

Increasing labour productivity is considered to be a major object of the brigade system. As the Chairman of the USSR State Committee on Labour and Wages has put it:

A major area of the effort to achieve a cardinal increase in labour productivity is the strengthening of collectivist principles and the effective utilization of the brigade form of the organization of labour and incentives. We see the basic task here as uniting the development of the most progressive types of brigades with measures for improving the system of the management of socialist enterprises. This organic unification will be achieved primarily through the contract form of the organization of labour and pay.[80]

Labour productivity is improved by workers themselves having an incentive to 'shed surplus labour'. If production is overfulfilled

with less than the assigned number of workers, supplementary pay
is increased by 1 per cent for every percentage overfulfilled up to
a limit of 10 per cent.[81] The wage fund for the brigade is not
reduced if the number of workers falls below that authorized in the
contract.[82]

A study of brigade contracts in the Gomsel'mash production
combine in one quarter of 1979 found that the total workforce had
declined by 9.1 per cent on average; output per worker had
increased by 13.2 per cent and the maximum and minimum
earnings had risen by 1.7 per cent and 8.3 per cent respectively
(comparisons made with previous year). Some brigades had
reduced the labour force from 10 per cent to 13 per cent a year
whilst maintaining the volume of production.[83] A survey of 21
enterprises in Irkutsk reported in 1982[84] found that, in
comparison with individual piece-workers, the brigade form of
organization had 20 per cent higher labour productivity and
turnover was 40 per cent lower.[85] A report of a brigade in the
building industry working in Siberia found that the average wage
was 476 roubles (compared to 300 roubles for a comparable
group), fewer workers were employed (80 compared to 400 of
another comparable administration). The *brigadir* remarked to the
*Pravda* correspondent:

it seems to me that in Western Siberia it's possible to reduce the number of
construction workers by a least one-third, if not by one-half. . ... Why should we
keep people on if we can't properly provide them with work? We're paying a high
price, and I don't mean wages—we're corrupting the workers, accustoming them
to an easy living. This applies not only to workers but to the managerial staff as
well.[86]

Hence brigades are a method of legitimating reductions in the
workforce. Indirectly, the acceptance of responsibility by the
brigade for *khozraschet* reduces the numbers of administrative
personnel: documentation is reduced and so is the need for norm-
setters, quality control inspectors and sector chiefs.[87] The Vice-
Chairman of the USSR State Committee on Labour and Social
Questions points out that foremen under the brigade system should
be capable of a larger workload and should be able to supervise
two or three brigades—i.e. 50–75 workers instead of 25.[88]

With the introduction of brigades at Kaluga, labour turnover
dropped to a quarter of its previous level. Productivity grew

enormously in the first year of work with the new brigades, it rose from 15−20 per cent, a third of the increase in labour productivity was claimed to be due to the brigade methods, but wages rose much less (at just over the average for the industry).[89] Similar results have been claimed at different times for other industries. In the building industry, a famous brigade named after the builder N.A. Zlobin was formed in the early 1970s and it succeeded in building a 14-storey block of apartments in 155 days instead of 235. The Soviet press is full of accounts of the successes of brigades. B. Molodtsov, writing in *Pravda* about the Orekhovsk cotton factory, reported that after the introduction of brigades, hourly output increased by 4−5 per cent, labour discipline was much improved and idle-time was down 2−3 per cent.[90] An account of the Elektrosignal factory in Novosibirsk recounts that with the introduction of a complex brigade system, lagging behind plan targets ceased. In one shop targets were subsequently fulfilled by 50 workers instead of 65, the number of rejects also declined; in another shop, with 15 per cent fewer than the planned number of workers, output rose 5.6 times and wages doubled.[91] In 1985, it was reported that a brigade in Vladimir saved 2617 person days (20,800 roubles) in a year, and workers in the brigade received 316 roubles in bonus.[92] In the Ukraine, a review of brigade activity found that when it was introduced absenteeism and labour turnover fell, and productivity rose. At another factory where experiments with brigades were tried, productivity was 2.7−4 times higher than the republican average. Turnover dropped from 13.5 per cent in 1975 to 10.8 per cent in 1979.[93] In one factory, labour turnover had declined from 27 per cent to 15 per cent.[94] I. A. Lanshin (Chairman of the Central Committee of the Trade Union of Workers in Construction and the Building Materials Industry) has claimed that the introduction of brigade methods in building would increase productivity by 3.1 per cent. He advocates the setting-up of brigades of 40−60 workers.[95] A study of the work of more than 1000 brigades by NII truda and Gostomtrud, reporting in 1983, found that in the year of formation, brigades on average improved labour productivity by 5−6 per cent, in the next year it usually rises 6−8 per cent and in the third year, 8−9 per cent. For workers not in brigades in these branches, labour productivity only improved 2−3 per cent.[96] It was found that in the brigade system, wages rose less than productivity: prior to the introduction of brigades the coefficient of productivity increase to wage increase was 1:72, afterwards it was 1:65;[97] also the average level of worker grade (*razryad*) increases from 3.1 to 3.5 with the movement to brigade status.[98] Workers, it may be assumed, have greater opportunity and incentives to raise their levels of skill.

## DIFFICULTIES IN FORMING BRIGADES

Articles in the Soviet press indicate, nevertheless, that the introduction of the brigade system is not without difficulties. Sometimes brigades will be set up only in a 'formal' sense without any changes in organization and accounting.[99] Quite often management does not see the advantage in introducing them. There are often no improvements in economic indicators after their introduction—rises in labour productivity, for instance, may be achieved through working overtime.[100] The administrative context is often not conducive to the effective operation of the brigade system. Irregularity in the supply of materials, the breakdown of machinery and inefficient servicing leads to the non-fulfilment of the output targets.[101] In January 1985 an article in the trade union newspaper, *Trud*, pointed out that the productivity of brigades in building was slowing because of the shortage of supplies and unevenness of delivery. Sometimes (the same writer points out) equipment costs rise during the plan period and subsequently bonus payments are reduced.[102] The logic of the brigade system is that *all* members will be penalized because they are commonly tied to the planned output. Thus collectives often break up and revert to the former individual norms because under such conditions fewer workers will be penalized if the product is not completed.

Changes in enterprise organization are essential to ensure that brigades, when introduced, operate efficiently and effectively. Sometimes after the changeover to a single contract insufficient technical preparation is made and initially productivity and wages drop; this leads to distrust of the new methods.[103] The optimum size of brigade must be related to the process of production, and the mere copying of practice of other brigades (say Kaluga) will lead to poor results.[104]

The advantages of brigades are lost if only part of the enterprise is organized. In 1980, one-shift brigades predominated, and a third of brigades had fewer than five workers. This effectively excludes workers from participation in the management of production, as they concentrate narrowly on their work tasks.[105] The importance of vertical or intershift (*skvoznye*) brigade structures is often emphasized as a means of gaining increases in productivity,[106] but this is often difficult to achieve. Sometimes factory chiefs set up an 'exemplary brigade' and *brigadir* in order to impress higher authorities.[107] Some enterprises also have a poor evaluation of the potentiality of the system.[108] The introduction of brigades creates a powerful form of worker association which may criticize the administration, for a whole group of workers becomes aware of, and has a material interest in, efficient management. It therefore becomes more arduous for the management than dealing with individual workers who may become resigned to breaks and interruptions in production.[109] Hence management may be reluctant to adopt the brigade system and have a negative evaluation of it.

Sometimes the brigade system operates to subvert the planning system. Rather than brigades being conditioned in reaching output targets, they attempt to negotiate levels of plan assignments.[110] Auxiliary workers (storemen, stock handlers) are also often excluded from the scheme. In 1982, for example, only 10 per cent of auxiliary workers were in brigades. White-collar and engineering-technical workers are usually excluded from the brigade system, though a Party-government resolution of December 1982 called for large all-purpose brigades to include engineering and technical personnel and production organizers.[111] It is often suggested that their pay should also be dependent on the success (or failure) of brigades.

One of the main reasons for opposition to the brigades is that some workers fear that collective responsibility and a levelling of pay will reduce their status on the shopfloor.[112] In an attempt to explain the reluctance of workers to form brigades, Bronshtein studied the characteristics of workers in brigades and those who did not wish to work in them. The average age of workers opposed to joining brigades was 11 years older than the factory average. They also had longer than average length of service at the factory. They were skilled workers, earning on average 295 roubles (67 roubles more than the average factory wage). The level of education was lower than average. These workers had the well-paid (*vygodny*) jobs, they had good relations with the foremen, received low targets to increase productivity and, due to their experience, enjoyed a high status in the collective. Such workers used their influence to minimize rises in annual output norms and rises in productivity.[113] Hence it would appear that a sort of 'aristocracy' of labour with high levels of skill, wages and experience has a material interest in opposing the brigade system. To overcome such problems it is often contended that such organization should be extended to encompass the whole factory as a brigade system.[114]

A more negative evaluation of the operation of the brigade system has been made by Nina Maksimova on the basis of visits to five machine tool and ferrous metallurgy enterprises.[115] The thrust of her article is that the brigade system develops 'instrumental' mercenary attitudes among brigade members who become estranged one from another. Some brigades do not want untrained workers because initially they lower productivity; the increased speed of operations leads some workers purposely to disrupt production to earn rest periods. After initial hikes have been made in productivity, further increases become progressively harder and brigades again begin to conceal reserves. Working out the coefficient of labour participation creates friction among the brigade members, as disagreements arise about the relative efficiency and personal contributions of different members, and subjective evaluations frequently occur. Participation in brigade meetings and by the *brigadirs* were often inadequate and management often usurped the position of *brigadir* or chose brigade leaders to their liking.

The inertia of management in introducing, and of the workers in accepting, the brigade system is to be overcome through the activity of the Party organization. The Party factory group has a particular role to play in combating inertia and demanding a new style of leadership from the management.[116] The 1982 resolution calls upon republican and lower Party organizations to get going the brigade form of organization. Party primary groups in enterprises should help to mould 'a healthy moral and psychological climate, [to develop] labour and public awareness, [to instil] in the collective's members a lofty responsibility for the

fulfilment of plan assignments and adopted socialist pledges . . ..
[T]he primary [Party] organizations at enterprises should set up
Party commissions for monitoring management's activity in
introducing the brigade form of labour and heightening its
effectiveness.'[117] The trade unions have been called on to be more
vigilant in bringing to task managers who break agreements.[118]

## EVALUATING BRIGADES

Press reports and individual accounts of the difficulties of
industrial organization are useful in portraying perceptions of
correspondents, but one can never be sure of their
representativeness. A number of studies have been made by
sociologists which have attempted to examine empirically and
objectively the progress of the brigade system. A study in
1982–83 by Ille and Sinov[119] of nine machine tool factories
located in eight cities interviewed 1684 workers in 211 brigades
and 329 representatives of the shopfloor administration. They
found many deficiencies in the organization of brigades. Of those
surveyed 54.2 per cent said that they had not learned to use their
rights in the brigades. (It has been reported, for instance, that the
administration distributes wages and defines the parameters of
KTU.)[120] About 40 per cent of those surveyed considered that the
administration was not interested in giving workers real rights to
control the management, and 30 per cent thought that the
administration encouraged participation but ignored their
suggestions.[121] Participation in the shop councils was also
irregular: a quarter of workers polled had not been to a meeting in
the previous year, and 40 per cent had not attended more than three
or four times. However, the majority of workers surveyed found
that in the brigade system work was more varied, interesting and
testing. Another study of workers in the Kostroma electric supply
found that 75 per cent of manual workers and 72 per cent of
engineering and technical workers approved of the transfer to the
brigade system; 50 per cent thought that pay and work safety had
improved, 40 per cent thought that norming, participation in
production and relations with the foremen had improved. In
addition, those interviewed thought that work efficiency could be
enhanced by improvements in work conditions (72 per cent), pay
(64 per cent) and organization of labour (59 per cent).[122]

E. I. Khrishchev has reported on research conducted at 20 industrial enterprises in Kishinev, Moldavia in 1976 and 1982.[123] Between 1976 and 1982, it was found that the number of respondents favourably disposed to the development of the brigade method increased (80 per cent in 1982 compared to 69 per cent in 1976). The researchers compared the respondents' attitudes to various aspects of labour: they were analysed into three categories: high, middle and low levels of satisfaction. Some of the data are shown in Table 8.1. The totals of categories (high, middle and low) sum to 100 per cent; only 'low' and 'high' satisfaction is shown in the table.

*Table 8.1:* *The Distribution of Workers by Degree of Satisfaction with Different Aspects of Labour Activity in Production Brigades in Enterprises in Moldavia, 1976 and 1982. (% of total surveyed)*

| | Level of Satisfaction | | | |
| | High | | Low | |
| Aspect of Labour Activity | 1976 | 1982 | 1976 | 1982 |
|---|---|---|---|---|
| Relations to labour collective | 52 | 79 | 18 | 11 |
| Relations to administration | 60 | 64 | 19 | 16 |
| Level of safety | 81 | 70 | 13 | 18 |
| Content of labour | 51 | 64 | 22 | 16 |
| Organization of labour | 71 | 60 | 21 | 26 |
| Participation in management | 40 | 52 | 31 | 24 |
| Perspective of growth of production | 39 | 59 | 19 | 17 |
| Level of payment of labour | 58 | 56 | 18 | 27 |
| Level of mechanization of labour | 42 | 56 | 26 | 23 |
| Organization of material supply | 50 | 55 | 27 | 25 |
| Physical stress | 43 | 52 | 36 | 31 |
| Hygiene at workplace | 41 | 51 | 39 | 34 |
| Nervous and psychological stress | 52 | 44 | 30 | 34 |

*Source*: E.I. Khrishchev, *Sotsiologicheskie issledovaniya*, no. 3 (1984), p. 54.

Table 8.1 shows that attitudes toward various aspects of labour by brigade members had improved between the two dates. By 1982, 79 per cent of brigade members had a high evaluation of the labour collective (52 per cent in 1976) and only 11 per cent had a low evaluation (18 per cent in 1976). The content of work, relations to the administration, participation in management, the 'perspective' on production all had higher positive scores in 1982 than in 1976. However, more workers felt that there was greater danger and there was more dissatisfaction with pay (27 per cent had a low satisfaction level in 1982, compared to 18 per cent in 1976), the level of nervous stress also rose ('high' satisfaction fell from 52 per cent in 1976 to 44 per cent in 1982). The more negative aspects may have been caused by some resentment at changes in wage differentials which were not compensated by increases in earnings, and the greater stress may have been due to a higher work rate and more complicated tasks. Khrishchev notes that less than half of the surveyed workforce had a high level of satisfaction on this score. This confirms the views of Maksimova, cited above.

The survey analysed changes by type of work unit. Over the six-year period, it was found that in brigades with a mixture of trades (*kompleksnye*), the levels of grade increased by 18 per cent, in single trade (*spetsializirovannye*) brigades it rose 14 per cent, and for those not working in brigades, only 6 per cent.[124] Greater initiative with respect to innovation was shown in the mixed trade brigades where 20 per cent of those surveyed had made suggestions, compared to only 8 per cent in single trade brigades.[125] Similarly, the brigade system led to greater demands on the part of their members compared to individual workers. The numbers of brigade workers dissatisfied with the activity of the permanent production meetings rose by 15 per cent (7 per cent for individual workers), people's control groups, 19 per cent (7 per cent) and with informational meetings and meetings with the director, 26 per cent (4 per cent). Khrishchev argues that the brigade method gives workers a greater awareness and interest in the affairs of the whole factory, whereas 'individual' workers focus on their own conditions and pay.[126]

Another study carried out in the Urals, soon after the introduction of brigade methods, compared brigade members and workers on individual piece-work jobs. It was found that the former were more dissatisfied with production conditions than the latter.[127] Table 8.2 shows that of brigade members 25 per cent were dissatisfied with the planning of work, 42.4 per cent with the condition of equipment, 33 per cent with the organization of work, and 32 per cent with the rhythm of work, those on piece-work were correspondingly more satisfied on all these counts.[128] The authors point out that such dissatisfaction is caused by poor organization of the brigades. Also when work is organized on an individual basis, organization is something abstract and only impinges when the individual's work is interrupted, in brigade methods, however, organization becomes magnified, as all administrative miscalculations affect the non-completion of the final project.

*Table 8.2:* Workers' Attitudes toward Various Aspects of the Production Situation (% of those surveyed)

|  | Brigade Members | Piece-workers |
|---|---|---|
| *Not satisfied with:* |  |  |
| Rhythm of work | 31.5 | 14.5 |
| Working conditions | 24.8 | 19.9 |
| Organization of work | 32.8 | 14.7 |
| Condition of equipment | 42.4 | 29.8 |
| Possibilities for occupational advancement | 18.3 | 14.5 |
| How work is planned | 24.9 | 15.1 |

*Source:* L.N. Kogan and A.V. Merenkov *Sotsiologicheskie issledovaniya,* no. 1 (1983), p. 90.

The brigade system acts collectively as a pressure group on management and exerts more influence than the sum of individual workers' grievances. Management subject to poor planning may resist the introduction of brigade methods because they are a threat to inertia.

Workers in brigades had a higher estimate of the use of their knowledge and abilities than those working individually. Their evaluations also increased over time, as may be seen from the data shown on Table 8.3.

Evaluations of various aspects of activity in work by three different forms of labour organization (mixed brigades, single-trade brigades and individual work) are shown on Table 8.4. The data cited refer to those with 'high' levels of satisfaction. The

*Table 8.3:    Evaluation by Workers of the Use of their Knowledge and Ability under Different Forms of the Organization of Labour. (% of those surveyed)*

| Form of Work | Estimate of Utilization of Knowledge and Ability | | | | | |
| | High | | Middle | | Low | |
| | 1976 | 1982 | 1976 | 1982 | 1976 | 1982 |
| --- | --- | --- | --- | --- | --- | --- |
| Individual | 32 | 18 | 40 | 36 | 28 | 46 |
| Single Skill Brigade | | | | | | |
| (Specialized) | 52 | 42 | 40 | 38 | 8 | 20 |
| Mixed Skills Brigade | | | | | | |
| ('kompleks') | 39 | 55 | 24 | 35 | 37 | 10 |

*Source*: E.I. Khrishchev, 'Sotsial'no-ekonomicheskaya effektivnost' brigadnogo podryada', *Sots. issled*, no. 3 (1984), p. 58.

results show that, in 1982, the mixed brigades had higher scores on nearly all indexes compared to the single-skill brigades and individual workers; conversely, those working outside brigades had lower levels of satisfaction than those in them. One exception may be noted: this concerns quality, in which individual workers excelled more than the other two groups. In order to fulfil output norms, those working in brigades may have had to 'rush' work, leading to poorer quality. In the mixed brigades, the index of good quality work only rose 4 points (from 56 to 60) between 1976 and 1980, and in the single-skill brigades it actually fell (from 78 to 64).

Considering the changes over time, a consistent pattern may be discerned of generally rising levels of satisfaction in the mixed-skill brigades, an uneven profile in the single-skill brigades and a decline in levels of satisfaction by those working outside brigades. One exception may be noted: those not in brigades improved considerably the deployment of advanced skills (a rise from 32 in 1976 to 51 in 1982). Of the workers surveyed in 1982, 73 per cent had a firm opinion about the brigade form of labour, 60 per cent considered that this form of organization and stimulation of labour undoubtedly contributed to the improvement of labour discipline and the improvement of the quality of work.[129]

*Table 8.4: Proportion of Workers with High Indexes in Various Dimensions of Work, by Different Forms of Labour Organization (%)*

| Index of Quality of Work | Mixed Brigades | | Single-Skill Brigades | | Working Outside Brigades | |
|---|---|---|---|---|---|---|
| | 1976 | 1982 | 1976 | 1982 | 1976 | 1982 |
| Fulfilling the tasks of shifts | 52 | 65 | 81 | 64 | 63 | 54 |
| Quality of products | 56 | 60 | 78 | 64 | 92 | 72 |
| Labour discipline | 70 | 84 | 65 | 54 | 49 | 55 |
| Efficient use of materials | 40 | 48 | 58 | 42 | 66 | 42 |
| Utilization of equipment | 59 | 68 | 72 | 34 | 52 | 36 |
| Participation in management of production | 59 | 55 | 20 | 26 | 16 | 18 |
| Participation in 'rationalization' | 23 | 16 | 21 | 12 | 26 | 3 |
| Mastering innovation | 38 | 45 | 30 | 33 | 42 | 36 |
| Diffusion of advanced skills | 41 | 60 | 40 | 44 | 32 | 51 |
| Participation in social activities | 60 | 73 | 22 | 33 | 23 | 36 |
| Aspiration to raise level of qualifications | 42 | 62 | 72 | 51 | 60 | 24 |

*Source*: Khrishchev, p. 58.

## CONCLUSION

Considered in the context of western developments in management and work organization, the brigade system has many positive attributes. Despite some drawbacks, the brigade system, if implemented, is likely to be an economic and social advance and will lead both to enhanced productivity and greater worker satisfaction. It combines the need for greater worker satisfaction and participation with economic stimulation which meets both the needs of the enterprise to improve productivity and the worker to benefit from the gains of productivity. While forms of worker participation in the USSR have been criticized as being inadequate by western writers, they do in practice involve very much more control over the job situation than do western experiments.[130] In the West workers *resist* management.[131] All schemes for worker participation (western and Soviet) are advocated within the context of production goals set by management. The brigade system combines job enlargement, job enrichment, job rotation, control of the work setting and participation in the design of the job process and the distribution of wages. The expectations for satisfying work are probably higher in the USSR than in the West and such schemes therefore would seem to be more appropriate.

The obstacles to the introduction of such 'semi-autonomous' groupings are quite different from the pressures in the West. In the USSR, the market does not have the same limiting effects. Enterprises are not subject to market pressures, and wage costs do not have comparable significance (they only imperfectly reflect demand and supply, and rises in wages or in prices do not lead to lay-offs or redundancies). Formal worker resistance to regrouping of skills orchestrated in the West by trade unions does not occur in the USSR. The dominant ideology sustains the notion of a unity of interest between management and employee. This is buttressed at all points by the Party organization (and by the trade unions). While resistance by workers to managements' attempts to raise the intensity of efforts occurs, there is an absence of any counter-ideology and organization sustaining worker opposition to the semi-autonomous group. Similarities with western types of resistance lie with management and with an 'aristocracy' of well-placed workers. The former sees the develpment of semi-autonomous groups of the brigade type not just as a challenge to their authority, but as a source of criticism of inefficiency and ineffectiveness. Individual workers with experience and authority in the enterprise likewise regard brigades as threats to their own status and privilege. The greater emphasis on an increased pace of labour effort through brigade pressure is likely to lead to some resistance on the part of workers who put a greater emphasis on the work place as a social community.[132]

## REFERENCES

1. This term is derived from the teaching of F. W. Taylor (an American born in 1856).
2. Craig R. Littler, 'Understanding Taylorism' *British Journal of Sociology*, vol. 29, no. 2 (June 1978), pp. 185-202.
3. John E. Kelly, 'Understanding Taylorism: some comments', *British Journal of Sociology*, vol. 29, no. 2 (June 1978), pp. 203-7; Henri Savall, *Work and People: An Economic Evaluation of Job-Enrichment* (Oxford: Clarendon Press, 1981), pp. 14-18.

4. Kendall E. Bailes, 'Alexei Gastev and the Soviet Controversy over Taylorism, 1918-24', *Soviet Studies*, vol. 29, no. 3 (July 1977), p. 378.
5. This contrast is brought out for Russia by Zenovia A. Sochor, 'Soviet Taylorism Revisited', *Soviet Studies*, vol. 33, no. 2 (1981), p. 248, and for capitalist societies by Kelly, *loc. cit.*
6. Savall is *not* here discussing the USSR (*op.cit.*, pp. 14-15).
7. G. Kozyrev, *Pravda*, 7 December 1984; abstracted in *CDSP*, vol. 36 no. 49 (1984), p. 5.
8. See the account in Sochor, pp. 250-1.
9. Bailes, p. 379.
10. Ibid., p. 380.
11. Ibid.
12. Ibid., p. 386-7.
13. Ibid., p. 390. See also Sochor, pp. 250-4.
14. Lenin emphasized that the Bolshevik government had 'to teach the people how to work': 'The Immediate Tasks of the Soviet Government' *Collected Works*, vol. 27, p. 259. Preobrazhensky also shared this view and attributed the 'dearth of a work ethic to the Russian national character'. Sochor, p. 257.
15. Cited by Sochor, p. 259.
16. Savall, pp. 18-21.
17. L.N. Kogan and A.V. Merenkov, 'Kompleksnye brigady: mneniya, otsenki, opyt, vnedreniya', *Sotsiologicheskie issledovaniya*, no. 1 (1983), p. 86. Brigades operate in agriculture and industry, only the latter is considered here. For an overview of the formation and operation of brigades, see M.V. Veller and A. Ya. Daugello, *Brigadnaya organizatsiya truda* (1983). For a short review of brigades in agriculture, see V. Gaevskaya, 'Kollektivny (brigadny) podryad v sel'skom khozyaystve', *Voprosy statistiki*, no. 2 (1985), pp. 37-42. As for agriculture: in 1983, 19 per cent of workers in state farms were in brigades and 17 per cent in collective farms. For an account in English, see D. Dyker, 'The Collective Contract and the 'Link' in Historical Perspective', RFE-RL 36/84, 20 January 1984. For an account by M. S. Gorbachev of the importance of the collective contract in agriculture, see *Pravda*, 19 March 1983. Translated in *CDSP*, vol. 35, no. 12 (1983), pp. 2-3.
18. O.F. Balatski, 'Tsel' - konechny resul'tat', *EKO*, no. 3 (1978), p. 151.
19. A. Dovba and A. Andrianov, 'Brigada - osnovnaya forma organizatsii truda', *Sots. trud*, no. 5 (1981), p. 92.
20. B.I. Fedorov, 'Skvoznye brigady—budushchee proizvodstvo', *EKO*, no. 2 (1980), p. 75.
21. For an experiment in industry in 1971, see L. Poklonski, 'Brigadny podryad v mashinostroenii', *Kommunist*, no. 5 (1977), pp. 42-3.
22. 'Brigadnaya forma organizatsii i stimulirovaniya truda', *EKO*, no. 3 (1980), p. 222.
23. L.N. Kogan and A.V. Merenkov, 'Kompleksnye brigady: mneniya, otsenki, opyt vnedreniya', *Sotsiologicheskie issledovaniya*, no. 1 (1983), p. 86.
24. L. Poklonski, 'Brigadny podryad v machinostroenii', *Kommunist*, no. 5 (1977), p. 42.
25. For a statement on the brigade system and the payment of wages, authorized

by Goskomtrud and the Secretariat of the Central Council of Trade Unions, see *Sots. trud*, no. 4 (1981), pp. 76-81. L.I. Brezhnev was an advocate of brigades and at the 17th Congress of Trade Unions, he called for their widespread introduction: *Trud*, 17 March 1982.

26. *Pravda*, 29 August 1979. Translation in *CDSP*, vol. 31, no. 30 (1979), p. 1.
27. *Smenny* (literally of the shift).
28. i.e. *skvoznye*, through several shifts.
29. A. Dovba and A. Andrianov, 'Brigada—osnovnaya forma organizatsii truda', *Sots. trud*, no. 5 (1981), p. 93.
30. Dovba and Andrianov, p. 92.
31. 'Razvitie brigadnoy formy organizatsii i stimulirovaniya truda', *Planovoe khozyaystvo*, no. 7 (July 1983), p. 102. The optimum size varies by industry and production process. Kulagin points out that in the machine tools, metal and wood working industries, the optimum numbers are 7−15 people for a one-man shift brigade, 14−30 for a two-shift brigade and 21−45 for a three-shift brigade. G.A. Kulagin, *Potentsial brigady* (1983), p. 52.
32. *Narkhoz v 1984g* (1985), pp. 143-4.
33. Ibid., p. 144.
34. In 1980, there were 1.068 million brigades with 10.765 million members, *Narkhoz v 1983g*, p. 132.
35. 'Razvitie brigadnoy formy organizatsii i stimulirovaniya truda, *Planovoe khozyaystvo*, no. 7 (July 1983), p. 103.
36. T. Baranenko, 'Rezervy ekonomikii rabochey sily', *Voprosy ekonomiki* (1980), no. 5, pp. 51-62, abstracted in *Problems of Economics* (February 1981), p. 18. Recommendations for introduction of the brigade system in industry, approved by the State Committee on Labour USSR and the Secretariat of the Trade Unions are published in *Ekonomicheskaya gazeta*, no. 1 (1984), p. 19.
37. A. Solodukha, 'Brigada i khozraschet', *Trud*, 15 April 1982.
38. 1.8 per cent in USSR Ministry of Meat and Dairy Industry, 2.5 per cent in the USSR Ministry of Food Industry and 3.7 per cent in the Ministry of Machinery for Light Industry and the Food Industry and for Household Appliances. Yu. Batalin, *Pravda*, 4 September 1984, summarized in *CDSP*, vol. 36, no. 36 (1984), p. 5.
39. M. S. Gorbachev, speech to Stakhanovites, *Pravda*, 21 September 1985. Translation in *CDSP*, vol. 37, no. 38 (1985), pp. 10-12.
40. Gorbachev, 21 September 1985, *loc. cit*, p. 11.
41. M.V. Veller, A.Ya. Daugello, *Brigadnaya organizatsiya truda*, (Moscow, 1983), pp. 7-11.
42. Baranenko, pp. 21-2.
43. The supplement to *Ekonomicheskaya gazeta*, no. 4 (1984) shows how it may be calculated. The brigade council notes each month the report of the *brigadir* which documents latecomers, early leavers, those with poor quality work and other deficiencies. It then confirms the KTU for each member of the brigade. O.F. Balatski, 'Tsel'—konechny resul'tat', *EKO*, no. 3 (1978), p. 156. This article contains examples of the calculation of individual workers' wages, p. 157. Some brigades, however, do not accept KTUs as they are too

complicated to work out. N.N. Oleynik and S.P. Gafanovich, 'Ot eksperimenta k praktike', *EKO*, no. 3 (1978), p. 164.

44. V.S. Petukhov, 'Oplata truda v brigadakh' *EKO*, no. 11 (1982), pp. 180-1.
45. Based on a study of over 1000 brigades in industry. I. Shapiro, 'Razvitie brigadnoy formy organizatsii i stimulirovaniya truda', *Planovoe khozyaystvo* no. 7 (July 1983), p. 104. Confirmed for USSR by Yu. Batalin, 'Effektivnost' brigadnogo truda', *Sovetskaya Rossiya* (December 1983), p. 1.
46. S. Koslov, 'Zarabotanny rubl', *Trud*, 30 April 1982.
47. For examples see C.R. Littler and G. Salaman, *Class at Work* (London: Batsford, 1984), pp. 80-90. H. Savall, *Work and People* (Oxford: Clarendon, 1981) pp. 60-3. Paul Thompson, *The Nature of Work* (London: Macmillan, 1983) pp. 138-44.
48. For an example from Volkswagen, see Littler and Salaman, pp. 82−3; on experiments in France, see Savall, pp. 64-71.
49. O.F. Balatski, 'Tsel'—konechny resul'tat', *EKO*, no. 3 (1978), p. 150.
50. A. Pavlov and E. Gavrilenko, 'Vybor iz dvukh zol ili put' treti?', *Literaturnaya gazeta*, no. 11 (17 March 1982).
51. The system was introduced in Kaluga in the early 1970s. *Literaturnaya gazeta*, no. 19 (1978), p. 11 and no. 20 (1978), p. 11. The Kaluga experiment was copied extensively in other industries. See the account by the minister of the ship building industry, M. V. Egorov, *Ekonomicheskaya gazeta*, no. 45 (1980), abstracted in CDSP, vol. 32, no. 46 (1980), pp. 7-8. By the end of the eleventh Five Year Plan, it was planned that the shipbuilding industry would have 75 per cent of its workers in brigades.
52. On Kaluga, see V. Chernov (chairman of the brigade leaders' council), *Ekonomicheskaya gazeta*, no. 45 (November 1980), abstract in *CDSP*, vol. 32, no. 46 (1980), pp. 7-8.
53. V. Shokun and E. Andryushchenko, 'Razvitie brigadnoy organizatsii truda v respublike. Chto pokazal analiz', *Sots. trud*, no. 3 (1981), p. 31.
54. M. V. Veller and A. Ya. Daugello, *Brigadnaya organizatsiya truda* (1983), p. 29.
55. Ibid.
56. In Minstroydormash, a 66-hour course on various aspects of the brigade system has been devised. V. Chudin, 'Razvitie brigadnogo metoda: sotsial'no-ekonomicheski i organizatsionny aspekty', *Partiynaya zhizn*', no. 3 (1983), p. 15.
57. Yu. Batalin, 'Effektivnost' brigadnogo truda', *Sovetskaya Rossiya*, (9 December 1983), p. 1.
58. B. Molodtsov, 'Upravlyaet brigada', *Pravda*, 17 November 1983, p. 2.
59. M. V. Veller and A. Ya. Daugello, *Brigadnaya organizatsiya truda* (1983), p. 28.
60. V. D. Bronshtein, 'Podvodnye kamni na puti k brigadnoy organizatsii truda', *EKO*, no. 7 (1982), pp. 134-5.
61. G. A. Kulagin, *Potentsial brigady* (1983), p. 55.
62. 'Tipovoe polozhenie o proizvodstvennoy brigade, brigadire, sovete brigady i sovete brigadirov' *Sots. trud*, no. 4 (1981), pp. 80-1.
63. G. A. Kulagin recommends that each brigade has its own party group, trade

union group and komsomol group; in small brigades the party and trade union organizers should participate. *Potentsial brigady* (1983), p. 54.

64. O.F. Balatski, 'Tsel—konechny resul'tat', *EKO*, no. 3 (1978), p. 154.
65. L. Poklonski, 'Brigadny podryad v mashinostroenii', *Kommunist*, no. 5 (1977), p. 45.
66. 'O brigadnoy organizatsiy', *EKO*, no. 11 (1982), pp. 173-5.
67. Ibid.
68. M. V. Veller and A. Ya. Daugello, *Brigadnaya organizatsiya truda*, (1983), p. 12.
69. V. Chudin, 'Razvitie brigadnogo metoda: sotsial'no-ekonomicheski i organizatsionny aspekty', *Partiynaya zhizn*', no. 3 (1983), p. 16.
70. Veller and Daugello, p. 12.
71. A. Levikov, 'Kaluzhski variant v Penze', *Literaturnaya gazeta*, no. 14 (6 April 1983), p. 12.
72. Ibid.
73. Ibid.
74. V. Chernov (chairman of the brigade leaders' council), *Ekonomicheskaya gazeta*, no. 45 (November 1980). Abstract in *CDSP*, vol. 32, no. 46, pp. 7-8.
75. L.N. Kogan and A.V. Merenkov, 'Kompleksnye brigady: mneniya otsenki, opyt, vnedreniya', *Sots. issled*, no. 1 (1983), p. 88.
76. T. Baranenkova, 'Reserves for Economizing the Workforce', *Problems of Economics* (February 1981) pp. 19-20. Translation of 'Rezervy ekonomii rabochey sily', *Voprosy ekonomiki* (1980), no. 5, pp. 51-62.
77. A. Tkachenko, 'Sotsial'no-vospitatel'naya rol' brigadnoy organizatsii truda', *Partiynaya zhizn*', no. 5 (1983), p. 28.
78. V. D. Bronshtein, 'Podvodnye kamni na puti k brigadnoy organizatsii truda', *EKO*, no. 7 (1982), p. 134.
79. Kogan and Merenkov, 'Kompleksnye brigady . . .', p. 86.
80. Yu. Batalin, *Pravda*, 4 September 1984. Summarized in *CDSP*, vol. 36, no. 36 (1984), p. 5.
81. 'Brigadnaya forma organizatsii i stimulirovaniya truda', *EKO*, no. 3 (1980), p. 221.
82. 'Dogovor brigadnogo podryada', *EKO*, no. 7 (1982), p. 129.
83. T. Baranenkov 'Rezervy ekonomii rabochey sily', *Voprosy ekonomiki* (1980), no. 5, pp. 51-62. Abstracted in Problems of Economics, February 1981, p. 21. Many other reports of the non-replacement of leaving workers and rising production due to the brigade method are to be found in the Soviet press. See for example, *Trud*, 22 October 1983, p. 2.
84. Bronshtein, pp. 132-9.
85. Ibid., p. 133.
86. G. Erlykov, *Pravda*, 27 April 1983. Text in *CDSP*, vol. 35, no. 17 (1983), p. 12.
87. Bronshtein, p. 133.
88. B. N. Gavrilov, *Ekonomicheskaya gazeta*, no. 47 (November 1980). Abstract in *CDSP*, vol. 32, no. 47 (1980), p. 9.
89. Data cited by N. Kozlov, *Ekonomicheskaya gazeta*, no. 45 (November 1980). Abstract in *CDSP*, vol. 32, no. 46 (1980), pp. 6-7. Overall in industry

during the tenth Five Year Plan, labour productivity rose by 17 per cent and the wage fund by 28 per cent.

90. B. Molodtsov, 'Upravlyaet brigada', *Pravda*, 17 November 1983, p. 2.
91. E. Solomenko (*Pravda* correspondent), 'Shipy i rozy', *Pravda*, 6 December 1983. For another account of the Elektrosignal factory, see 'Brigada na proizvodstve: segodnya i zavtra', *EKO*, no. 10 (1981), pp. 58-73.
92. N. Moskovtsev, 'Zarplata i premiya', *Trud*, 1 February 1985, p. 2.
93. See other examples in V. Shokun and E. Andryushchenko, 'Razvitie brigadnoy organizatsii truda v respublike. Chto pokazal analiz', *Sots. trud*, no. 3 (1981), p. 27. A report of the effects of the brigade method at the Frunze bicycle factory noted that breaches of labour discipline declined from 30-40 per day in 1975 to 3 or 4 on average in the early 1980s, labour turnover was also reduced to 6 per cent. A. Levikov, 'Kaluzhski variant v Penze', *Literaturnaya gazeta*, no. 14 (6 April 1983), p. 12.
94. M.E. Ille and V.V. Sinov, 'O razvitii samoupravleniya v brigadakh', *Sots. issled*, no. 3 (1984), pp. 63-4.
95. I.A. Lanshin, *Ekonomicheskaya gazeta*, no. 10 (March 1982). Abstracted in *CDSP*, vol. 34, no. 9 (1982), p. 9.
96. 'Razvitie brigadnoy formy organizatsii i stimulirovaniya truda', *Planovoe khozyaystvo*, no. 7 (July 1983), p. 100.
97. Ibid.
98. Ibid., p. 101.
99. 'Optimal'ny variant', *Trud*, 8 December 1983. Complaints about 'formalism' are widespread, and have been voiced by Yu. Batalin (Chairman of Goskomtrud), 'Effectivnost' brigadnogo truda', *Sovetskaya Rossiya*, 9 December 1983, p. 1.
100. V.P. Nezhdanov, 'V poiskakh "Zelenoy ulitsy"', *EKO*, no. 11 (1983), p. 88.
101. See accounts in 'Brigadny metod i radost' i ogorcheniya', *Sotsialisticheskaya industriya*, 15 December 1982.
102. Yu. Pogrebnyak, 'Strasti vokrug podryada', *Trud*, 23 January 1985, p. 2.
103. L. N. Kogan and A. V. Merenkov, 'Kompleksnye brigady: mneniya, otsenki, opyt, vnedreniya', *Sotsiologicheskie issledovaniya*, no. 1. (1983), p.90.
104. See the interesting article by I. Rudoka on the difficulties of defining the optimum size of brigade unit. 'Kollektivnaya organizatsiya: vremya stanovleniya. Kakoy byt' brigade?', *EKO*, no. 7 (1982), pp. 115-20, and A.A. Gorel'ski, 'Chto takoe brigadny khozraschet', *EKO* no. 7 (1982), p. 128-31.
105. Account of seminar on brigades in the engineering industry, N. Kozlov, *ekonomicheskaya gazeta*, no. 45 (November 1980). Abstracted in *CDSP*, vol. 32, no. 46, p. 6.
106. 'Brigadny metod . . .'.
107. A.A. Gorel'ski, 'Cho takoe brigadny khozraschet', *EKO*, no. 7 (1982), p. 126.
108. Examples given from the Ukraine, V. Shokin and E. Andryushchenko, 'Razvitie brigadnoy organizatsii truda v respublike. Chto pokazal analiz', *Sots. trud*, no. 3 (1981), p. 29.

109. This point has been made by the minister of one of the machine tool ministries. V. Chudin, 'Razvitie brigadnogo metoda: sotsial'no-ekonomicheski i organizatsionny aspekty', *Partiynaya zhizn'*, no. 3 (1983), p. 14. A. Dovba and Andrianov, 'Brigada—osnovnaya forma organizatsii truda', *Sots. trud*, no. 5 (1981), p. 98.

110. A.A. Gorel'ski, 'Chto takoe khozraschet', *EKO*, no. 7 (1982), p. 127.

111. *Pravda*, 4 December 1983. Summarized in *CDSP*, vol. 35, no. 49 (1983), p. 13.

112. L.N. Kogan and A.V. Merenkov, 'Kompleksnye brigady: mneniya, otsenki, opyt, vnedreniya', *Sots. issled* (1983), no. 1, p. 87.

113. Bronshtein, pp. 136-7. Bronshtein also points out that in 19 of the 21 factories studied, bonuses under the industrial piecework system could be granted as a supplement to income, without the production plan being fulfilled for the section or workshop. Under the brigade system, more effort has to be made to fulfil the plan, as bonus is only payable on completion of the end result rather than on various pieces of it.

114. This has been done at the Volga automotive plant (VAZ) and the Kaluga turbine plant. Kogan and Merenkov, *op.cit.*

115. Nina Maksimova, 'Brigady na pereput'e', *EKO*, no. 8 (1985), pp. 151-99.

116. A. Tkachenko, 'Sotsial'no vospitatel'naya rol' brigadnoy organizatsii truda', *Partiynaya zhizn'*, no. 5 (1983), p. 29.

117. *Pravda*, 4 December 1983. Abstracted in *CDSP*, vol. 35, no. 49 (1983), p. 13.

118. Yu. Pogrebnyak, 'Strasti vokrug podryada', *Trud*, 23 January 1985, p. 2.

119. M.E. Ille and V.V. Sinov, 'O razvitii samoupravleniya v brigadakh', *Sots. issled*, no. 3 (1984), pp. 59-64.

120. A.A. Gorel'ski, 'Chto takoe brigadny khozraschet', *EKO*, no. 7 (1982), p. 125.

121. Ille and Sinov, p. 61.

122. *Problemy ispol'zovaniya vysvobozhdeniya rabochey sily na predpriyatiyakh* (Ivanovo, 1982), pp. 93-6.

123. E. I. Khrishchev, 'Sotsial'no-ekonomicheskaya effektivnost' brigadnogo podryada', *Sots. issled*, no. 3 (1984). In 1976, more than 1200 people were surveyed and in 1982, 1300. These included 2000 members of brigades and 500 personnel working in administration (*rabotnikov apparata upravleniya*).

124. Ibid., p. 56.

125. Ibid.

126. Ibid., p. 57.

127. The research was conducted in the early 1980s at one of the largest factories in the Urals: 55 per cent of the workers were in brigades. Twenty per cent of the brigades were studied and those survey included a sample of workers in 50 'complex' (multi-trade) brigades.

128. L. N. Kogan and A.V. Merenkov, 'Kompleksnye brigady: mneniya, otsenki, opyt, vnedreniya', *Sots. issled*, no. 1 (1983), p. 90.

129. Khrishchev, p. 58.

130. Paul Thompson does not give sufficient attention to the participatory

activities of workers under socialism. *The Nature of Work* (London: Macmillan, 1983) pp. 217-27. Elizabeth Teague shows the limits of workers' power: 'The USSR Law on Work Collectives: Workers' Control or Workers Controlled?', in D. Lane (ed.), *Labour and Employment in the USSR* (Brighton: Wheatsheaf Books, 1986) pp. 242-4. On western forms of participation, see Savall, pp. 91-6.

131. On Britain see I. Maitland, *The Causes of Industrial Disorder* (London: Routledge, 1983) chapters 4 and 6 and Paul Thompson, *The Nature of Work* (London: Macmillan, 1983) pp. 167-70.

132. As one brigade member put it to Maksimova, 'We don't now talk while we work . . . and we don't get together afterwards for a drink'. (*loc. cit*).

# 9 Full Employment and Labour Shortage: The Direction of Change

In the foregoing analysis, it has been demonstrated that in distinction from capitalist societies, a very high rate of labour utilization is a feature of the Soviet economy. We may conclude that the Soviet labour market is characterized by: (a) the employment of a large proportion of the population leaving no 'reserve army' of unemployed or self-employed; (b) the under-utilization of labour at the place of work—'hoarding' or maintenance of labour reserves, and (c) a market shortage of labour: the labour market is a 'seller's market'. Labour utilization in the USSR is not characterized by mass unemployment. The main disutility is in various forms of underemployment. By underemployment one has in mind conditions in which persons are in paid employment but their labour is not used efficiently: they may be idle for all or part of the time, or their level of skill is higher than required in the job they do. The Soviet economy may be characterized as one of labour shortage and labour under-utilization. Shortage may be defined as a state in which effective demand for labour (or the number of jobs) outstrips supply. Labour 'shortage', however, is complicated by considerations of the efficient use of labour, by whether the supply of jobs is inflated, and by whether the requirements of production may be met by fewer workers. Such considerations involve technical, managerial, educational, psychological and cultural criteria.

Here I shall turn from empirical analysis to consider explanations of the full-employment low-wage economy character-istic of the USSR. First, I shall examine three general approaches to the socialist full-employment economy; second, I shall develop my own sociological paradigm (including elements from all three of these paradigms): and third, I shall indicate some probable developments in terms of reform in the USSR in the coming decade. In explaining the level of full employment (i.e. the 'quantity' of people at work) one should also take into account the nature of employment (i.e. the 'quality' of work). One needs to grapple with three distinct dimensions of the labour market: full employment at a macro-level, underemployment at a micro-level, and a general chronic shortage of labour. The effects of the Soviet labour market give rise to a strong bargaining position of labour at the place of work and to a regime of 'soft' labour discipline.

One may distinguish three explanations of the high though inefficient labour utilization rate in socialist societies. The first regards full employment as a positive consequence of government policy. A second interprets the labour market in terms of over-full employment and emphasizes the inefficient under-utilization of labour. A third considers the labour market in terms of systemic contradictions.

## THE GOVERNMENT POLICY APPROACH

The structure of the Soviet labour market and its ensuing problems are explained by many writers in terms of government policy. A socialist economy, it is argued, rests on public ownership and planning and ensures the maximum utilization of labour power. Workers are not left unemployed which is a social cost, but are utilized gainfully at work. Government policy under planning has a goal of providing work. The policy of a fully employed but low-paid workforce is a response both to the ideological imperatives and to the requirements of modernization under conditions of state ownership of the means of production and central planning. It fulfils the economic need to utilize the workforce, and at the same time it provides employment implementing the political objectives mentioned earlier. In the early period of Soviet power, industrialization and economic growth was the primary objective of the Soviet government, but once full employment had been achieved, it became a sacred element in Soviet social policy. The duty to provide full employment is derived from the legitimating ideology of Marxism—Leninism. From this point of view full employment cannot be abrogated without seriously weakening the integrity of Soviet society. The provision of full employment and the overcoming of alienation at work are legitimating factors for the regime in the world order. Soviet statesmen as well as philosophers and journalists point to the fact that 'the majority of representatives from the capitalist world, no matter what their political views or class background, recognize that the right to work is a great achievement of socialism. . . . Soviet society is a society of people at work' (*lyudi truda*).[1] There is an international dimension to internal policy: the weakening of a policy of full employment (perhaps more so than a decline in the rate of economic growth) would cast in doubt the Soviet claim to be a socialist state. The political framework, in which the Communist Party is legitimated as the expression of the interests of the working class, ensures that full employment is a priority. In essence, full employment is considered to be a consequence of socialist planning.

Shortage of labour and the under-utilization of labour are regarded by this school of thinkers to be imperfections—the unintended consequences of planning are due to 'lack of fit' between labour supply and labour demand. V. Medvedev, criticizing western conceptions of a 'deficit economy', considers that 'shortage' is not an innately inherent characteristic of a planned economy.[2] Deficits persist because of disproportions in planning and non-fulfilment of plan targets. Labour shortage occurs because of disruption in the system of production in which managers hoard labour reserves. The remedy is not merely adjustments of supply and demand but reform of the planning mechanism involving the liquidation of the discrepancy between money appropriations and material resources to coordinate the money supply with the improvement of labour productivity.[3] A. Kotlyar conceives of 'labour shortage' as a non-antagonistic contradiction which may be resolved through the strengthening of the planning mechanism.[4] Movement to 'intensive' production with rising productivity will lead to the reduction of the number of people employed in production; in time, a shift of labour to services will take place and a shortening in the length of the working day will occur.[5] Full employment of labour, however, will be ensured. Other sources of labour shortage are demographic considerations (fluctuating levels of birthrate, mismatch between geographical areas of industrial development and labour supply) and the education system 'lagging behind' changes in technology leading to an inappropriately skilled workforce; labour discipline and socialization are inadequate. Organizational methods are poor and enterprises are given too slack a wages fund or fail to improve productivity. Improvements in planning the size, training and discipline of the labour force are seen to be antidotes to the inefficient and wasteful use of labour. This line of reasoning is taken by most economic reformers in the USSR who believe that the existing structures need perfecting rather than changing in any significant way.

## THE NEED FOR A MARKET

Some western writers also explain labour shortage as due to deficiencies in the planning of labour but they see such deficiencies as an inherent part of the planning system.[6] Thus a second approach is to fault the system of planning as such. To raise labour productivity and the efficiency of labour some Soviet specialists and most, if not all, western economists, advocate the use (or greater use) of the market. Labour shortage and under-utilization are caused, it is argued, by wages being too low and insufficiently differentiated by market forces. Overemployment is a cause for sorrow not rejoicing. If the price of labour reflected supply and demand, there would be no chronic shortage at a macro-level (though 'frictional' unemployment would persist): a higher cost to the enterprise would stimulate its more efficient use and reduce overmanning, higher wage incentives would increase labour productivity. Wages would more accurately reflect the contribution of the worker to output, and labour mobility would be enhanced; real 'shortages' would be ended through the inflow of workers seeking higher wages. Wage differentials would reflect economic needs not political priorities. The development of a proper labour market would lead to the shedding of surplus labour, a pool of unemployed and the seller's market in labour would become a buyer's one. These policies involve major changes in the system of planning and the dismantling of a command economy. The forces of the market would replace many of the activities which are now subject to administrative control. The present high rate of labour utilization would fall; fewer people would be employed but they would be more effectively used and better paid.

It cannot be doubted that the 'market' in economics and politics has been a major innovation accompanying the rise and consolidation of capitalism both as a form of economy and in terms of bourgeois democracy. It has enlarged the area of individuals' positive freedom through giving more choice. However, the market has costs. The market militates against other values—those of community, and of control of the environment. As R.E. Lane has cogently argued, it restricts opportunities: amenities, privacy, cultural goods, safety, cleanliness and public goods generally.[7] Fulfilling market-generated needs reduces other forms of gratification and well-being—family, love, health, friendship.[8] It works against equality: choice is limited by unemployment under capitalism and labour markets are themselves socially stratified. Market capitalism has not secured full employment for the labour force. In Japan where there is job security in industry, this is limited to a relatively small proportion (18 per cent of the labour force) of 'permanent employees'. The registered unemployment rate of 2.5 per cent grossly under-represents the real level of unemployment—26 per cent of all female workers are part-time; in 1974, unemployment rates of 10 per cent for men and 40 per cent for females have been calculated. There is a large secondary labour market with low wages, high turnover, the absence of unionization and lack of unemployment insurance.[9] The market may generate needs for work and income that cannot be fulfilled and thereby create dissatisfaction. Market forces in the arena of the industrial enterprise severely limit job redesign and worker participation both of which, if introduced, would increase production costs. More important from a Marxist standpoint, impersonal market 'laws' put their outcomes outside direct human control. The market is the antithesis of a Marxist–Leninist worldview which sees conscious political control shaping human destiny, rather than impersonal economic forces. The market economy is a value in itself: as Milton Friedman has made explicit, the free market promotes a 'largely free society'.[10] Lurking behind 'free market' analyses are ideological preferences.

Reliance on the market is an unlikely and undesirable strategy to coordinate factors of production and to improve productivity and labour efficiency in the USSR. This is for three main reasons: experience of market societies has led western governments to intervene to promote public welfare, the ideological mental set of the Soviet leadership is alien to the market and the Communist Party will maintain its political control.

## SYSTEMIC CONTRADICTIONS

A third explanation of the present labour situation is in terms of systemic contradictions. Writers adopting this stance reject the assertion that the high levels of labour utilization are an intended result of planning. Planners, they argue, have little control over recruitment and labour supply. They have been unable to eradicate labour shortage and 'unemployment on the job', and their attempts at increasing labour productivity have not been successful. The working of the economic mechanism in socialist states leads to shortages not only of labour but also of other goods; a feature of the system is its incapacity to supply commodities in relation to effective demand. Concurrently, resources are not efficiently used—labour and capital are under-utilized. The operation of the economy is seen as the unintended consequences of individuals' and institutions' actions. Such writers would seek independent laws of a socialist economy in the same way as western economists and sociologists assume that capitalist economies have their own internal logic leading to depression and under-utilization of resources—particularly, labour unemployment.

It is important to stress that the socialist economy operates in quite a different political, administrative and ideological environment and consequently the laws or processes of capitalist economies cannot be applied. The major differences may be itemized as follows: (1) public ownership and planning give the socialist government a greater role over the economy and a responsibility to provide work for the citizen; (2) the ideological constraints make chronic unemployment an unacceptable economic and political cost; (3) demand and supply are not responsive to price as in capitalist economies; hence in the absence of significant structural change, 'freeing' the price system, in the sense of making it more like a western market one, will not resolve the pathologies of the labour market noted above.

In such a system a labour shortage concurrent with underemployment at the workplace is a systemic contradiction: it is, to quote Kornai, a 'consequence of the economic mechanism and of the institutional framework'.[11] This school of economists does not make any normative pronouncements about reform of the system; rather it is concerned in a behavioural sense to expose the operation of the economy.[12]

Janos Kornai is the best-known exponent of this approach.[13] He contrasts a 'resource-constrained' market for labour in socialist states with a 'demand-constrained' one under capitalism. The demand for labour is determined by the supply, the plan for labour is based on the forecast of employment constraints.[14] The plan consumes all available labour in the forecast which creates a shortage of labour. The system has an 'investment hunger' which uses resources and labour reserves.[15] Employers, to counter this deficit, inflate their demands for labour as expressed in their planned estimates. This in turn leads to 'unemployment on the job': 'the more frequent and intensive the labour shortage, the greater will be the internal slack, namely the unemployment on the job.'[16]

Effects of the labour shortage are the loosening of labour discipline, the deterioration of work quality and the lessening of workers' diligence. The security of employment gives rise to irresponsibility in anyone susceptible to it. Absenteeism exacerbates the shortage. Output becomes erratic and supply of commodities and services falls short of demand. Deficits characterize the wholesale market. Insufficiencies of supplies, materials and services in turn lead to slackness on the job,[17] creating 'storming' when they become available. Securing ample labour reserves, therefore, is a logical response by employers to meet their output targets. This hoarding tendency in turn increases the labour shortage and unemployment on the job making a vicious circle.

Kornai rejects the view that a policy of full employment may be explained solely in terms of government policy in socialist states: 'It is true that much depends on employment policy . . . yet an explanation of the process . . . depends on considerations deeper than mere government policy. It follows necessarily from the *system*; for if the system is resource-constrained, an almost unlimited hunger and expansion drive *must* prevail and then the potential reserve labour *must* be absorbed sooner or later.'[18]

It is when Kornai comes to analyse the political and social framework that his explanation is inadequate. He points out that the tolerance level of employment is a 'social phenomenon'.[19] Once 'given', only marginal changes are possible. Unemployment, he argues, cannot fall much below the minimum level caused by 'friction'. Employment, he notes, is not just work for a wage but is 'a way of life'.[20] Hence in socialist states, there is no fear of 'genuine' unemployment, only fluctuations around the normal participation rate.[21] He asserts that the state of the labour market has changed permanently under socialism—the behaviour of sellers of labour is *'characterized by guaranteed employment'*.[22] There is a 'control mechanism that drives [the] system . . . back to a normal state following deviation from it'.[23] Having dismissed the explanation of full employment as being due 'solely to a description of government policy measures', he insists that it be traced to 'intrinsic social forces'.[24] It is precisely here that Kornai's argument is lacking. While he makes reference in a general way to the institutional framework, he does not analyse the relationship between polity and economy.[25] Kornai emphasizes that 'definite social relations and institutional conditions generate definite forms of behaviour, economic regularities and norms'.[26] His focus is on the forces operating on the industrial enterprise and in the economic sphere, yet he lacks a macro-analysis of what shapes 'the forces operating on the enterprise' and determining the nature of the economy which give rise to 'shortage'. The role of values, the nature of exchange between economy and polity, and the legitimation process involving loyalty and solidarity are not dealt with in his work. It is precisely these areas, however, that shape expectations and are powerful constraints on the operation of the economy. It is to this wider social and political framework that I now turn.

## A SOCIOLOGICAL APPROACH

Whilst Kornai and others argue that employment and labour shortage are systemic characteristics of state socialism, their accounts lack analysis in terms of the social system. They describe the economic mechanism, but evade the societal and political dimensions. One reason for this, I suspect, is that Marxism is a systemic theory of society and in state socialist societies, a legitimating ideology. If the traditional Marxist model is brought into question by having insufficient power to explain the operation of the economy, then its role as a legitimating ideology is cast in doubt. Also, if the 'economic mechanism' is at the root of the inefficiencies of the system (rather than political institutions and ideological preferences) then *economic* reform is required to put things right (as opposed to systemic changes in power, property and ideological relations). In addition, economists by training have insufficient interest in, and knowledge of, theories of *society*, rather than models of the economy. When economic models break down, which they must do when applied to activity beyond their frame of reference, analysis relies on making discrete observations.

An attempt will be made here to develop a sociological model of the socialist labour market which may also be applied to other aspects of the economy. Full employment has to be explained in terms of values, forms of political and social integration, the fusion of politics and economics, as well as through the processes of the economy. The objective is to highlight the exchanges between the economy and its social and political environment.

The framework of societal analysis suggested by Talcott Parsons may be utilized. This involves four analytically distinct sub-systems of society: (1) the economy, (2) the polity, (3) the societal community, and (4) the cultural system. The *economy* needs little comment: it is concerned with production and distribution of commodities and services, labour is the major resource which turns natural objects into use-values. The *polity's* functions are to make decisions for the mobilization of resources, for the definition, making and attainment of society's goals. The *societal community* has to do with maintaining social control and integration including norms, law and coercion. The integration system has the role of coordinating the various parts of the system. The *cultural system* represents the goals which motivate people in society, and these are derived from the overriding values. The four sub-systems may be illustrated by four boxes designated by the letters A (adaptation), G (goal-attainment), I (integration), L (latency) (see Figure 9.1).

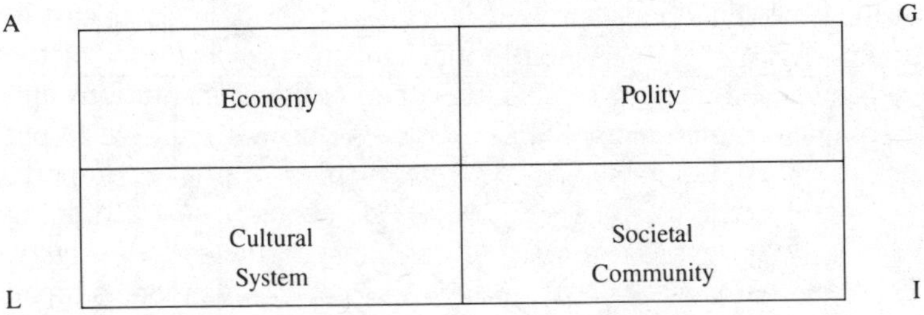

| A | | | G |
|---|---|---|---|
| | Economy | Polity | |
| | Cultural System | Societal Community | |
| L | | | I |

*Figure 9.1  Dimensions of society*

These analytical categories apply to all societies. Complex exchanges take place between these four sub-systems. But various societies have different ways of making such exchanges. First, I shall consider the interchanges described by Parsons which characterize a market system (he has in mind the USA); and second, I shall suggest how this model may be applied to socialist societies. From economic analysis, the notion of a moving equilibrium is applied to adjustments which continually happen. Parsons has described his scheme as one of 'the analysis of dynamic equilibriating processes'. (He notes, however, that equilibrium under capitalism does not always occur—exceptions are hyper-inflation and chronic shortages; wars, slumps and mass unemployment may also be added.) Exchange takes place between these systems in a way analogous to an economic model consisting of inputs (factors of production) and outputs (products) between each system. Links are established between the sub-systems through different media. Money serves as a medium for the economy, power for the polity, influence for the integrative sub-system and commitments for the cultural system. The principles governing the four systems are: integrity (for the value system), solidarity (for the integrative system), effectiveness (for the polity) and efficiency (for the economy).

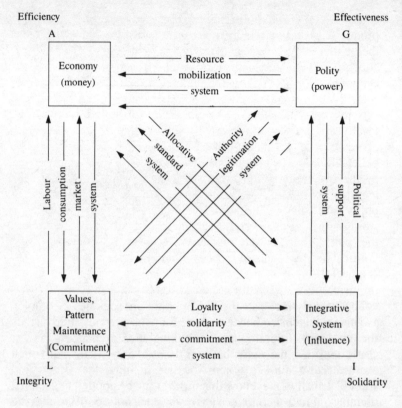

*Figure 9.2   Systems of society*

Figure 9.2 summarizes these exchanges and illustrates the appropriate media. There are six systemic sets of exchanges which characterize all societies. (The detailed categories are shown in Parsons.)[27] Under capitalism, the labour consumption market system (the L–A exchange) is distinguished by an exchange of labour capacity (work) for wage income: money, used to purchase commodities, is the essence of the individual's commitment to work.[28] In other words, motivation to work is satisfied by wage income. The resource mobilization system (A–G) is maintained through exchanges of money and power. The polity maintains the conditions for effectiveness, it controls the level of credit and the price of money (interest), the level of capital investment is determined by the polity. The economy in return maintains productivity and thereby increases the level of goods available to the collectivity. The allocative standard system (A—I) is concerned with the assertion of claims to resources by the economy against standards for such allocation. The integration of society requires that claims have to be prioritized; entrepreneurial activity plays an important role in innovation. The loyalty/solidarity/commitment system (the L—I exchange) expresses the exchange between values and integration. The beliefs in property, private enterprise and individualism are given by the overriding value system and they ensure solidarity. The legitimation system (G—L) summarizes the exchange between the polity and values. The terms of the legitimation of activity in western society are expressed through democratic procedures in the polity, and private ownership of economic enterprises. Political loyalty is ensured when these conditions are met. Loyalty is a necessary condition for the effectiveness of the polity, which in turn ensures its role in mobilizing resources (G—A) and contributes to solidarity (G—I).

This concludes my brief exposition of the Parsonian model of the economy under capitalism. As far as the economy is concerned, a few salient points may be highlighted: individual motivation for work is provided by wages; demand is superior to supply; priorities and budgeting are controlled through allocations of money in return for productivity. Such exchanges are performed through differentiated institutions, money is a crucial unit of account and medium of exchange.

## EXCHANGES IN SOCIALIST STATES

These types of exchanges do not occur in socialist states. The chief differences may be itemized as follows (1) The values involving motivational commitments are different. 'Commodity demand' is not a prime motivational force under planning. (2) 'Wage income' in return for labour capacity does not have the same salience, as moral duty and psychological satisfaction are also considered to be motivating factors for work. Motivational commitment to labour is in moral and legal as well as financial terms. (3) In Parsons' scheme, affecting all the exchanges in and out of 'A', is the role played by the medium of money. The budget constraints in social-ist societies are extremely weak, money is a unit of account but it is not a medium of exchange as under capitalism. (4) Forms of legitimacy and authority are derived from the ideology of Marx-ism—Leninism and the Communist Party. (5) Production is not responsive to price, and price is insensitive to demand; this is the case in all commodity markets. (6) 'Inefficiencies' are characteris-tic of the economy and have become an accepted way of life. (7) The economy is publicly owned, it is organized and planned by administrative bodies. The allocation of resources takes place through administrative channels rather than a market. (8) There is no entrepreneurship in the sense of individuals marketing products or services in exchange for profit. (9) Flows of money (credit) and interest rates do not influence investment or production; accumu-lation of money does not lead to investment. (10) There is no pay-ment for risk (profit) and there is no bankruptcy.

In conceptualizing the role of the economy in a socialist society, however, Parsons' insights should be retained as a framework. It must be conceded that all societies have four functional dimen-sions, and differentiated ones need to have forms of exchange to maintain equilibrium. Compared to market-type societies, plann-ed ones of the Soviet type have a deceptively simple appearance. The main structural difference is the absence of differentiated institutions having relative autonomy. The Communist Party as an institution appears to be omnicompetent and in practice the func-tions defined above are not the concern of differentiated institu-tions. The 'inputs', 'outputs' and media are dissimilar in capitalist and socialist societies. The motivational commitment system is derived from the value system of Marxism—Leninism, though money and status for the individual also have a role. Integration through planning, law and education seeks to secure the values of the dominant Communist Party: harmony is sought through the notion of a classless society. (The complicating effects of tradition-al values, procedures and norms are excluded here, though I have discussed them elsewhere.)[29] Efficiency and effectiveness, the motivating values of capitalism, have less salience than those of integrity (of ideology) and solidarity.

The socialist system (see Figure 9.3) has some notable differen-ces compared to the capitalist. Parsons has made clear that Ameri-can society has the major 'collective goal' of the pursuit of

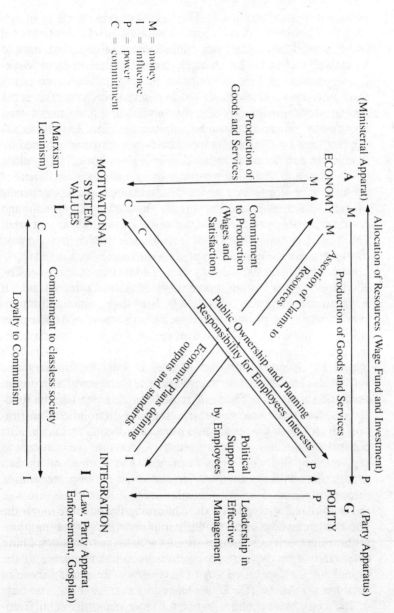

Figure 9.3 *State Socialism as a Social System*

economic productivity. The collective goals of a Marxist–Leninist party are comprehensive. Motivational commitments stemming from values include full employment and social welfare (the L–I exchange). 'Commitments' as media out of L are retained in this model. The exchange with the economy (I–A) involves a commitment to maximum production of goods and services: goals are defined in terms of supply, rather than commodity demand, as under capitalism. This has important implications for the conduct of affairs at enterprises: plans are fulfilled in output terms, rather than efficiency ones. The medium of coordination at I under capitalism is 'influence'; in socialist societies planning exerts power-like sanctions. Administratively ordered plans characterize the I–A exchange, rather than entrepreneurship and the influence of the interest rate as in market societies. Legitimation of authority (L–G) comes from public ownership and the expression of class interests which in turn have been derived from the value system of Marxism–Leninism. The economy is not a market-linked network of competing firms, but a system of enterprises controlled by Ministries which in turn are subordinate to the polity and the societal community (I). Money is still a medium out from A and wages are products which fulfil motivational commitments (A–L). However, money is not a means for accumulation and income in kind (social services, subsidies) reduces its potency; work is also regarded as a moral need and social duty. The polity penalizes those who do not work and by the same token the integration system prioritizes the provision of jobs. Goods are measured in monetary terms (A–G), but prices do not reflect scarcity. Claims to resources are expressed in financial terms (money is a unit of account), but capital markets do not allocate resources (it is not a medium of exchange).

The exchanges from G are determined by the medium of power. The Party apparatus is particularly important in aggregating plans for the allocation of resources (in line with its interpretation of the community's needs). Priorities in allocation of resources to the economy are specified by G (G–A). Responsibility for employees' interests (G–L) are shared by Party and trade unions, in the context of public ownership and planning. The Party leadership combines the allocation of resources with leadership in management (G–I).

The outputs from I differ considerably from capitalist states. Parsons has in mind 'influence' in the sense of 'constituent demands'[30] (I−G). In socialist states these demands are often suppressed. Under American capitalism, Parsons describes an action sequence of interest-demands → leadership responsibility → policy decisions → political support. (This is analogous to a perfect competition model of the economic market in which demand stimulates supply.) In socialist states, interest demands do *not* 'define the situation for political decision-making', as postulated by Parsons. Political support is sought, but it is not crucial to leadership. The legitimation system gives the polity authority to achieve general goals, irrespective of political support in a western electoral sense. The 'assertion to claims on resources' may not be reciprocated in the allocation of claims (I−A exchange). Claims may not be met. Shortages of commodities may ensue (i.e. the production of goods and services A−G may not coincide with the definition of outputs expressed at I). Ideology legitimates societal integration in terms of a classless society and the meeting of needs; market systems fulfil wants in terms of consumer demands which in turn may violate norms of equality and fraternity. Shortages may be a source of 'strain' (I−L) but, as Kornai concedes, shortages are an accepted part of life (as inflation is under capitalism) and do not have serious destabilizing effects. Consensus is maintained through a combination of social and welfare benefits coupled to the provision of employment in the context of a low productivity economy. The welfare state and full employment are linchpins in the loyalty/solidarity/commitment system and the political support system.

## THE FUSION OF POLITICAL AND ECONOMIC

The organization of political and economic institutions in the USSR has important effects on policies. In socialist societies there has been no clear institutional division between the economic and the political. In any society, the costs of economic efficiency in political terms may be measured in the weakening of public loyalty and social solidarity. But the accepted division in capitalist society between economics and politics diverts responsibility for unemployment away from the formal arena of politics.

Unemployment is legitimated in the West as being necessary for economic efficiency. Policies to reduce unemployment do so in the context of maintaining efficiency. Invariably they involve financial compensation for the loss of work but do not make the provision of employment a major policy goal.

In the USSR the greater fusion of politics and economics and the responsibility the state assumes for public welfare make it impossible for the government to ignore the social and political costs of economic change. If unemployment were to be a consequence of economic policy, its cost could not be shouldered by the working class, as the Party claims that the Soviet state is the expression of the interests of that class. The hegemony of the political over the economic in the USSR ensures the priority of loyalty and solidarity over economic efficiency and this entails a full employment policy.

The implication for policy and reform is that a reliance on market wage stimulation will not be effective unless the ideological priorities are also changed. Values, however, are notoriously difficult to alter. The role of the polity is to release resources to maximize output. This is ensured by the public ownership of the means of production and planning (the authority-legitimation system). The nature of the political support system is also different from that under capitalism. The polity is much more strongly anchored under the domination of the political party. Political support is certainly necessary, but there are few checks on leadership for 'effective management'. This may weaken solidarity and consensus. However, this is compensated by the stabilizing effects of full employment and social security. Unlike under capitalism, where the allocation of resources and the need for efficiency leads to employment uncertainty, under socialism efficiency in the economy is sacrificed for solidarity. And unlike in capitalist market societies where the amount of credit and the levels of interest may depress economic activities, in socialist societies it is the 'allocative standard system' that has been weakly developed. Administrative control of claims to resources is weak in face of the power to invest sanctioned by the polity. The loyalty/solidarity/commitment system is predicated on the creation of a classless society. The standards of allocation are in terms of maintaining loyalty: full employment is a priority rather than, as under capitalism, the striving for efficiency in the economy. It is in this sense that full employment is part of government policy. It would not be impossible to reduce the level of labour utilization and increase unemployment in the USSR. But the economic processes leading to present overemployment are not countered by the government because political values stress the importance of work and occupation: loyalty and solidarity are politically dependent on full employment.

Kornai and other commentators who argue for a 'systemic' analysis of socialist societies are correct in their general standpoint. My own approach has sought to outline the fact that full employment is systemic because it is closely linked (a) to the loyalty/solidarity system, (b) to motivational commitments, (c) to a supply resourced economy, and (d) to an output-maximization and politically determined resources allocation system. 'Shortages' are likely to be a consequence of such a system because integration is not fulfilled through the satisfaction of 'demands'. Any major change in the system of motivational commitments and integration processes would lead to the breakdown of the complex sets of institutional interests and exchanges. This would have to include greater individual sovereignty, an enhanced role to 'influence', the strengthening of standards of allocation involving the use of money as a medium— as a criterion of investment. A thorough use of the price system (affecting wages, capital and commodities) would destroy the present complicated sets of exchanges established under state socialism.

One can also look at the social system in another way—by consideration of group interests. The legitimating ideology can only be effective in terms of a social policy of full employment if there are dominant and subordinate groups in support of it, or at least, if the balance of political interests favours it. Compared to western capitalism, a wide range of groups in the USSR endorse a full employment policy.


## INTERESTS PROMOTING FULL EMPLOYMENT

Three main interests promote full employment under socialism: management, labour and Party. By contrast, in a market system, management is under pressure to cut labour costs to compete more effectively. Poor market performance leads to a decline of profits, possible takeover and bankruptcy. There is little financial cost involved in creating redundancy, the costs of unemployment are social costs which are not borne by the firm. In command economies, however, management has no incentive to shed labour. The more labour resources it has available, the better it can meet its output targets. Enterprises are not subject to bankruptcy or takeover. Surplus labour not only helps management to overcome production bottlenecks, but the size of the labour force is also a criterion of management's earnings. The ministerial apparatus superior to the enterprise also has plans to fulfil and, recognizing the need for 'slack', will not push for greater efficiency at the cost of supply uncertainty. Surplus labour is a social cost, not a financial one to the enterprise or ministry.

Labour itself is far more homogeneous than in the West. Trade unions do not have the power to bargain on behalf of privileged groups of workers (such as printers, or doctors of medicine). There is no impetus from organized labour in the USSR to break out of a low-pay economy, or to increase pay differentials. Unemployment resulting from labour costs being kept artificially high, as a result of union activity, does not occur. The masses of employed people have good reason to fear the consequences of unemployment. Many of the older workers have neither the motivation nor education to acquire new skills forced by technological change and they would be likely to suffer reduction of wages and status. Any prolonged form of unemployment would, in the absence of social security benefit, cause poverty. It is likely that labour, at the levels of the factory Party and trade union committees, as well the rank-and-file worker, favours a policy of full employment at the expense of economic efficiency.

The Communist Party as a political agency has no incentive to allow unemployment to develop. Any threat of mass unemployment, let alone public disturbances as have occurred in Poland, would weaken the Party's authority and would bring into question the USSR as a socialist state. The police and security services have a stronger voice in government decision-making than in advanced western states. Their concern with the prevention of public disorder also encourages a full-employment policy, as witnessed by campaigns instigated by Andropov against parasitism and their explicit views that unemployment causes crime (see above p. 57).

Another way of putting it is that certain groups' interests are met by present policy which would be undermined by a 'market-type' economic reform. The present system of planning gives the Party and government leadership prerogatives over the allocation of resources that would pass to 'the market'. A market-type system would not only diminish the political power of the economic Ministries and Party, but would be likely to divert resources to consumption and away from defence and welfare. A weakening of the right to employment would be opposed and feared by the mass of rank-and-file Party members and qualms about the effects of labour unrest (in a socialist society) are strong enough for the Party leadership to give priority to the maintenance of loyalty on the part of the working population albeit at the expense of economic efficiency.

## SOURCES OF CHANGE

The command economy described above is under pressure to change. The maturation of the economic, political and social system, its greater diversity, complexity and size, requires modification to the sets of exchanges described above. The Soviet Union has had a turbulent political history reflected in high levels of political insecurity and oppression during the time of Stalin. The instability associated with post-revolutionary regimes has led the political authorities to give priority to the maintenance of the solidarity system, and to channel resources into economic growth and defence. As B.P. Kurashvili has put it, historically the development of production relations in the USSR required the predominance of common (as opposed to individual) interests, it required direct state management and the disposal of resources by the state.[31] This has involved the hegemony of the polity with administrative control located at G (see Figure 9.3 above). Political power (P) has been the dominant medium of control with little use of other media—in terms of money (M), influence (I), commitment (C).

The greater political, social and economic maturity of the USSR has created the basis for greater diversity and the necessity for exchange. Reforms call for a greater role to be given to money, influence and commitment. The higher levels of differentials and the rise of articulate interests on the part of various occupational groups in the USSR has been noted by Kurashvili and by Zaslavskaya. The latter has called for greater open debate about priorities and has called for greater 'flexibility' and 'democracy'.[32] In terms of my model this involves the formalization of exchanges between G/I (the nature of effective leadership and political support), A/L (commitment to production through satisfaction and wages and production of goods and services), L/G (the relationship between public ownership and planning and employees' interests) and A/I (a realignment of claims to resources and outputs of economic plans). As noted in Figure 9.3 interchanges through the media of money, influence and commitment occur between economy, polity, society and cultural system. Zaslavskaya summed up the problem when she pointed out that the USSR's productive forces have changed significantly from the 1930s when the economic mechanism was set up, what is now necessary is making 'a rational calculation between administrative and economic methods of management under new conditions'.[33]

In the 1980s, the Soviet Union has a different order of priorities. These have been explicitly articulated by the leadership of Gorbachev. They involve a greater concern with efficiency and quality of life. There are also exogenous pressures: the need to adopt new technology to match the West's military effort, the greater awareness by Soviet citizens of the living standards in advanced capitalist countries and the relative underachievement of the Soviet economy in relation to them.

Gorbachev's policy reflects the initiative of professional groups ('specialists') with a vision of a different type of society—one more able to compete with the economic advance of the West; one more differentiated with greater individual choice and uncertainty; one in which change is institutionalized in the socioeconomic system. It involves greater 'flexibility' on the part of the workforce, entailing more job changing and a weakening of job tenure; it involves greater autonomy for work units (brigades) and for the industrial enterprise. Groups advocating these changes have been discussed above: they are made up of 'reformers' in government and Party hierarchies and particularly in academic institutes, especially in the Academy of Sciences.

They take their cues for change from the practice of the West and the policies adopted in other socialist countries, such as

Hungary.[34] They have the support of the younger, better qualified workers and professionals who will be able to compete and excel under a system encouraging initiative and independence. Such people are more 'consumer-oriented' and desire a higher quality standard of living. This policy, however, involves greater inequality in the distribution of resources and greater income differentials. It is a policy in favour of the strong—those who can compete successfully. Market principles and contractual relations, as advocated by Aganbegyan,[35] for instance, would be part of such a policy.

In terms of my model, the polity and economy have to become more differentiated to enhance efficiency and effectiveness. The resource mobilization system and the labour consumption system inherited from the period of rapid economic growth and political consolidation are now inappropriate. As Gorbachev puts it: 'The specific economic and political situation we are in, and the particular period of the historical process that Soviet society . . . [is] going through require that the Party and every member of it display their creativity, capacity for innovation and skill to transcend the framework of habitual but already outdated notions.' Later in his speech Gorbachev made explicit:

The forms of production relations, the system of running and managing the economy . . . took shape . . . in the conditions of an extensive development of the economy. Gradually they become obsolete, they began to lose their role as incentives and here and there they turned into impediments. Currently we are striving to change the thrust of the economic mechanism, to overcome its cost-intensive nature, to target it towards enhancing quality and efficiency, accelerating the progress of science and technology and the strengthening of the role played by the human factor.[36]

Communism is not only an ethic of work and industrial development, but it also aspires to the provision of abundance in terms of goods and services. In the contemporary Soviet Union, there is a peculiar combination of socialist welfare objectives and a growing western-style consumerism. The more demanding population seeks better forms of services and commodities, as well as more significant forms of participation and the use of non-working time. Pushed both by the need to keep up with the West and by a more urbane and demanding younger generation, the political leadership of the USSR will move policy in the direction of greater efficiency. Inefficiency is not legitimated by Marxism; it is not a virtue of a planned economy.

Economic reform will probably lead to greater differentiation of the political and the economic and to a greater stress on efficiency. The greater emphasis on economizing (and an improvement in quality) is brought out by the slogan: 'Pace, quality, thrift and organization'.[37] The role of money will be enhanced. Gorbachev has called for restructuring of the economy and for a critical examination of the relationship between 'goods and money'. In discussing the organization of agriculture, Gorbachev pointed out: 'The role of financial autonomy will be raised significantly, its final results must become the norm for all links in the agro-industrial complex. . . . The practice of bank credit must be substantially altered so that it provides incentives to raising the level of activity of collective and state farms.'[38]

Gorbachev calls for a 'radical reform' in economic management to raise 'efficiency and quality, to speed up scientific and technical progress, to develop the workers' interest in the results of their work and develop initiatives in a socialist sense of enterprise in each unit of the national economy and primarily in labour collectives.' Economic enterprises will be given greater autonomy: 'Enterprises and organizations should be given the right to market above-plan output, unused raw and manufactured materials and equipment and so on, independently. . . . It is finally time to put an end to the practice of petty tutelage of enterprises on the part of Ministries and Departments. . . . Ministries should concentrate on issues of technical policy, balance within industries and satisfying the requirements of the national economy for high quality output from their industries.'[39] The task of enterprises is 'to react responsively to the demands of consumers'.[40]

The exchanges between economy and the motivational system (the L−A exchange) will be strengthened in the form of exchanging money for goods and services. 'It is necessary for the size of an enterprise's wages fund to be directly tied to revenues from the sales of their products . . . We can no longer reconcile ourselves to the fact that the workers of enterprises producing useless products are . . . receiving . . . in full, both their wages and bonuses and other benefits.'[41]

I pointed out above that a market system could not effectively be grafted on to the present political order unless a change in values also occurred. The mobilizing principle of 'social justice' is likely to be used to legitimate the shifting of resources from administrative control to the market. M. N. Rutkevich[42] has pointed to the fact that the proportion of real income for manual and non-manual workers received through public consumption funds has increased from 25.2 per cent in 1960 to 28.9 per cent in 1984, and the proportion received by collective farmers has correspondingly risen more quickly—from 10.3 per cent to 19.2 per cent. Rutkevich argues that the principle of 'payment according to one's work' should be applied in this arena. He points out that income transfers through public consumption lead to inequality. Subsidies for the upkeep of certain activities (e.g. theatres, clubs, libraries) benefit some people irrespective of their contribution to society. He argues—rather like opponents of the welfare state in western countries—that a *minimum* level should be provided by the government and that people should pay for themselves above this. This would involve, for instance, progressively higher rents for more desirable accommodation and housing. Charges would be introduced for certain kinds of educational courses (foreign languages, typing, music). The provision of medical services and other welfare services varies according to the place of work of an employee. This form of injustice, according to such writers, could be remedied by allowing more people to buy these services on the market. In this way real income would be shifted from payments in kind to money income which would be an 'incentive for increasing the labour activity of personnel and labour collectives'. It might further be argued that the 'defence of workers' interests' would be weakened with a movement to market type bargaining: trade unions under capitalism have experience of wage bargaining unknown in socialist countries where their tasks have traditionally been mainly integrative.

Such views, however, have to be implemented in the context of the legitimating principle that people under socialism give according to their abilities. Furthermore there is an implication in Marxist ideology that with the development of the material basis of communism, people should receive 'according to their needs', rather than to 'their deserts' as the market would reward them. T. Zaslavskaya has addressed this concept in relation to social justice.[43] Here Zaslavskaya argues that a socialist state has to 'create the optimal conditions for the full-fledged social development of each person'. This calls for *greater* state provision to enable all children to enjoy relatively equal starting conditions to develop their abilities. The unequal access to higher education by higher social groups and the unequal distribution of cultural resources (between urban and rural) entail greater collective provision. Zaslavskaya advocates that 'a substantial portion of the expense of raising children should be placed on the state'. By adjusting welfare payments in this way, a more equitable level of well-being would be achieved by raising the standards of families with many dependent children. The distribution of occupations is such that in many localities it is impossible to match the potential of people to jobs available (in some rural schools most girls become milk-maids). The supply of jobs should be organized to fulfil human aspirations. This procedure is again contrary to the development of a western-type free labour market and is in opposition to the ideology of many of the economically-oriented reformers.

The 'acceleration' of social change in the 1980s will, in the sphere of labour, lead to redeployment of the labour force at a much greater rate than hitherto. Both Gorbachev and Kostakov have estimated that from 12 to 19 million existing jobs will be lost through the intensive development of the economy.[44] The need for greater efficiency to maintain higher levels of output, however, is unlikely to lead to structural unemployment. The supply of jobs is already inflated, the length of the working week may be reduced, and the system of planning is able to ensure the provision of sufficient jobs at a macro-level to accommodate the labour force.

It is likely that the need for efficiency will lead to some weakening of the principle of solidarity. However, for reasons adumbrated above, a full-employment policy under present conditions of planning will continue, albeit at the cost of economic inefficiency. Some market features are likely to be adopted. Policy will mitigate the worst effects of underemployment. Changes are likely to involve greater administrative control over the number of workers' places, a tightening of the wages fund, greater incentives for management and workers to make surplus labour redundant, the lifting of the responsibility from enterprises to find work for redundant workers, greater reliance on labour exchanges to place them in new jobs and finally, the payment of wages for extended periods to workers made redundant. A distinction between job security and full employment will be made entailing the weakening of the former and the maintenance of the latter. One is likely to have a situation of full employment at the macro-level with greater job insecurity at the micro-level.

As I have illustrated on Figure 9.3, state socialism as a social system does not have the *same* kinds of reciprocated exchanges as under capitalism. It is possible, however, for reciprocated exchanges to develop under state socialism and to enhance its efficiency and effectiveness. *Within-system* reform will entail an increased role to money: as a medium of exchange for commitment (the A−L exchange), for the production of goods and services (the A−G exchange). The system of motivational values (Marxism−Leninism), types of integration and political priorities (planning and Party hegemony) require modernization—being brought up-to-date in a world of a consumer society and high technology. The problem for the Soviet leadership is to decide what kinds of policy are consistent with a Marxist framework of motivational values, patterns of integration and socialist management. Merely copying some elements of a market capitalist economy may create distortions and weaken solidarity. As far as employment and labour are concerned, the adoption of a western-type labour market would undermine public ownership and planning, the present forms of social integration, the legitimacy of the leading role of the Communist Party and it would (intentionally) weaken the bargaining position of employees. From the point of view of practical politics, 'economic reform' is limited by the systemic properties (including the values) of the socialist system. A movement away from a full-employment/low-wage policy would have serious destabilizing consequences for the present political system and the political leadership. Economic reform cannot simply copy western processes which are organically part of a different social and political infrastructure. Reform is likely to be piecemeal, to take place within the existing structures and procedures of planning.

# REFERENCES

1. A.S. Ivanov, 'Pravo na trud i obyazannost' trudit'sya', *Pravda*, 18 March 1983.
2. V. Medvedev, 'K voprosu o sbalansirovannosti narodnogo khozyaystva', *Planovoe khozyaystvo*, no. 9 (September 1983), p. 28.
3. Ibid., p. 31. This involves an economic reform of the planning mechanism, which is outside the scope of this book.
4. A. Kotlyar, *Ekonomicheskie nauki*, no. 3 (March 1984), note 4. See also above Chapter 8.
5. Kotlyar, ibid. See also V. Kostakov, *Sovetskaya kultura*, 4 January 1986.
6. Susanne Oxenstierna, *Labour Shortage in the Soviet Enterprise* (Stockholm: Institut for Social Forskning, 1985), pp. 35-9.
7. Robert E. Lane, *The Dialectics of Freedom in a Market Society*, (University of Illinois at Urbana-Champaign: Dept. of Political Science, 1979), p. 10.
8. Robert E. Lane, 'Markets and the Satisfaction of Human Wants', *Journal of Economic Issues*, vol. 12, no. 4 (1978), p. 808.
9. A. Ernst, *Japan's Unvollkommene Vollbeschäftigung* (1980) pp. 501-2.
10. *Capitalism and Freedom* (Chicago: University of Chicago Press, 1962), p. 9.
11. J. Kornai, 'Shortage as a Fundamental Problem of Centrally Planned Economies and the Hungarian Reform', *Economics of Planning*, vol. 18, no. 3 (1982), p. 103. P. Hanson develops a systemic approach, 'The Serendipitous Soviet Achievement of Full Employment'; while D.M. Nuti acknowledges the social policy choices available to governments his model is also a systemic one: 'Systemic Aspects of Employment and Investment in Soviet-Type Economies', both in D. Lane (ed.), *Labour and Employment in the USSR* (Brighton: Wheatsheaf Books, 1986).
12. J. Kornai describes his approach as a 'descriptive-explanatory theory', *Economics of Shortage* (Amsterdam: North Holland, 1980), vol. A. p. 15.
13. Ibid. The following is drawn from chapter 11, vol. A.
14. Ibid., p. 254.
15. Ibid., p. 260.
16. Ibid., p. 255.
17. Ibid.
18. Ibid., p. 261.
19. Ibid., p. 248.
20. Ibid., p. 237.
21. Ibid., p. 250.
22. Ibid., p. 252. Italics in original.
23. Ibid., p. 265.
24. Ibid.
25. Ibid., p. 13.
26. Ibid., p. 569.
27. Talcott Parsons, 'On the Concept of Political Power', in R. Bendix and S.M. Lipset, *Class, Status and Power* (London: Routledge, 1967), p. 263.

28. A simple diagrammatic representation of the exchanges is given in T. Parsons and N.J. Smelser, *Economy and Society* (London: Routledge, 1956), p. 68.

29. 'Towards a Sociological Model of State Socialist Society', in Simon McInnes *et al.*, *The Soviet Union and East Europe Into the 1980s* (Ontario: Mosaic Press, 1979).

30. 'On the Concept of Political Power', p. 242.

31. B.P. Kurashvili is the head of the sector on the theory of state management of the USSR Academy of Sciences' Institute of State and Law, see *EKO*, no. 5 (May 1985). Abstract in *CDSP*, vol. 37, no. 41 (1985), pp. 1-2.

32. T.I. Zaslavskaya, 'Ekonomika skvoz' prizmu sotsiologii', *EKO*, no. 7 (1985). Kurashvili also calls for greater independence of individuals and institutions. (*loc. cit.*).

33. See discussion between E. Manucharova and T.I. Zaslavskaya, *Izvestiya*, 1 June 1985.

34. An interdepartmental commission, chaired by Ryzhkov, the head of Gosplan, has been set up to study the experience of reform in other East European Countries. O.T. Bogomolov, *Pravda*, 14 March 1983, p. 4. Cited by Ed. Hewett, *Soviet Economic Reform: Lessons from Eastern Europe*, unpublished paper, NASEES Conference (Cambridge: 1984), p. 1. Reports from this commission appear regularly in *Ekonomicheskaya gazeta*.

35. See his article in *Trud*, 28-29 August 1984. Translation in *CDSP*, vol. 36, no. 36 (1984).

36. Gorbachev, Report to 27th Party Congress, 25 February 1986, reported in *Pravda* on 26 February. English versions available in *CDSP*, vol. 38, no. 8 and BBC *Summary of World Broadcasts* (SU/8193/C/1).

37. Gorbachev, *Pravda*, 21 September 1985.

38. In his conference speech he says: 'It is time to overcome prejudices relating to commercial and monetary relations and their undervaluation in the practice of planned management of the economy . . . A healthy functioning of commercial and monetary relations on a socialist basis is capable of creating the situation and the conditions of management under which the results will entirely depend on the quality of work of the collective and on the ability and initiative of managers' (*loc. cit.*).

39. Ibid.

40. Ibid.

41. Ibid.

42. *Voprosy istorii KPSS*, no. 1 (January 1986). Abstract in *CDSP*, vol. 38, no. 5, pp. 4-5.

43. *Sovetskaya kultura*, 23 January 1986. Abstract in *CDSP*, vol. 38, no. 5 (5 March 1986), pp. 1-4.

44. See above p. 165.

# Index